Arkansas Hillbilly

One Man's Memoir of a Blessed Life

By Carl J. Barger

Strategic Book Publishing and Rights Co.

Strategic Book Publishing and Rights Co., LLC
USA | Singapore

For information about special discounts for bulk purchases, please contact Strategic Book Publishing and Rights Co. Special Sales, at bookorder@sbpra.net.

ISBN: 978-1-68181-890-0

Book Design: Suzanne Kelly

PROLOGUE

From the day I was born in the little community of Higden, Cleburne County, Arkansas, I was considered a hillbilly. I was told as a kid growing up in the Ozark Mountains that city folks referred to us as "hillbillies." We were defined as poor folks who were uneducated, went barefoot, chewed tobacco and/or smoked rabbit tobacco, dipped snuff, cursed, smelled bad, wore overalls, drank moonshine, and talked funny.

After pondering how we were perceived by outsiders, I decided a better description was that a hillbilly was a practical person, often very wise, with good common sense, and able to work hard to provide for his or her family. I liked my definition better. Another thing city folks didn't know about us was that we were a caring people who were mostly happy and content with that which God had blessed us. If we liked a person, we would give him the shirt off our back.

We didn't worry much about tomorrow as long as we had shelter over our heads, beds to sleep in, and food on the table. We made our living by the sweat of our brow.

When I think of the hard times we experienced and all the hard work we did growing up in the Ozark Mountains, I'm reminded of two things that bring to light the life of a hillbilly. The first is a song that Hank Williams Jr. recorded, "Country Boys Can Survive." If anyone knew how to survive, country folks did.

The second thing is a quote from a Charles Dickens's novel, *A Tale of Two Cities*. I believe this quotation exemplifies what it was like during the time I was growing up in Cleburne County. It goes like this: "It was the best of times, it was the worst of times, it was the age of wisdom, it was the age of foolishness, it was the epoch of belief, it was the epoch of incredulity, it was the season of Light, it was the season of Darkness, it was a spring of hope, it was the winter of despair, we had everything before us, we had nothing before us."

Although Dickens's *A Tale of Two Cities* was written about a revolution in 1859 between two cities—London and Paris—I still think it is a good way to describe the time when I was raised.

I hope my stories will make you laugh and cry as I share memories of the hard times as well as the good times. Between these pages, which span the early 1900s to 2016, are the struggles my parents and ten siblings experienced working as a migrant family, plus stories of how my father and mother survived the great depression through hard work, faith in God, and true grit. I also explain my inward drive to rise above poverty, my goal to overcome the stigma of how people perceive hillbillies, and what motivates me to achieve my goals, dreams, and a better life.

Within these pages is the story of how I and my wife, Lena, were blessed with two babies through adoption and, after fifteen years of marriage, how God blessed us—and surprised us!—with a biological son. I also share the joyful story of searching and finding my two adopted children's biological parents and the heartwarming experience of bringing them together.

I firmly believe that having faith in God, making wise choices, and focusing on Jesus Christ are key elements for one to have a blessed life.

CHAPTER 1

Our Family Begins

My mother was born in an old log house in the small community of Settlement near Shirley in Van Buren County, which is now part of the town of Fairfield Bay. Her father, Elias Samuel Totten, came to Settlement in 1901 from Olney, Richland County, Illinois. He received a land grant for one-hundred-sixty acres of rocky ground. After building his log cabin, he went courting to find himself a wife. He met my grandmother, Nancy Jane Bradford, at a square dance in Shirley, Arkansas. My grandmother was half Cherokee. It wasn't long before they were married and started their family.

Grandfather needed boys to help him on the farm, but God decided to send girls instead. My grandmother gave birth to six girls and one boy. The first girl, Magdalene, died as an infant. After Magdalene's death, Grandmother had five additional girls before having her only son, Samuel Devon Totten. My Aunt Martha was the oldest, followed by my mother, whom they named Mamie Ann. After Mamie came Aunt Gladys, Aunt Pearl, Aunt Lorene, and Uncle Samuel Devon.

As soon as Mamie and her sisters were old enough, they went to work for their father, my grandfather. Since he didn't get his boys, his girls took on the role of boys. They worked hard from daylight to dark. Grandmother made each of them bonnets so their skin wouldn't blister. Their hands cracked and bled from hoeing and harvesting thousands of rocks they carried from the fields so that Grandfather could raise cotton and corn.

At the age of fourteen, my mother met my father, Edward Barger, at a square dance in Shirley. It was love at first sight.

He was twelve years older than Ma. He had been married once before and had gotten a divorce. There were no children born to that marriage.

After a four month courtship, my grandfather gave his permission for Mamie Ann to marry Edward. Because of the hard work and her life style, Mamie was quite mature for her age. The hard work had prepared her for what lie ahead in her marriage.

Ma was about five feet six inches tall. She had long black hair that came down to her waist. She and her sisters were forbidden to cut their hair, because Grandpa Totten believed their long hair was their glory. Ma honored his wishes, and not one time in her eighty years did she get her hair cut. According to Pa, Ma was a good square dancer and when she danced, her long black hair bounced up and down.

When Ma and Pa married in Shirley on August 26, 1922, Ma weighed every bit of ninety-six pounds. According to Pa, he fell in love with her blue eyes and long black hair. He always said, "I got me the best looking girl in Van Buren County." According to Pa, Ma could outwork any other woman in the Settlement community.

Ma believed in God and insisted that her children be raised in a Christian home. She and my older siblings walked to church every Sunday. Pa had been saved, according to Ma, but he usually wouldn't go to church unless one of us kids had a role in a church program.

At the age of sixteen, Ma gave birth to her first son, Harvey Eugene Barger. After Harvey, two years later, she gave birth to Chester. After Chester, came her first daughter, Imogene.

All three of my elder siblings were born within a quarter mile of the Indian Rock House, which was a wide-mouthed shallow cave and a popular place in the Settlement area. At one time, Indians lived in the Indian Rock House. In fact, Pa courted Ma on top of the cave before they were married. The Indian Rock House has since become a tourist attraction. People have come to see it from all parts of the world. It is now part of the Indian Hills Golf Course at Fairfield Bay.

Both Harvey and Chester attended a one-room schoolhouse near the Davis Special Cemetery, not far from the Indian Rock House. The little school house was built by my grandfather, Elias Samuel Totten. Today it is recognized as a historical landmark in Arkansas.

When Harvey and Chester started school, Ma walked to school with them until she felt comfortable letting them walk by themselves. After Imogene was born, Pa and Ma moved to the community of Higden, Arkansas, where Betty, Loudeen, Willie, Jimmy, Roy, Carl, Ella Mae, and Leona Faye were born. Ma lost one girl at birth; they named her Marie. Our family was like two different families in age. Ma had exactly six boys, and six girls. Leona Faye and I hold the distinction of being the youngest girl and youngest boy in our family. I am the ninth child in order of birth, while Leona Faye is the twelfth.

I feel certain some of our neighbors felt Ma and Pa would eventually lose some of us to starvation, but that didn't happen—we all survived. According to Ma, the depression era was the hardest period of survival. Money was extremely scarce during those times. When the depression hit, Harvey, Chester, and Imogene were teenagers. Harvey and Chester were old enough to hold down a man's job at the local sawmill, which was owned by Mr. Reinhold Frank Dudeck. The wages they earned were absolutely necessary in contributing to the survival of our family. Pa also cut and skid logs for Dudeck's mill.

Harvey and Chester both dropped out of school after completing the sixth-grade at the two-room schoolhouse at Post Oak. A six-grade education wasn't considered bad during that era because the highest grade taught at Post Oak was eighth grade.

Pa's and Ma's educations were limited also. Pa completed the sixth grade, and Ma completed the fifth grade. As years passed, Ma and Pa both improved their education by reading and practicing their math skills. They read everything from a Sears Roebuck catalog to *Grit* newspapers. Pa was a good manager. He knew math pretty well and was always able to calculate accurately when it came to buying land or conducting business.

By age sixteen, Harvey and Chester were going off to potato and wheat harvests in Kansas. They sent some of their wages home to help Ma and Pa with family expenses.

My older sisters were a big help to our parents as well. They were strong and worked like boys. All three of my older sisters—Imogene, Betty, and Loudeen—helped Pa with his logging. They could skid logs and pull a crosscut saw as well as some men in the community.

Pa borrowed money from Jerome Johnson, president of the Cleburne County Bank, to purchase land. As the owner, he and my older brothers and sisters cut the timber off the land. Pa took the money from the sale of timber and paid off the bank note. After the timber was cut, Pa sold the cleared land for a good profit over what he paid for it.

My sisters were a big help to Ma. They were helpful when it came to cooking, washing clothes, washing dishes, cleaning house, and babysitting us younger children. This help gave Ma some much needed rest. All in all, my parents did the best they could to raise us. We were poor, but we didn't know it because almost everyone in the Higden community was equally poor.

CHAPTER 2

My Early Years

From the first three years of my life, I have no memories. I only know what my mother told me. I used to worry about that, but now realize it isn't uncommon for a child not to remember the early years of life. What I do know is that I had a wonderful, loving, and caring mother, who nursed me from the time I was born until I was one year old.

Ma breastfed all her children up to their first birthday. She believed a mother's milk played an important role in a child's physical and mental development. She believed her milk was better than cow's milk in fostering good healthy growth in children. Most of the mothers in the Ozark Mountains breastfed their babies as well.

According to Ma, I was a good boy and always obeyed her. She didn't have to spank me or scold me. She said I would go off by myself and play imaginary games. That, I don't doubt, because to this day I still fantasize and imagine things. I have the ability to create hypothetical situations and events and play them out in my mind. One of the good things about playing something out in your mind is, if you don't like it you can change it. That makes good common sense to me.

On August 17, 1943, my mother gave birth to me in an old log house. The old house consisted of a combination living room/kitchen and three bedrooms. Two of the bedrooms were located across the open dog trot and were heated by a pot-belly woodstove in the winter.

My brothers and sisters shared the two bedrooms, sleeping sometimes three to a bed, while my parents claimed the bedroom adjoining the living room and kitchen. The living room had a large fireplace which heated Ma and Pa's bedroom as well as the kitchen. Ma wanted the convenience of waking up to a warm kitchen before having to get up and fix breakfast for her big family.

I remember our house was really hot during the summer months. The only fresh air coming in was by open windows, the dog trot, and screen doors. As a child, I remember helping my brothers and sisters carry mattresses outside where we slept some nights under a big oak tree. It was much cooler outside than inside.

Sleeping outside gave us an opportunity to admire God's canopy. On most hot nights, the sky was clear, and we could see thousands, maybe millions, of sparkling stars, too many to count. Living inside the city limits, the same cannot be said today: light from artificial sources hides the natural light from many stars. Sleeping outside, the moon was beautiful also. On a clear night, the moon lit up the sky and the earth as well. Many nights we didn't need our lanterns to guide us to the outside toilet.

My favorite part of sleeping outside was watching the moon. Do you know that if you look hard enough, you can see a man in the moon? I know that may sound silly, but I've seen that man time and time again.

When I was about five years old, my folks built a new house. About this time, and for several years thereafter, I had this recurring dream that I was being awakened by rain drops hitting me in the face. These dreams occurred as the result of what happened to us in our old house. Every time we had a hard rain, the old shingle roof would start leaking, and rain drops would hit me in the face. Ma would come in our bedroom, get us out of bed, and have us move our bed to a dry area as she put dish pans under the leaks.

During the winter months, I remember sleeping under what seemed to be tons of quilts with two of my brothers, Jimmy and Roy. Since I was the youngest, Ma insisted that I sleep in the middle. She didn't want my older brothers pulling the quilts off me.

There were other things I remember about the old house. There was a porch running across the front of the house. I remember watching chickens underneath the porch through cracks in the wood. I also remember Ma and Pa spitting tobacco and snuff into their empty pork-and-bean cans while we sat eating popcorn or parched peanuts as we listened to the Grand Ole Opry or a boxing match on a battery-operated radio. Pa loved boxing. His favorite boxer was the great Joe Louis, who was the heavyweight champion of the world for most of the time between 1937 and 1949, the longest period of any heavyweight champion.

When it came to country music shows, our favorite performers were Hank Williams, Roy Acuff, Loretta Lynn, Little Jimmy Dickens, and Minnie Pearl.

We didn't have electricity until we moved into our new house. Prior to that time, we used lamps and lanterns to read by and navigate around the house and out to the toilet. Our new house was much larger and nicer than the old one and included four bedrooms. It had a living room with a big pot-belly stove and a large dining room with a big table and a bench on each side. At the ends of the table were straight back chairs where Ma and Pa sat.

Pa wanted Ma to have something new for her new home so he bought her a new cook stove. The stove had a bread warmer and a water tank to keep water hot for washing dishes and bathing. The wood section of the stove was much bigger than Ma's old stove. The larger wood section held enough wood to allow Ma ample time to cook an entire meal without having to add more wood. The oven had a double rack which allowed her to bake more things at one time. The oven had a temperature gage on the door to let her know how hot the oven was. Ma thought she had died and gone to heaven to have such a nice new stove.

Our new house still did not have running water, but the back porch was screened in and had a newly dug well. We were happy that we didn't have to go outside in bad weather to draw water from the well. During rainy and cold weather, we had a big five-gallon bucket on the back porch for the purpose of relieving ourselves. I never really enjoyed using it, but it beat going to the outhouse in cold rainy weather.

Our new house was located on a one-hundred-sixty-acre farm about two miles west of Higden, a quaint little town located on the west side of the Little Red River. Those living within the city limits of Higden often boasted that they lived in the best little town in the Ozark Mountains.

Higden was a thriving little town, especially after the M&NA (the Missouri and North Arkansas Railroad) began making daily stops at the depot. The little town had a mayor and a city council that made their laws. They had a sheriff who enforced the laws. There were two churches: Baptist and Church of Christ. There were two grocery stores, a post office, one gas station, a blacksmith shop, a four-room school, and one boarding house.

To get to Higden from where we lived, we had to cross a suspension bridge that stretched east and west across the Little Red River. The bridge had a wooden floor with cracks big enough to easily see the water below. The bridge was supported by two, large, steel cables connected with large concrete blocks at both ends of the bridge.

I was told that Frank Dudeck was responsible for getting the bridge constructed. He needed a bridge to transport his logs from the western part of Cleburne County to his sawmill in Shiloh, Arkansas.

The swinging bridge made it possible for wagons and automobiles to come and go to the other small communities of Stark, Edgemont, Shiloh, Prim, Drasco, Batesville, Clinton, and Heber Springs.

Every Sunday, come rain or shine, Pa hitched our two old mules to the family wagon, in which Ma and we kids would go to the Church of Christ in Higden for the service. We didn't have an automobile then, and our main source of transportation was the wagon.

My brother, Willie, was the oldest boy left at home so he was given the responsibility of handling the mules and getting us to church on time.

We continued to go to church in Higden until I was sixteen. It was at that little church in Higden that I accepted Jesus Christ as my Lord and Savior. I can remember it so clearly. It was on Mother's Day. The Holy Spirit had been convicting me for several weeks, but I wouldn't yield. The thought of accepting Christ was pretty scary because to do so in our church and many other protestant churches in the South, one had to come forward at the end of a service and pray to receive Christ. By doing so, one was admitting publicly that one was a sinner. Importantly, one was also committing to turn over a new leaf and to live as sin-free as possible.

The day I was saved was different for me for some reason. The call of God's Holy Spirit was stronger than ever before. My chest felt as if it were going to explode. I was gripping the pew in front of me with my entire might as my heart continued to race faster and faster. I bowed my head and prayed. I wanted to be saved so badly but feared that I wouldn't be able to live as a Christian. I knew in my mind and heart what I needed to do. The Holy Spirit was stronger than I had felt any time before. He seemed to say, "Carl, don't put this off any longer."

As the second verse of the invitation started, our pastor said, "Those who need to step forward and accept Jesus Christ need to do it now. Come right now and meet your savior." Then it happened, and it was so fast. I released my hands from the pew in front of me, stepped out in the aisle, and practically ran down the aisle. Our preacher took my hand and asked if I wanted to be saved. I said, "Yes, I do, I want to accept Jesus Christ as my savior." He prayed with me, and Jesus Christ came into my heart. I felt a big burden leave my body. It was as if a hundred pounds of weight had been lifted from my chest. As I turned to look at the audience, I saw two of my older brothers, Jimmy and Roy, coming to accept Christ as well. Had I been a positive influence on my older brothers?

The Church of Christ believed that new converts needed to be baptized on the day of their conversion. So, at two o'clock in the afternoon that same day, our preacher baptized Jimmy, Roy, and me in a big pond on the outskirts of Higden. I shall always remember that day. The wind was blowing, and the water was cold, but my burden was light. The Holy Spirit was in my heart, and He's been there since the minute I accepted Jesus Christ.

After the baptismal service, I heard Ma say to her friends, "Today is the best day of my life. Having my three sons saved and baptized is the best Mother's Day gift I've ever received. Praise the Lord!"

CHAPTER 3

Migrant Years

When Willie and Jimmy obtained their legal driver's license, our life style changed from a stay-at-home farm family to a migrant-working farm family.

I was six years old when we made our first trip to Benton Harbor, Michigan.

This was the beginning of our laboring years as migrant workers. The trips to Benton Harbor would continue until I was seventeen years old. My life would drastically change during those twelve years.

During our first year in Benton Harbor, we worked for three different German-American farmers. All three farmers had large farms that joined each other. Mr. Grandwhisky's farm bordered Art Goosey's farm to the west and Bud Piggott's farm to the north. All three of these farmers raised basically the same fruit and vegetable crops. Because we were a large family, we made good money picking strawberries, raspberries, cherries, tomatoes, cucumbers, peaches, apples, and asparagus.

During our first year to Benton Harbor, we lived in small cabins on the Carl Grandwhisky's farm. The small cabins had electricity, water, gas cook stoves and small beds and cots. Just like back home in Arkansas, we shared an outside toilet with migrant workers from Alabama and Georgia. I hated the sharing of the outdoor toilets.

After that first year on Carl Grandwhiskey's farm, we spent the next three years on Art Goosey's farm.

Art Goosey was an All American football player for Notre Dame. We enjoyed getting to know him and doing things with him. I can still remember the weekend he took us to South Bend, Indiana, for a tour of the Notre Dame campus. I was so fascinated by the huge football stadium and basketball arena. Some of the campus buildings were huge and beautiful, with large clocks at the top so students could keep up with the time and not be late for class, or at least that was Art's story on why the clocks were on the buildings. I never knew if Mr. Goosey was just kidding around with us about the clocks.

He was a happy-go-lucky kind of guy, a bachelor who never wanted to get married, although we all thought he flirted around some with our oldest sister, Imogene. Everyone knew that he treated her extra special.

Mr. Goosey loved showing us around. I believe he sensed we had lived a deprived life back in Arkansas and wanted to expose us to some finer ways of life. He fed us a big meal after our tour of Notre Dame. I loved Art Goosey. He was a good man who went out of his way to show us a good time. He didn't look down on us because we were poor. He accepted us as we were and helped us to see some amazing things at Notre Dame.

While working for Mr. Goosey, we picked both sour and sweet cherries. I hated all aspects of picking sour cherries. On a hot day, the juice from the cherries made things really nasty.

At the end of a working day picking cherries, we'd go immediately to the big water barrel that sat on a big platform near the packing shed. The big barrel stored water to be used in spraying fruit trees for insects. It was so refreshing to jump into the big barrel of water. The barrel was about six feet deep and had a circumference of ten feet. It turned out to be one of our favorite places to relax and keep our bodies clean. It was a far cry better than taking a bath in a big galvanized washtub.

Picking cherries was dangerous but exciting. We used long wooden ladders that reached to the top of the big cherry trees. We were expected to get the cherries at the top, so we'd climb right to the top of the ladder. At times, the limb that the ladder was resting on would break, and our ladder would fall to another limb. We hung on for dear life until the ladder came to rest. Yet, in all the years we picked cherries, we never fell off a ladder.

We boys were the only ones allowed to harvest cherries as Ma wouldn't let the girls anywhere close to a ladder. All in all, cherry picking was my least favorite job in harvesting fruit, and I was always eager for cherry picking time to end.

After spending three years on Art Goosey's farm, we spent the next seven years on Bud Piggott's farm. His farm was mid-way between a little town called Millburg and Benton Harbor. While working for Mr. Piggott, we picked strawberries, raspberries, asparagus cucumbers, tomatoes, and peaches.

Bud was a lot like Art Goosey except Bud was married. He and his wife, Dorothy, had six daughters. They tried unsuccessfully to have a son, but God blessed them with beautiful, hard-working daughters instead. His six daughters ranged in age from five to seventeen.

Apparently, because Bud always wanted a son, he treated me like a son. He took me to market with him, bought me food and drink, and talked politics with me. Bud loved politics. He told me he had considered many times running for office. He was always concerned about the national debt. He would say, "The national debt is going to bring America to its knees someday. We've got to get politicians in Washington who realizes that the national debt is killing us." I can only imagine how disturbed Bud would be about the national debt today. At its current level of almost nineteen trillion, the debt must be a thousand times greater today than back then.

Like Art Goosey, Bud liked to entertain us. He threw parties on the lawn of his home and cooked us meals and made homemade ice cream.

Bud was the one who took us on our first trip to an amusement park, which was in the Benton Harbor area on Lake Michigan. It was my first time to see a lake as large as Lake Michigan. It is so large one cannot see the opposing shore. We had lots of fun swimming, riding the big waves, riding the roller coaster, and eating ice cream. Each of the seven years we went to Benton Harbor, Bud transported my whole family and his daughters in a big, two-ton truck to the amusement park at Lake Michigan.

Even though our work at Benton Harbor was very hard, we loved our time there each summer. We were blessed in so many ways. The travel was exciting, and the things we did were educational as well. I will always be indebted and grateful to Art and Bud for taking their time to show us hillbillies a different side of life, one that we'd never experienced in Higden, Arkansas.

Most years when we were working as migrants, Pa stayed behind to plant and harvest corn and hay crops for our farm animals. Ma was the one who accompanied us to Benton Harbor. I can still remember her keeping our money in her overalls, which she wore while working in the fields. Bud paid us in cash. Ma kept the cash in a wallet in the front compartment of her overalls. She slept with the wallet underneath her pillow at night. She guarded that wallet like a prized possession. I guess it truly was a prized possession because it contained every penny of the money we earned picking fruit. I remember how the wallet got bigger and bigger each time Bud paid us.

Bud tried unsuccessfully to get Ma to let him take her to the bank in Millburg to open a bank account. Ma always depended on Pa to handle the finances, and she didn't trust banks, not one bit. She was always nice to Bud but declined his offer to open a bank account. She would say, "Bud, I appreciate your offer, but I think I'll just keep this money right here," patting the wallet compartment.

After returning to our home at Higden at the end of each fruit harvest, Ma would take the wallet out of her overalls and throw it on the bed and say to my Pa, "There it is, Ed, now go pay our debts!"

Pa was amazed at the amount of money we made. It took him about thirty minutes to count it. He counted it over and over until he was satisfied that he was correct. He then took the money to Mr. Jerome Johnson at Cleburne County Bank in Heber Springs. About half of the money went to make payments on our family's truck and farm notes. What was left went into a savings account.

Looking back on my experiences as a migrant worker, I'm reminded from time to time about one of my all-time favorite movies, *Grapes of Wrath*, written by John Steinbeck. I can easily identify with the people in that movie. I catch myself relating to those Oklahoma folks in a special and admiring way. Those eleven years we spent as migrant workers have truly been a humbling experience for me. Years I shall never forget. Experiences that helped me get where I am today.

CHAPTER 4

Fun and History

Living in the Ozark Mountains had its advantages. As kids, we created our own entertainment. One type of entertainment was going swimming and fishing in the Little Red River. Each year after we returned to Higden from Benton Harbor, we spent the rest of the summer helping Pa on the farm and playing. We loved spending time at our favorite swimming hole on the Little Red River.

One of our favorite things at the swimming hole was swinging on a rope as high as we could and then dropping off into the deep water. Someone on the bank of the river would push the person on the rope until he reached his desired height, and then he dropped into the river. Some of us were brave enough to turn flips in the air before we landed in the water.

Another pastime was looking for Indian arrowheads. Over the years, we found many. Later in life, I learned that the Cherokee Indians once lived in that very same location, not far from where Pa raised corn. We kids played hide and seek on a ridge that consisted of a number of small caves. Although the caves were good hiding places, being inside them was a little scary. We found several animal droppings, which Pa said were from bears. All the time we were growing up and playing in the caves, I never spotted a single bear. I now believe Pa was just trying to scare us. When I grew older, I learned that the droppings were from deer.

Right above the bluff area near the river was another forty acres my family owned. Thirty acres of this property were used for raising hay and provided a pasture for the farm animals as well. That same thirty acres included a big hog pen, a big barn, and a big garden.

A creek ran through the forty acres and was fed by an all-weather spring that never went dry. The spring emptied water into a big water hole we called the Blue Hole, which was about the size of a large swimming pool. We kids learned to swim in the Blue Hole. In the summer, several of our friends would come to visit us, and we'd take them to the Blue Hole to swim. We didn't own bathing suits so we skinny-dipped.

The spring that fed water into the Blue Hole was our main source of refrigeration. We kept our milk and milk products in the spring to keep them from spoiling.

As a young boy, I became interested in knowing more about my ancestors. Pa never talked much about his family. Since he was forty-five years old when I was born, I didn't feel comfortable asking him about his life growing up and before he met Ma.

At the time I became interested in knowing more about Pa, my second-oldest brother, Chester, was living near us. He was married to Letha Smith, and they had a daughter, Johnnie Sue, and a son, Ronnie.

I felt relaxed around Chester and decided I'd ask him some questions about Pa and Ma. Chester and my oldest brother, Harvey, these two being the oldest in the family, knew Pa better than any of the rest of us.

My first question to Chester was, "Chester, do you know where Pa was born?"

"Yes, I do. He was born in Orrick, Missouri, which is located in Ray County, but later moved with his family to Bates City, Missouri. He was eighteen years old when he and our grandparents came to Higden from Bates City."

"Why didn't I know that?"

"Well, if Pa wanted you to know that, he probably would have told you."

"I don't know, Chester. Pa and I don't talk much."

"I guess since Harvey and I worked side by side with him as kids, he talked to us more. Don't feel bad, Carl, I wanted to know the same thing about Pa. If I hadn't asked, I don't think he'd have told me either."

"What else can you tell me?"

"Well, I know he was the oldest in his family. I believe he had an older brother named Willie who died from a fall from his horse. He's buried in the Concord Cemetery in Bates City."

"How did Pa and our grandparents get to Higden?"

"Pa said they came in two big covered wagons. He drove one team of mules and Grandfather drove the other."

"What was Grandfather like?"

"He was a little man who liked his whiskey. According to Ma, he'd get drunk and stay out all night."

"Do you know why Pa and our grandparents came to Higden?"

"According to Pa, his aunt, Sarah Barger Thompson, sister to Grandpa, was already here and offered to sell Grandpa some of her land."

"Is that where Grandma Elizabeth Barger lives today?"

"Yes, it is. As a boy, Harvey and I spent lots of hours playing on Little Sugar Loaf Mountain. Their farm was at the base of the Sugar Loaf."

"Can you tell me anything else about Pa?"

"I'm going to tell you one other thing about Pa, but you must promise me you won't ever tell anyone. Will you promise me?"

"I promise," I said.

"After coming to Higden, Pa married a lady who lived in the Stark community. I'm not going to mention her name, but I will tell you what happened. According to Pa, she was lazy and wouldn't cook or do anything that a wife should do. Pa said all she wanted to do was sleep.

"Pa decided he would teach her a lesson. One cold morning he got up, went and got a bucket of cold water, and dumped it on her while she was asleep in bed. She moved out of the house, and Pa got a divorce. He later married Ma."

"Why didn't I know this?"

"Carl, there are some things that are better not mentioned, especially the story I just told you. We were always grateful Pa and his first wife didn't have any kids."

From that day forward, if I wanted to know something about my family's genealogy, I would go and ask Chester.

CHAPTER 5

The Whipping

Pa was a quiet man who seldom got mad and seldom whipped any of us kids. Whipping children was a common practice in this place and time. When Pa did whip us, however, he whipped too hard. I can personally attest to that.

One day Pa took me with him and Jimmy, my fourth-oldest brother, to plow the corn crop that was planted on twenty acres of our eighty-acre bottom land. This land was very rich and good for farming as it ran right along the east side of the Little Red River.

On that particular day, my job consisted of hoeing weeds out of the corn and keeping Pa and Jimmy supplied with fresh water. By two o'clock in the afternoon, the sun was beating down on all three of us. We were out of water, so Pa told me to run to the house and bring back a fresh jug of water.

On my trip up the rocky steep path leading to our house, I had to walk right past our hog pen. As I was walking by, I heard one of the old sows making a weird noise. I stopped and looked, and low and behold, she was giving birth to piglets. Although I was raised on a farm, I had never seen a sow giving birth. I stood there for several minutes just watching our old sow have one pig after another. If I counted right, she ended up having twelve pigs. As the pigs were born, they were in a slimy sack. They wiggled and wiggled until they broke the sack open. As the sack opened, at first the pig looked like a white ball. It wasn't long before the piglets stretched out and made their way to their mother where they began to nurse. Because I was fascinated by the birthing of new life, I completely forgot about my purpose for coming to the house. Realizing that I had made a grave error in judgment, I thought to myself, "Oh shoot, Pa will kill me!"

I ran to the house, put the well bucket in the well, pulled out a gallon of water, filled the gallon jug, and made a dash for the bottom eighty as fast as I could.

As I approached the field, I saw Pa standing behind his old mule, Dan, wiping sweat from his brow with his long-sleeved work shirt. He looked up at me coming and started shaking his head in disgust. I knew right then, I was in deep trouble. As I handed him the jug of water, I said, "Pa, I'm really sorry!"

He was truly thirsty. He drank about half of the jug of water without stopping. He put the lid back on the jug and pointed toward Jimmy, who was plowing nearby.

"You take Jimmy the rest of the water," he said.

As I approached Jimmy, he stopped plowing and reached for the jug. He too was starving for water. After drinking about a fourth of the water, he stopped and said, "Little brother, you are going to get your ass whipped." He handed me the jug and shook his head, and said, "I'm sorry for what awaits you under that big oak tree."

I turned and looked. Pa was under the oak tree motioning for me to come over there. As I headed his way, I saw Pa take out his pocket knife and cut a long switch from a nearby bush. I knew then that Jimmy was correct. I was in for a whipping.

After I reached the big oak tree, Pa didn't say a word. He just took the switch and started hitting me on the legs and back. It hurt badly. He was overcome with anger and forgot how many licks he had given me. I was crying as loud as I could when Jimmy came running up to Pa and said, "Pa, stop it, I think he's had enough!" If it hadn't have been for my brother, Pa might have killed me.

Pa stopped when Jimmy grabbed his arm. Pa was huffing and puffing by then and screamed for me to leave his presence and return to the house. I gladly obeyed him and ran as fast as I could up the steep path leading to our house. The pain from the whipping was awful. I cried all the way to the house. When I got home, I went immediately to the bedroom that I shared with Jimmy and Roy. I threw myself on the bed face down.

Ma heard me crying and came in to check on me. She could tell that my crying was from pain. She came over and sat on the edge of the bed, and placed her hand on my back. I cried out, "Ma, it hurts bad!"

Ma pulled my shirt up and saw the stripes on my back.

"Who did this?" she asked.

"Pa whipped me," I said.

"Your Pa did this to you? Why would he do such a thing?" she asked.

As I continued crying, I tried to explain what I had done and why Pa whipped me. I confessed that I was at fault, but Ma was furious! She went to the family medicine cabinet and brought back some ointment. "Pull your shirt off, Carl!" As I stood up to take off my shirt, she asked to see my legs. I slowly unbuckled my belt and let my blue jeans fall to the floor. I heard her say, "Oh, my God!"

Pa's whipping had left big whelps on my legs as well. After Ma put ointment on both my back and legs, she instructed me to lay down on the bed and rest. She said, "Don't lay on your back, son."

It wasn't long before Pa and Jimmy returned to the house. Ma was waiting for Pa. I had never seen her angry with him before that day. She tore into him, grabbing him by the arm and pulling him into the bedroom where I was lying.

"I want you to see what you've done to your son. Stand up, Carl, and drop your pants."

I did exactly as Ma instructed. When I did, Pa moaned, "Oh, what have I done?"

"You have beaten your son, that's what you've done," Ma replied. "You should be ashamed of yourself. You should get down on your knees and ask the good Lord to forgive you, and ask your son to forgive you, too. What were you thinking, Ed Barger?"

Ma always called Pa Ed, whereas his full name was Edward.

"I'm so sorry, Carl. I didn't know I was hurting you so bad. Please forgive me," Pa said, as he started crying.

That made things worse. I had never seen my pa cry. I felt sorry for him but was still angry with him for whipping me so hard. I finally said, "It's all right, Pa."

He came over and hugged me and said, "I promise you, I'll never do this to you again." I cried more!

Pa stood by his word. He never whipped me again. In fact, after that beating, our relationship as father and son improved significantly.

My relationship with Ma had always been good. She seemed to understand me better than anyone else.

Ma was good to share stories and events of the past with me. She knew I was very interested in our family's history. One of the things she shared was the day I was born. She said, "You caused me much grief when you were born. It was mid-afternoon on August 17, 1943. I'm telling you, it must have been the hottest day of the summer. The temperature was a hundred and five degrees in the shade. I'll be honest with you, Carl, I was so glad when you were finally born. I thought I would die of a heat stroke giving birth to you."

She went on to say, "Someday, you must thank your Grandma Bradford and Mrs. Mary Stark for helping bring you into this world. I don't know what I'd done without them."

My grandma, Nancy Jane Bradford, and Mary Stark were two of the best mid-wives in Cleburne County. Between the two of them, they delivered more babies than Dr. Thomas Birdsong, our family doctor.

Dr. Birdsong had trained a number of women in Cleburne County to be midwives. Like Grandma Bradford and Mrs. Stark, they were skilled at birthing babies. It was a good thing, too. It wasn't humanly possible for Dr. Birdsong to be present for every baby born in Cleburne County.

As a child, I was rambunctious, full of wild spirit, and sometimes downright mischievous. Some might describe me as a little devil in disguise. When I misbehaved, Ma would say, "Carl, you caused me pain and agony bringing you into this world, I don't need you to cause me more pain today.

Now, get outside and play. I don't need your horseplay in this house!"

When Ma looked at you a certain way, you better "git and git fast." She didn't warn you a second time!

CHAPTER 6

Chicks, Chores, and Chewing Tobacco

As a child, I remember our local mailman, Joe Hawkins, driving up to our front door and delivering cardboard boxes full of baby chicks. Pa bought Rhode Island Reds. Those little chicks would grow up and make us some good tasting meals and lay lots of eggs.

Between the ages of eight and sixteen, my main job was splitting and bringing in pine kindling for starting fires in Ma's big wood stove and for the large potbelly heating stove in the living room. Within only a few minutes, that big stove could put out enough heat to warm the entire house.

I was also responsible for churning butter. There is a certain art to churning butter. First, Ma filled the large churn with milk. When the cream came to the top, it was ready for churning.

Churning was accomplished with a tool called a dash. It was a heavy, round-handled wand made of wood, about three feet long. The dash had a cross-like framework attached to the bottom. The handle fit through a round hole in the middle of the churn's clay lid. The lid sealed the churn's milk compartment so the cream and extra milk wouldn't slosh out from the top during churning.

To make butter the dash was moved up and down in the churn until the butter coagulated. Until I mastered the art of churning, there were times I felt my arm would fall off.

I also was responsible for drawing water from our family's well on a daily basis for drinking, cooking, and bathing. Every morning I would draw enough water to fill a large galvanized tub. We would set the tub of water out in the sun so we could have warm water for baths at the end of the day. Several of us had to use the same tub of water. Needless to say, no one enjoyed being the last one to bathe.

There were certain things I didn't like about drinking water from the bucket. For one thing, everyone had to drink from the same water bucket. We did so with either a lightweight tin dipper or a gourd dipper. What made things really bad was that both Ma and Pa chewed tobacco and dipped snuff.

I especially didn't like seeing the snuff and tobacco juice running out the corner of my parents' mouths. I never got accustomed to seeing Ma and Pa taking a drink from the dipper. They would swish out their mouths with water before drinking and then put the dipper right back into the water bucket. When I decided to take a drink from the dipper, I always made sure I threw the first dipper of water away. My reasoning was I would get rid of the tobacco and snuff taste before my lips touched the dipper.

Although I hated the smell of tobacco and the nasty looking snuff, one day my curiosity got the best of me. That day I took a big chaw of Pa's Bull of the Woods and crawled underneath the house. The house had a crawl space, and I got as far under the house as I could. I didn't want anyone to know I was chewing tobacco. I hated the taste. It wasn't long before my head started spinning. I felt the need to vomit, but couldn't. I spit out the tobacco as soon as I felt my head spinning, but that didn't help. I just lay there and suffered and prayed, "Lord, help me! I promise, I won't ever chew tobacco again. I don't want to die. Please, Lord, help me!"

The family missed me and sent my brother, Roy, out to find me. When Roy came around to the back of the house, he heard me groaning and moaning. He looked under the house and called out my name. I heard him, but I was really weak. "Roy, help me," I said weakly.

"What's wrong with you, Carl," he asked.

"I'm so sick, Roy. Please help me."

I was a good sized kid by this time. The only way Roy could get me out was to pull me out feet first.

After my rescue, Roy saw tobacco juice coming out the corner of my mouth. He said, "I know what's wrong with you. You've been chewing Pa's Bull of the Woods, haven't you?"

"Roy, promise me, you want tell Pa. He will beat me dearly. Promise me you want tell," I pleaded.

"I'll make a deal with you. I won't tell if you will do my chores for a week."

"One whole week? You've got to be kidding me," I said.

"Take it or leave it, Little Brother!"

"Well, okay, I'll do it, but you can't ever tell anyone about this. Promise me!"

When I got on my feet, I fell back down. I was as dizzy and as wobbly as a newborn colt. I couldn't keep my balance. But Roy reached down and took me by the hand and said, "Put your arm around my neck. We'll walk around until you get this out of your system." I was so thankful and proud to have Roy as my brother.

I've always appreciated Roy for saving my butt that day. Pa would have whipped me, but good. Roy found Pa's Bull of the Woods pack and put it back on his bedroom dresser before he ever knew it was gone. We both feared Pa would notice the missing tobacco, but he never mentioned it, at least not to us.

CHAPTER 7

Cotton Picking, Whooping Cough, and Potions

When I was about five years old, Ma made my first burlap sack for picking cotton and gave it to me. Every school year after the first six weeks' grading period, the school administration dismissed classes for six weeks so that students could help with the cotton harvest. There were several farmers in Cleburne County who raised cotton, especially in the Miller and Shiloh communities. The local cotton gin was owned and operated by Dick Hunt, who was also the owner of a big mercantile store in the Lone Pine community.

Since Pa never planted cotton, our big family packed our big GMC truck with bedding, cooking utensils, and other needed items and traveled to Monette, Arkansas, in Craighead County for the annual cotton harvest.

From the time I was five years old until I was seventeen, we picked cotton for a farmer by the name of Claude Neely and his father-in-law, Lee Milligan. Each year we stayed in Mr. Milligan's old house near the cotton field. The old house had two bedrooms, a living room, and a kitchen/dining room. With all our mattresses on the floor, there was hardly room to tiptoe between them. The house had no toilet and no running water. We had to get our water from a well and pump outside the house.

After dark, we boys would go to the pump area with washcloths, towels, and a bar of soap. We would remove our shoes and clothes and take sponge baths. Some nights we were too tired and skipped the sponge baths. That was a big mistake. That's when sand trickled down from our bodies and made its presence known in our beds.

Ma cooked our meals on a two-burner butane stove. We had no oven, so we had to buy sandwich bread to eat. I sure missed my mother's homemade biscuits.

Ma and my older sisters washed our clothes in a big galvanized tub using a scrubbing board and soap to get the stains out. After washing our clothes, they squeezed out the excess water with their hands and pinned the wet clothes on a clothes line supported by two-by-four wooden posts. Depending on the wind and humidity, it took several hours for the clothes to dry.

There were two things that I literally hated about picking cotton at Monette. First, I hated going to bed nightly in a gritty bed. There was little room between the mattresses, so when we pulled off our blue jeans, a good deal of sand found its way into our beds. It was very uncomfortable trying to sleep in a bed with sand.

On Saturdays Imogene, Betty, Loudeen and Ella Mae washed the sheets. I always looked forward to going to bed on Saturday nights after Ma had put the clean sheets back on our beds.

The second thing I hated was getting up early. Ma would get us up before daylight and feed us breakfast. It was important to start picking cotton as early as we could see the bolls of cotton. Cotton weighs more when it is wet. The dew on the cotton didn't dissipate until the sun came out and dried the dew away. Since we got paid by the pound, we tried to pick as much cotton as possible in our first sack. It always weighed the most.

Because of our large family, we made good money during the six weeks of cotton harvesting. We were paid three to four cents a pound for every pound we picked. Almost all my older siblings could pick at least three hundred pounds of cotton a day. It was not until I was fourteen, though, that I accomplished picking three hundred pounds. One of my sisters, Loudeen, was the cotton-picking champion of our family. She could pick up to four hundred pounds of cotton on a daily basis.

Ma insisted her daughters not lift anything heavy, so we boys got the responsibility of carrying their sacks of cotton to the weighing station. We'd pick the heavy sack up, throw it over one shoulder, and carry it to the weighing station, sometimes a long distance away. I now know how hard that was on our backs. As I am writing this, I am seventy-two years old. To this day, all my brothers and I have back problems.

The weighing station was a big wagon with large sideboards reaching about five feet above the main base of the wagon. It was a real challenge to pull a one hundred pound sack of cotton over the sideboards to empty the cotton into the wagon. I always had to have assistance from the person on the ground that weighed the cotton. He would get under the sack on the ground and push it upward as I pulled. It would take all my strength, but we would finally succeed in getting the sack over the sideboards so I could empty the cotton from the sack into the wagon. Picking cotton by hand was a big and difficult job, but the hardest part was dumping those hundred-pound sacks of cotton.

I hated going to the cotton patch more than anything we did as migrant workers. It was a nasty job. Our hands bled the first two weeks because of the sharp cotton burs puncturing our fingers and palms. It normally took two weeks for calluses to form, thereby preventing further damage to our hands.

After six weeks, we returned to our home in Higden and continued our schooling at Post Oak, a two-room schoolhouse for grades one through eight. The rock building was built by the U.S. government's Works Progress Administration (WPA) program near the beginning of the Great Depression. The building stands to this day. The interior of the building has been renovated into a worship center, and today the building is the home of a Baptist church.

When I turned six, Jim, Roy, and I rode a red horse with a white blaze forehead to school daily. We called him Big Red, even though his coat made it look like he was wearing white stockings just above his hooves. He was a gentle horse and could be trusted to get us to and from school each day.

My brother, Jimmy, being the oldest on Big Red, was given the responsibility of handling the reins. Because I was the youngest, Ma made sure I rode in the middle, with Jimmy in front and Roy in back. She didn't want me to fall off. Roy was the one who had to worry about falling off, however. I will never forget when Roy did fall off Big Red. We were riding home from school, traveling down a narrow lane leading to our house, when a copperhead snake spooked Big Red. It happened so quickly that Big Red reared on his back feet forcing Roy off. He fell on the hard ground. Luckily, he did not break anything.

After Jimmy got control of Big Red, he said to Roy, "Get that big rock over there and kill that damn snake." Jimmy was known at times to let a few bad words slip out of his mouth. This was one of those times. Roy did as Jimmy instructed. After killing the snake, Roy decided to walk the rest of the way home.

I got my first paddling in school while attending first grade at Post Oak. I was very mischievous, not mean, but full of spirit. I can still remember the incident clearly. Two of my friends and I decided to scare three neighboring girls by throwing rocks at the outside toilet. We waited until they had entered the toilet before throwing the rocks. We had no intention of hurting any of them, but, lo and behold, one of the girls, Jean Stark, came running out of the toilet screaming. I had already released one of my rocks, and it struck her in the head. I was thankful it was a small rock. Jean ran inside and informed our teacher, Mrs. Smith, that one of the boys throwing rocks had hit her in the head. She was crying like she was dying. I thought she was being overly dramatic until I saw the big knot on her forehead. Needless to say, it didn't take Mrs. Smith long to parade us into her office where she seemed to joyfully administer three licks each to our tender buttocks.

Mrs. Smith was small in stature, but let me assure you, she could swing a wicked paddle. I cried, and so did my friends, LaVaugn Davis and Wayne Stark. However, we learned a great lesson that day—to respect the outside toilet and those who entered in.

Not only was my butt hurting, but I had to live with the anguish thinking about what was going to happen to me when I got home. In that era in rural Arkansas, in our family and many others, it was a standing rule that if you got in trouble at school and received a paddling, you would get another when you got home.

In our family, if we failed to fess up and tell Pa and Ma about the whipping and they found out from another source, we would get double punishment. I knew that Mrs. Smith's paddling wasn't the only sting I'd feel that day.

In all my days living at home, I never thought this rule was fair. Yet it was like a rule written on stone tablets around our house, and that rule was consistently enforced in our family all the years of my siblings' and my public education.

When I was six, an epidemic of whooping cough hit our community and county. The Barger family was not exempt from the epidemic. Ma, Roy, and I all contracted the disease. We were awfully sick!

Dr. Birdsong quarantined us and instructed Pa not to let anyone near us, except those who were attending us. He gave Pa some medicine with instructions to give it to us every three hours. He also left aspirin for our fevers. We didn't know it at the time, but Dr. Birdsong told Pa that we might not survive the epidemic. There were some families in our community who had already lost family members.

All three of us were running high fevers, and our throats were so sore we could barely swallow. My mother was sick and weak to the point that she couldn't get out of bed. Pa and Loudeen even had to assist her in using the potty.

Ma had some old fashioned potions she believed in. One was gargling with warm salt water at least four times a day. She had Loudeen make another potion consisting of Vicks Vapor Rub, hog lard, and turpentine. Loudeen melted the three items together on the kitchen stove, dipped large cotton socks into the potion, squeezed out the excess potion, and tied the socks around our throats. The warm sock felt good. It helped soothe our throats and open our breathing passages.

Another treatment Ma used to help with our coughing was whisky. She instructed Loudeen to pour four ounces of whisky in a glass, add sugar, and stir until the sugar dissolved. She then had Loudeen give us a tablespoon of that concoction every two hours. It really helped with our coughs. It left a warm feeling in my throat, and I looked forward to the next dose.

Especially when we were sick, Ma believed in drinking lots of water and fruit juice. She insisted we drink eight glasses of water in a day's time. Because of all the extra water I drank, I had to make frequent visits to the big five-gallon bucket.

Ma's father, Elias Samuel Totten, died during this same whooping cough epidemic. Like us, he was a very sick man. Ma, Roy, and I were so weak we couldn't attend Grandpa's funeral. Ma grieved for days over the loss of her dad. She had always been strong and available during time of need, but this time, she wasn't able to do anything but lie in bed and grieve.

At some point Ma, Roy, and I turned the corner and began improving each day. By the grace of God, Ma's potions, Dr. Birdsong's medicine, and Loudeen's special care, we all survived the epidemic.

Once a year every year in our household, one of two events occurred that we kids literally hated. Those events have always been embedded in my memory, and I've questioned many times what scientific good came from either of them.

Ma believed strongly in both Black Draught and Chill Tonic. She believed that certain impurities get inside one's body and cause certain diseases. So once a year, to get rid of these impurities, Ma would give us a big dose of either Black Draught or Chill Tonic. I'm here to tell you that if it didn't kill you, it would certainly cure you. These tonics were given to us on Saturday mornings so we wouldn't be hindered in going to church on Sunday.

Ma would give us the tonics and tell us to drink a full glass of water. I would gag and try to throw it up, but for some reason, I never could. My sister, Ella Mae, was different. Every time she took her tonic, she would vomit. But Ma would keep giving it to her until it stayed down. In about an hour after we took it, we would meet each other coming and going to the outhouse for relief. If by chance someone was already in the toilet, we would have to go out behind the barn. Oh, what a miserable time that was!

Most every family in the Ozark Mountains practiced this annual event. These two tonics were stronger than the laxatives we have today. For some reason, the Black Draught and Chill Tonic were taken off the market. I never knew why, but my guess is that somebody may have died from their use.

Another event from my childhood is still embedded in my mind as well. This event occurred when all my siblings and I came down with the chicken pox. Again, Ma believed in the Ozark Mountain rituals that were passed down from generation to generation. According to this one, sitting in front of a chicken house and letting chickens fly over you would soften the effects of chicken pox.

At night, after the chickens went to roost, Pa went down and closed the front door of the chicken house so the chickens wouldn't be able to get out the next morning. After breakfast, Pa and Ma told us that we were going to the chicken house to participate in this ritual. Some of my older brothers had some knowledge of what was going to happen and began to complain.

"Do we have to?" Willie asked.

"Yes, you do," Ma said.

"This is really stupid," Willie said.

"Willie, just because of your complaining, you will sit in front," Pa said.

That was an experience I shall never forget. We sat down in front of the chicken house doorway. Then Pa went in and chased the chickens through the open door. All of us were afraid that when the chickens flew over us their spurs would hit us in the face; we buried our faces in our hands for protection.

I'm here to tell you, when those chickens came flying through the door, they went in all directions. Some flew to the west, some to the east, and some directly over us to the south. I've never experienced so much chaos. Some landed right in the middle of us. My sister, Ella Mae, was crying from her fear of the chickens. The chickens stirred up lots of dust that landed on us.

I must confess, Ma seemed to be right once again as we all ended up with a mild case of chicken pox. No one but God really knows if our mild cases were due to the chicken ritual, but Ma had no doubts.

It is my theory, and always will be, that the fear of those chickens flying over us scared us so badly, it frightened the chicken pox right out of our bodies.

Ma knew this lady in our community who could remove warts by reading scriptures from the Bible. The lady would tie a knot with sewing thread, place it around the wart, and repeat some kind of chant over and over. She would then remove the thread and place it under a rock. After a few days, the wart would disappear.

She removed warts from several of my brothers and sisters over the years.

My sister, Loudeen, had freckles when she was a child and teenager. There was some kind of potion Ma used with Loudeen to remove the freckles. I remember removing water from a hollow tree stump to make the potion. Then she would have Loudeen wash her face in it over many days. I don't know what Ma added to the tree stump water, if anything, but after washing with it for a certain period of time, the freckles went away. Don't ask me for the potion's formula, because I was too young to remember. I just know that it worked.

CHAPTER 8

Rusty Nail, California, and Strawberries

When I was about five years old, Ma and Pa decided to build a new house. Those who came to help them were Buster Bittle, a neighbor; Harvey, my brother; and J. D. Stark, my brother-in-law who was married to my sister, Betty.

About this time, my oldest brother, Harvey, purchased a used Model T Ford. He was so proud of it and loved showing it off by giving us rides around the pasture. We had never ridden in any car before, so this was a real treat.

One morning, as Harvey was getting ready to go to work at Dudeck's sawmill, he went out to crank his car. To start early Model Ts, one had to manually crank the engine. After cranking over and over with no success, Harvey began kicking the tires while saying some choice swear words.

Ma hollered at him and said, "Harvey, you cussing that car ain't gonna do you any good at all, and kicking it is not going to hurt that car."

Harvey was so mad. He picked up a big rock and threw it through the front windshield, shattering it to pieces. He stomped and raved and finally sat down from exhaustion.

After he calmed down, he grabbed his dinner bucket and off he went walking to DuDeck's Sawmill. He had earned enough money at the mill to purchase the old car. Although he was frustrated and mad, he knew he had to go to work or be fired.

After he arrived at work, Harvey shared with his foreman why he was late. His foreman laughed and said, “Did you check to see if the car had any gas in the tank?”

“No, Sir, I didn’t think about that!”

“Well, maybe you need to take a gallon of gas home with you today and see if that might be your problem.”

It was five-thirty in the afternoon when Harvey returned home from work. We saw him coming over the hill carrying a one-gallon container of gasoline. After arriving home, he checked the gas tank. We heard him cussing. Indeed, the car was out of gas.

As we watched Harvey crank the old car, it sputtered like it wanted to start, but didn’t. He was about to lose his temper again when Willie said, “Harvey, why don’t you get in your car and let us push you. Maybe the car will start if we can get up enough speed for you to clutch it.”

“Well, it’s worth a try,” Harvey said.

We got behind the car and started pushing it down a hill. Harvey popped the clutch, and the car started. After gas got to the carburetor, it ran like a charm.

Harvey learned a valuable lesson that day about dealing with automobiles. Some of his hard-earned money went for the purchase of a new windshield.

After that particular incident, Harvey worked to control his temper. He realized that patience pays more dividends than losing one’s temper. He learned that money goes further when one trumps emotion with reason.

When I was seven years old, Pa and Ma decided to move to Exeter, California, to harvest fruit. Ma’s sister, Pearl Mayben, lived in Exeter, a quaint little town near Portersville, California. Ma’s oldest sister, Martha Cupler, lived in Rio Osa, California. Between the two, they convinced Ma that lots of money could be made with large families picking fruit and cotton in and around Exeter and Rio Osa.

What Ma’s sisters didn’t tell her was that California had begun enforcing the Child Labor Law. School-aged children had to attend classes during school hours and were only available to work in the afternoons after school and on weekends.

It didn't take my parents long to figure out that, without our help, their expectations of getting rich from picking fruit and cotton in those beautiful fruit and cotton fields around Exeter, California, weren't going to happen.

We children still made pretty good money when we were allowed to work, but nothing like we made when working full time. We spent less than a year in California before Pa decided to move our family back to Arkansas. It was sad for Ma to leave her sisters behind, but she knew that Pa's decision was for the best.

California was a wonderful learning experience for me. The only other state I had lived in besides Arkansas was Michigan. I enjoyed traveling and seeing all the different landscapes. I loved Okie, the little sub-community of Exeter, where my family and Aunt Pearl's family lived. Okie was a quaint little place made up mostly of people from Oklahoma who had come there during the depression to harvest fruit. There were only three streets in Okie, and all three ran north and south.

Lloyd and Lois Mayben, my twin cousins, had some of the same interests that I had. We were all in the second grade at Exeter. Every Saturday we would go up and down the streets in Okie selling or trading our comic books.

Dealing in comic-book selling, trading, and buying was the biggest thing to do as kids in Okie. I loved comic books, and every child I knew in the neighborhood had some. I was not a big reader of regular books, but I loved reading comic books. They could be read in a single session, unlike big books, and one could really get involved in keeping up with Dennis the Menace, the Lone Ranger, Superman, and other favorite comic book characters.

Porterville and Exeter were located in a valley surrounded by beautiful mountains. Concrete canals ran along the bottom of the mountains. These canals were full of water and used by the farmers for irrigating their fruit orchards and cotton fields.

On several occasions, my cousins, brothers, sisters, and I went hiking in the mountains. There were several locations along the trail where we could sit and look out over the beautiful valley below. The valley came alive with beautiful, lush orange groves, cotton fields, peach and apple orchards, and many other types of fruit trees. It was like a picture of paradise that was good for everyone's soul.

Exeter had a movie theater that we sometimes went to on weekends. My cousin, Helen Mayben, worked in ticket sales and got us a family rate. I was living in California the first time I went to the movies. I was in awe of the big theater screen.

I can still remember the first movie I saw in Exeter: *Superman*. I loved that movie. I had never seen anything like it. I sat there trying to figure out where Superman got his powers to fly and pick up buildings, cars, and all that other stuff. It was certainly a mind-boggling and eye-opening experience for this little hillbilly from the Ozark Mountains of Cleburne County.

I loved the elementary school in Exeter as well. The curriculum was much broader than I had experienced back at Post Oak. The teachers used many educational movies as teaching aides. One such movie still stands out in my mind today. It was a film on tarantulas. I can still see those big hairy-legged creatures crawling everywhere. The teacher told us that most of them are harmless, but they still scare the heck out of me every time I see one.

After returning to Arkansas, I found myself repeating the second grade at West Side Public Schools. It wasn't because I was dumb, but because of the Arkansas Attendance Law. The State of Arkansas requires a student to attend a certain number of days before being promoted to the next grade. At first, I didn't like repeating the second grade, but later I realized it was in my best interest.

After completing the second grade at West Side, we Bargers resumed our migrant travels. In early spring, we traveled to Marshall, Arkansas, the strawberry capital of Arkansas.

Several in our community commuted daily to Marshall to pick strawberries. Marshall was a beautiful little town located in Searcy County. It was an economically deprived county, but farmers and ranchers there raised strawberries, cattle, and chickens. Ma used the money we made picking strawberries in Marshall each year to pay our expenses to Michigan.

The strawberry patches were located on hills with lots of rocks—flint rocks: very pretty, white, and slick. It was really unique how the farmers planted their strawberries. They'd lift up a flint rock, insert the strawberry plant into the hole, and place the flint rock over the root of the plant. It wasn't long before the plants began to grow, shooting sprouts in all directions. Because the strawberries lay on top of the flint rocks, they were not dirty and did not decay like strawberries that touch the ground.

To pick strawberries in Marshall, the workers had to walk to the bottom of the strawberry row with an eight-quart tray. They had to pick uphill while standing, bracing themselves from falling backwards. Almost all of the strawberry patches in Marshall were located on hills.

One of the best things to come out of Marshall was my sister-in-law, Norma Cooper. We picked strawberries for Dorsey and Helen Horton. Helen was Norma's older sister.

One day, my older brother, Willie, and I had gone to a local grocery store to buy some bologna, cheese, and bread for lunch. Willie was driving our new red Ford pickup. As we approached the packing shed, my brother Willie said, "See that pretty girl working in the packing shed?"

"Yes, I see her. What about her?"

"Watch and learn, Little Brother."

Willie pulled up in front of the shed and stuck his head out the window and said, "Hey, good looking, what's cooking?"

The girl smiled and said, "I don't know, what's cooking with you?"

That was the beginning of a short courtship. Willie married that girl from Marshall, Arkansas.

CHAPTER 9

Fantasies, Television, and Dares

The migrant way of living taught me valuable life principles, principles I've been able to use to improve my quality of life. It was a rough existence, living in not-so-perfect housing and with limited hygiene standards, yet we survived.

I can still remember my last year in Benton Harbor, Michigan. I had been picking strawberries all morning and was exhausted. My knees were hurting from the hours I had spent crawling on the ground. As I tossed fresh red strawberries into the eight-quart strawberry cart, I began to fantasize.

To pass the time away, I fantasized a lot. Most of my fantasies were related to either being one of the greatest actors of all time, even greater than the great Spencer Tracy, who won a record four Oscars at the Academy Awards.

I also spent a lot of time fantasizing about sports. I loved basketball and baseball and hoped to play those sports in college someday. Anyway, I decided to quit fantasizing and have a good talk with God.

I said, "God, there has to be something better for me than being a migrant worker the rest of my life. I'm sure, with your powers and wisdom, you're well aware of my desire to do something else with my life. I'm asking for your blessings, Lord. I really don't have anything particular to ask for, but something maybe easier and more engaging than migrant work. Lord, it can be anything that will get me up off these aching knees. Something, Lord, in which I can make a real difference in my life as well as the lives of others. If you will do this Lord, I'll be eternally grateful, and I'll serve you the rest of my life."

I counted on my Lord to know my heart and my thoughts and for Him to know I would serve Him whether he helped me or not. I've always believed God has a purpose and place for each of us, and I accepted that through my faith in Him. I guess I was hoping the all-knowing Lord, with His undying love for me, would react kindly to my request.

The year I had this talk with the Lord was the last year my family and I went to Benton Harbor, Michigan, to harvest fruit.

In 1957, Pa and Ma built another new home, with a grocery store and a gas station on a one-acre piece of property on Highway 16, in the Stark community, about eight miles from Heber Springs, Arkansas.

About the time we moved into our new home, Pa bought the family our first television, which came with an antenna. At times, we had to go out and turn the antenna to get good reception. On clear days we could get four channels. Our family thought television was the best invention this side of heaven. It brought a new dimension to our lives and frequently presented life from a different perspective than what we had previously experienced.

Before television, we were quite uneducated about what was going on in other parts of the world. Pa and Ma didn't have to worry about screening any of the television shows we watched. During this era, curse words, sexual scenes, and violence were not allowed on television.

Some of our favorite shows were *The Roy Rogers Show* (which also starred Roy's wife, Dale Evans), *I Love Lucy*, *The Red Skelton Show*, *The Ed Sullivan Show*, *The Lawrence Welk Show*, *The Gene Autry Show*, and sports shows like boxing, baseball, and wrestling. I guess you could say we liked everything.

My oldest sister, Imogene, lived next door to us. Her three children—Joy Ann, Linda, and Tommy—spent more time in our house than in their own. They were great kids. Joy Ann was the oldest and four years behind me in age. She was my shadow. Everywhere I went, she was right behind me. I loved her then, and I still love her today.

One day after school, when my sisters Ella Mae and Leona Faye and I walked through the front door, we noticed that Ma, Pa, and Roy were watching *The Edge of Night*, a popular soap opera, featuring Mike and Sarah Carr. Mike was a lawyer, and his wife, Sarah, was a housewife. It wasn't uncommon to walk in the front door and see our parents watching *The Edge of Night*, but this day was different. All three of them were crying. Ella Mae looked at me, and I looked at her. We didn't know what was going on. I finally said, "Hey, what's going on?" Ma was crying so hard she was actually boohooing, literally.

"Will someone tell us what's going on?"

Ma finally looked at me and said, "Sarah just got killed."

Since I knew soap operas were not true to life, I started laughing. That was a big mistake! I also proceeded to tell them that it was only a television show. That was my second mistake. The third mistake was definitely the wrong thing to do. I tried to tell them she wasn't really dead, and she'd be back on another show.

Ma had taken all of my smart mouth she could handle. She picked up a tennis shoe and threw it at me with all the force she could muster. She looked at me and said, "You get out of here! Now! Go shoot some basketball!"

I didn't dare say another word. I left immediately and did exactly as Ma had ordered. I had struck a nerve. I didn't realize they were so deeply involved with *The Edge of Night*.

When we first got the television, I would get amused at Pa when he'd be watching a western and see some actor who was killed in another show. Pa would say, "This can't be! That guy was killed in a show the other day!" I tried to explain to him that he hadn't really been killed; he was just playing a different role or a different character. I never was able to figure out if Pa was just playing with me about the television stars.

Pa loved wrestling on television! He couldn't get enough of it. Wrestling in those days was so fake, but many of the older people in our community, like Pa, thought it was genuine and super good.

Besides playing basketball, there wasn't much to do in the little community of Stark. We went to the movies on Saturdays in Heber Springs and to church on Sundays.

It was during my sophomore year that I got hooked on rock and roll music. Elvis Presley was my favorite actor and singer. I know it might sound funny hearing it from a male admirer, but he was truly my idol. He was the king of rock and roll. Every time one of his movies came to the GEM Theater in Heber Springs, I was there. Every time I went to see one of his movies, I noticed that we boys were outnumbered by the girls in attendance. At Elvis's movies, like *Jail House Rock* and *Love Me Tender*, the girls would literally fall out of their seats with emotion.

It was during my sophomore year that I fell from grace and started dancing. I loved dancing. My neighbors, Martha Stark and her daughter, Jean, loved rock and roll as much as I did. They watched the *Steve Steven's Show*, which featured teenagers dancing every Saturday out of Little Rock, Arkansas. Martha took it on herself to link Jean and me up as dance partners. We went to several local parties and danced. We had gotten pretty good, and Martha thought we were good enough to go on the *Steve Steven's Show*.

Even though the *Steve Steven's Show* originated from Little Rock, young people from all over Arkansas went to dance on his show and compete in dance contests.

There was one thing that prohibited our appearance on this live television show. I was a member of the Church of Christ, and our church didn't believe in dancing. If I were seen dancing on the *Steve Steven's Show*, I would be an embarrassment to my family and the church. I might be kicked out of the church as well. After analyzing the situation, I decided I had to decline the opportunity to go to Little Rock to compete. Although I wanted to go badly, I knew I had made the right decision. I didn't want to be a stumbling block to those that considered dancing a sin.

When we lived on Highway 16, we became friends with neighboring boys who were not afraid to do almost anything.

I thought on several occasions that if they met the devil, they would not be afraid to fight him.

The most popular, and perhaps the most dangerous game we boys played, was Chicken. One of us would do something and then dare someone else to do the same thing. If one refused, he was labeled a chicken. I think I was the champion when it came to being labeled chicken.

I never thought of myself as being very smart in book learning, but I had good common sense. I think I learned or inherited that from Ma. When it came to the game of Chicken, I found it to be too dangerous for my blood on several occasions.

The most dangerous thing my friends did involved climbing the big bluffs that ran along the sides of the Little Red River. They would climb all the way up to the top of the bluff, find and climb a tall tree, jump out and catch a tree limb, and then, with that momentum, shimmy down the tree until they were on the ground. To me this activity was complete idiocy. I could just see myself missing the tree limb and someone having to scoop up my brains that had splattered all over the ground from a fall of thirty-five feet. Every time they played that game, my two brothers, Jim and Roy, participated. I prayed for their safety each time they jumped out onto one of those limbs. I guess I valued my life more than they did. I loved life and surely didn't want to contribute to my death before my time.

Another thing I refused to do at first, was to bend a young persimmon tree over and, while three or four boys held it down, grab the top of the tree, after which the others would turn the tree loose. The tree would immediately spring back with amazing speed and leave the person at the top hanging on for dear life. That was some kind of thrill. If one didn't hold on tight, however, he would take a big fall and probably break several bones, maybe his neck! Fortunately, no one ever got hurt. I took that dare one time, and that was enough!

There weren't many things we boys couldn't and wouldn't do. We made our own entertainment as we played and, with the grace of God, we survived. Some of the things we did were at odds with the common sense I wrote about in the pages above.

On the other hand, learning from my friends', brothers', and my own mistakes may have contributed to the common sense I have.

There were other Chicken-type games we tried that weren't so dangerous, at least not life threatening. One of those dares was to inhale while smoking a cigarette. I had smoked a cigarette before, but never inhaled.

My friend, Lynn Stark, took me to the woods one day and dared me to inhale. I took the dare. I thought, *What harm could come from inhaling one small puff on a cigarette?*

Lynn rolled the cigarette with Prince Albert tobacco. He took a match, lit the cigarette, took a big puff, and inhaled it. Soon, the smoke started coming out of his nose. He made it look easy. He handed me the cigarette and said, "Now, take a big puff and suck it in."

I took a big puff and breathed it in. I knew quickly I had done something terribly wrong. There was no smoke coming out of my nose. I began to cough. I was in deep trouble. Lynn, seeing that I was strangling, started hitting me on the back. I literally thought I was dying. Lynn's quick response worked, and I eventually returned to my normal self.

"Carl, what happened?" Lynn asked.

"I did what you did, and it didn't work for me."

"You didn't do it right! You were supposed to hesitate until the smoke started coming back from your lungs and then blow it out through your nose."

"I don't care! You can have your smoking. It's not for me!"

Lynn laughed and said, "Someday you will get the hang of it!"

"Don't count on it, friend!" I said.

I decided right then and there that I was going to be a non-smoker. Since that day, I've never again tried inhaling cigarette smoke.

Lynn later dared me to drink moonshine. I don't know exactly where he got the moonshine, but it wasn't very hard to find it among hill folks. Once again, I took the dare. He took a big swallow and said, "Boy, is this ever good!" He handed me the jar, and I took a big swallow. Immediately, I thought my insides were on fire. That stuff burned me all the way down to my gizzard. Why on earth did I let him talk me into drinking that awful stuff?

Again, I learned a great lesson. I have always avoided both smoking and drinking from those first tries to the present.

The Chicken games continued from time to time with a dare from my friend, Lynn Stark. The last dare I can remember taking from him was peeing on a live electric fence.

One day we were crossing a field that led back to his house. Mr. Walter Stark, Lynn's father, had erected an electric fence to keep his cows from leaving a certain pasture. The fence was about waist high. In times past, we had crawled under the fence to avoid touching it. On this particular day, however, Lynn was feeling his oats and dared me to pee on the fence. I was so dumb about scientific things so I said, "All right, I'll take your dare!"

Since I needed to pee anyway, I didn't see any harm in peeing on the fence. As I relieved myself, I was immediately knocked backward with a strong painful shock. I had never in my live felt such pain; it shot through my entire body. I screamed as I fell backwards to the ground. I was so mad that I wanted to kill Lynn. For reasons that remain obscure to me, Lynn had some kind of influence over me. He almost always was able to get me to do things that I shouldn't have done and wouldn't have with anyone else. However, the fence escapade was the last time I accepted one of Lynn's dares. We continued to be the best of friends up to the day my parents moved to yet another new home in Pearson, Arkansas. After our move, I saw very little of my good friend, Lynn Stark.

CHAPTER 10

Moving and Improving

In the summer of 1960, we moved into our new house in Pearson, a small community located eight miles from Quitman and eight miles from Heber Springs. The way the school districts were drawn up, our residence was in the Quitman school district.

The location of our new home was on a forty-acre farm that was about one and half miles south of Highway 25, which ran through Quitman and on to Heber Springs.

The only thing I didn't like about the location of our new home was the walk to the bus stop. Every morning, come rain, snow, or sunshine, my sisters, Ella Mae and Faye, and I walked to the bus stop, which was about a half mile from our house. We lived on a narrow dirt road that didn't have a place large enough for a bus to turn around, so we had to walk the half mile to catch the bus.

Our new house was the third—and the best—house Ma and Pa had built. They were both excellent carpenters. My mother learned a lot of her carpentry skills from her father, an excellent carpenter, who had built several houses for people in the their neighborhood.

Pa purchased an old two-story house in the Shiloh community, not far from where we lived in Stark. The house had a lot of good lumber, and its foundation was made of big square timbers similar to railroad ties, but larger. All houses in the city of Shiloh had to be moved because of the coming Greers Ferry Lake. In fact, all of what was Shiloh is now under water.

The lumber that came from the old house supplied most of the lumber needed to build our new house in Pearson. The only other materials we needed were some new rafters and tin for the roof. The new house had four bedrooms, a kitchen, a living room, and a new indoor bathroom. We also had electricity.

I was excited also, because this was the first time I would have my own bedroom. I no longer had to sleep with my brothers, unless we had company, of course.

I was also happy about the new indoor bathroom. Never again would I have to go outside to use the toilet. I hated going out in the cold, rain, and snow, especially at night when one needed a flashlight to see the path to walk to the toilet. Perhaps the best thing I liked about the new indoor bathroom was that I didn't have to use Sears catalog pages for wipes.

My brother Willie was responsible for our having indoor plumbing. He had moved to the big city of St. Louis, Missouri, to work. While he was there, he became *citified*, so to speak. He wanted my folks to enjoy the luxury of indoor plumbing. He bought Ma a new gas cook stove, the first one she had cooked on. This made her a very happy lady. I too was happy because I no longer had to cut kindling for her wood cook stove.

Willie arranged for the installation of a water pump in the well so she could have running water and a sink in her kitchen. All the new conveniences cut my chores in half. However, I still had to milk two cows every night. My brother Roy did the milking in the morning, since I was still attending high school.

The move to Pearson and enrolling in the Quitman Public School System was the best thing for me at that stage of my life.

When I attended West Side Public Schools, I developed a bad attitude. The number of whippings I received from Mr. Elmer Gathright, our superintendent and chief disciplinarian, were largely responsible for my stinking attitude. I went around school with a big chip on my shoulder. I developed an I-don't-care attitude toward my teachers. I became paranoid thinking they didn't like me and didn't care whether I passed or failed.

I didn't understand it at that time, but later I realized that I had brought all this on myself. It wasn't their fault; it was mine. They just had gotten fed up with dealing with me and my attitude on a day-to-day basis.

All I wanted to do was play basketball and make good enough grades to stay eligible.

The only two teachers who offered encouragement during my ninth-grade year were my basketball coach, Charles Brady, and my civics teacher, Mrs. Ann Mullins. Both seemed to see potential in me and motivated me to do better.

When I was in the tenth grade, I begin to see some change in my attitude. Mrs. Flossie Woods joined Coach Brady and Mrs. Mullins in motivating me. Mrs. Woods taught English. Before Mrs. Wood became my teacher, I was butchering the English language. I actually started making Cs and some Bs on my grammar tests. Every time I improved on a test, Mrs. Woods complimented me. I loved being complimented. That was a new thing for me!

I loved Mrs. Mullins's civics class. I loved studying government and had developed an interest in politics. Politics still intrigues me today. After developing an interest in civics, I decided I wanted to beat Lena Dollar, who had not made anything but As her entire life.

By the tenth grade, I had developed an interest in her, but she didn't know it. Her beautiful brown eyes, black hair, sweet smile, and dark complexion fascinated me. I admired her because she came from a poor family just like me, but she didn't let that stand in her way.

Her father, Leonard Dollar, died when she was nine years old leaving his wife, Milbra Mae Dollar, and four daughters. Lena was the oldest of the four, followed by Earlene, Virginia, and Patsy Ann. Lena's intelligence was remarkable. She could handle about any assignment a teacher dished out, and the teachers loved her. When they needed someone to assist them in an academic activity, they would ask Lena to help.

Because of her intelligence, I wanted to beat her at something. So, I set myself a goal to make an A in civics. I knew she would make an A, but I wanted my A to be a better percentage A than hers.

When the final grades were averaged, I was surprised and excited to learn that I had accomplished my goal. I had the highest average in class. Lena was second. That may have been the first A that I had ever made in school. I cannot begin to describe what that A meant to my mental state. It inspired me and made me want to do better in my other subject areas as well.

Over the years, I've concluded that the person most responsible for the turning point in my life had to have been Lena. Without my desire to beat her at something, my life may never have changed.

She presented the challenge of competition for me that led to my becoming a better student and maybe being perceived as a decent human being, at least in the eyes of my teachers.

CHAPTER 11

Coming into My Own

My enrollment in the Quitman Public School System was a blessing. It was the beginning of changes in my life that helped me develop both character and attitude.

Although, it was my first day in a new school, I felt pretty secure. I was like Ma in several ways. She never met a stranger. I wasn't shy and certainly didn't mind asking questions. I had asked my bus driver, Russell Davies, what I needed to do to get my baby sister, Leona Faye, enrolled in the elementary school.

He asked, "Have you been to any of the buildings on campus?"

"No, Sir," I said.

I explained to him that we had just moved to the Pearson community and had not had an opportunity to visit the Quitman schools.

"When we arrive at school, I'll show you where the elementary and high schools are located," he said.

"Thanks, Mr. Davies," I said.

I liked Russell Davies from the beginning, because he immediately took a liking to me. He loved basketball and was the basketball team's bus driver during basketball season. We started talking about basketball, and when he found out I had come from West Side, he said, "I may have watched you play basketball. What position did you play?"

"When I played, I was either a forward or center. I was the sixth in the lineup. Coach Brady played me often, but never started me unless one of his main players was hurt or sick."

"How is your outside shot, Carl?"

"That's my strong point. I'm pretty consistent with my outside shots. If I have a couple of seconds to get my shot off, I'll hit the biggest majority of my shots."

"If we had someone who could hit the outside shot, we'd have a good senior boys basketball team this year," he said.

"In that case, maybe I can be of some help to the basketball team," I said.

"Well, you've got the size for a basketball player. I'm betting Coach Solomon will be happy to see you sign up for basketball."

Upon arriving at school, Mr. Davies pointed toward the elementary school and said, "There's the elementary school. Go to the middle door, that's the principal's office. Someone will help you get your sister enrolled. You can come back here and go to the high school. The principal's office is to the left. Mr. Lonnie Rowlett is the principal. You tell him that Mr. Russell said you are special," he laughed.

After getting off the bus, Ella Mae and I accompanied Faye to the elementary school, where I helped her enroll. After leaving Faye at the elementary school, Ella Mae and I did exactly what Mr. Davies had told me to do: We reported to the crowded principal's office and were greeted by Mrs. Rowlett's secretary.

"May I help you?" she asked.

"Yes, Ma'am, my name is Carl Barger and this is my sister, Ella Mae. We are new students."

"Carl, you and your sister take these papers, go over there, fill them out, and bring them back to me," she said, pointing to two student desks next to the wall.

After filling out the papers, we went back to the counter and gave the secretary the papers. She looked the papers over and said, "I'll see that Mr. Rowlett gets these papers. You and your sister go on to the assembly. Mr. Rowlett will be giving everyone instructions during the assembly. After he's finished, he will tell new students what to do."

Ella Mae and I left the principal's office and went into a large auditorium full of students. The assembly had not yet started, for which I was very thankful. I would have been embarrassed to walk into an assembly while the principal was making a speech.

Ella Mae and I were standing by the wall looking for empty chairs, when someone touched me on the shoulder. I turned around to see a young man about my size smiling.

He said, "I'm Carroll Rhoades. You are new here, aren't you?"

"Yes, we are. We are rather lost right now," I said.

"Come with me. You and your sister can sit back in the back with me and some of my friends."

We followed Carroll to the back of the auditorium where some of his friends were sitting. I could tell right away that Carroll Rhoades had the respect of the other students. He introduced Ella Mae and me to his friends and we sat down. He took a seat by me and began to tell me a little about what was going to take place. He seemed to have a keen understanding of how we were feeling, being in a strange place.

"I hope we end up in some of the same classes," he said.

"I do to," I said.

"Do you play sports?"

"Yes, I play basketball and baseball."

"Me too," he said.

Mr. Rowlett entered the auditorium and introduced Mr. Olen Parrish, the school superintendent. Mr. Parrish welcomed everyone and encouraged us to do our best. After Mr. Rowlett's opening speech, he asked the new students to remain in the auditorium for additional information. The other students reported to their homerooms.

As Carroll was leaving, he said, "I'll look you up later and show you around." His friendliness was just what I needed. In my heart, I knew I was going to enjoy Quitman Public Schools.

Mr. Rowlett and two teachers helped us with our class assignments. Ella Mae, being in the ninth grade, would also be at the high school. I was happy that we'd be staying in the same building. She was a little on the shy side, so I would be there should she need me.

As it turned out, Carroll and I were in every class together. I was thankful for that!

With Carroll's help, it didn't take me long to get oriented to the high school. I learned quickly that if one wanted to have more time for lunch, one had to sprint as fast as one could to the cafeteria. The cafeteria was about the length of a football field from the high school. Those students who got there early didn't have to stand in line. They were able to get their food, eat, and have more time to socialize.

The high school was unique in several ways. It was a long building with a hallway down the middle that separated classrooms on each side of the hall.

The girls' and boys' restrooms were located at the end of the south entrance of the high school. Having outside restrooms made them hard to supervise. Lots of things went on in those restrooms that didn't always comply with school rules, if you know what I mean! When the smoke got thick, I thought of a line in a popular song, "Fe fi fo fum, who's that smoking in the auditorium? Charlie Brown! He's a clown!"

There was a concrete sidewalk that extended all around the high school and played a major role in determining who was popular among the students. If one wanted to be among the most popular boys with the girls, he would invite a girl to walk around the school with him. If she accepted the invitation and they walked around the building three consecutive days in a row, they were considered going steady.

There were some girls I liked, but I didn't want to get caught up in that three consecutive day thing.

Carroll and Tommy Bateman, another boy I became friends with, told me the girls considered me to be cool. I have to admit, it did something for my ego. It made me feel pretty good to be labeled a cool guy.

The first conflict I encountered in Quitman was when I beat a home town boy out of a starting position on the basketball team. The person had been a starter for two years. I can understand how he was feeling, but I felt I had earned the starting role.

Jimmy Solomon was our coach, and he didn't let community pressure determine who played or didn't play. He was fair with all his players. If I hadn't have earned my position, I certainly wouldn't have been starting.

Anyway, over a period of time, we resolved our differences and became good friends. I worked hard, and, like my older brothers, I could put some points on the score board. I was a natural outside shooter. I became that outside shooter that Mr. Davies had said was needed for Quitman to have a good team. Coach Solomon worked us hard. We were in excellent shape. As time went on, our team developed into a county championship team.

My old school, West Side, was traditionally strong in basketball and had won the Cleburne County Tournament more times than any other school in the county. But it was Quitman's time to shine. We beat West Side *at* West Side in the finals of the Cleburne County Tournament in my junior year. I was named to the Cleburne County All-Tournament Team, an accomplishment I probably wouldn't have received if I had stayed at West Side.

My favorite class was agriculture. Since I grew up on a farm, I thought I had some knowledge of the course content. I loved the agriculture teacher, Mr. Reedy Turney, who right away showed an interest in me. He encouraged me and motivated me to do the very best in everything I did. It was because of him that I learned to discipline myself when it came to academics and sports. It wasn't long before I went from a C average student to an A and B student at Quitman.

The sense of achievement really did something for me. As I've mentioned previously, I was not a very good student prior to moving to Quitman, mainly because of my attitude.

I also loved my American history teacher, Mrs. Ethel Groaner, who created a lot of interest for me. She made history come alive. She didn't try to lecture a lot, but got her students involved by discussion. I always liked discussions better than lectures.

Mrs. Groaner often called on me to help her get a discussion going on a particular subject. I think she knew I wouldn't object, because I loved to talk about historical events.

With Mrs. Groaner's and Mr. Turney's encouragement, I found myself in love with school. I even started thinking about the possibility of going to college. No one in my family had ever gone to college. My three older brothers, Willie, Jimmy, and Roy, were terrific basketball players and could have played college ball, but they all caught the love bug and got married instead.

During the district tournament, Quitman got beat in the semi-final game by two points. We were all heartbroken. The district was full of strong teams like Greenbrier, Mayflower, Plumerville, and Southside Bee Branch. I really don't think there was a weak team in our district. Although we lost the game to Mayflower, we were still proud of our accomplishment.

After we lost to Mayflower, Couch Solomon sat us down and gave us a strong pep talk. The first thing he said was, "I'm proud of all of you. Most of you will be returning next year. Let's set our goal to win the county and district tournaments and advance to state next year. Can we do that?" We were pumped up by his speech and shouted, "Win state, win state!" I was named a member of the all-district team, another honor I was quite proud of.

In the following spring, I made the starting lineup in baseball, playing third base. It was at that time that I begin to think I might be joining my brothers in the sports arena as a good athlete.

CHAPTER 12

The Beginning of a New Life

During my junior year, I returned to West Side to visit my friends at school. While I was there, Lena Dollar caught my eye. I had never seen anyone change as much as Lena had. She had really blossomed into a nice-looking young lady. I had always liked her from the second grade until I moved in the tenth grade, but she had shown me no interest. I think it was because of my bad attitude.

It was during this visit that I noticed something was different. As we were eating in the school cafeteria, I saw her looking in my direction. It appeared she was checking me out.

I asked my friend LaVaughn Davis if Lena was dating anyone. He said not to his knowledge. After lunch, I intentionally ran into her. We visited a while, and I asked her for a date. At first, I thought she was going to turn me down because of her body language. As I waited for an answer, my mind was telling me that she'd say, "Thank you, but I can't." She finally looked at me with a cute smile and asked, "When?"

I said, "How about this Saturday night?"

"I'll have to ask my mother, but I believe it will be okay."

"When can you let me know?"

"What is your phone number?"

I gave her my phone number, and she left for her scheduled history class.

Lena and I had our first date on Saturday night. We went to a movie in Heber Springs and later parked at the Lone Pine Church of Christ parking lot. Lone Pine is now part of Greers

Ferry, Arkansas. The Church of Christ building was where I attended church.

Parking was the most popular form of courting when I was growing up in Cleburne County. Normally, we would just sit around, listen to radio, talk about our friends, and discuss what we wanted to do after graduation. We both loved rock and roll and country music. We discovered quickly that we shared an interest in Elvis Presley. During the time we dated in high school, we saw several of Elvis's movies.

My favorite actress during the time Lena and I dated in high school was Natalie Wood. I loved her in *West Side Story* and *Splendor in the Grass*. In my opinion she and Elizabeth Taylor were the two best actresses who ever graced the movie screen.

I loved Elizabeth Taylor in *Rain Tree County*, *Cat on a Hot Tin Roof*, and, my favorite, *Suddenly Last Summer*. She later became my favorite actress of all time. I can still remember her soft, sexy voice. There will never be an actress who will top her magnificent talent and her true beauty on the big screen.

I used to fantasize that I played opposite Liz Taylor in a movie called, *Young Man, Bad Woman*. The only person I ever told that to was Lena, and she laughed hysterically.

I really enjoyed my first date with Lena and seeing another side of her from the one I saw in classes at school. I can't speak for her, but our first date was exciting to me. It was never boring, and time went by fast. So fast, that it was getting close to the hour that her mother told me to have her home.

We sat there for a long time just listening to country music and talking. Finally, I mustered up enough nerve to ask if I might kiss her. I was really surprised when she replied, "I thought you'd never ask." Gees, was I ever surprised! I had prepared myself for a big letdown. I just knew she was going to say, "Maybe next time."

Our first date, with that first kiss, certainly was a big boost to my ego, not that I really needed it, but it was good for my soul.

After returning Lena to her home, we parked in the yard and talked a little longer. It must have been longer than her mother wanted us to talk. Just as I was going to kiss her goodnight, the front porch light started flashing on and off. This was Milbra's way of telling Lena to get herself in the house. After one kiss there came another. Time meant nothing to us right then. Then it happened: The door opened, and we heard Milbra say, "Lena, you are not setting a good example for your little sisters. You need to come in!"

She looked at me and smiled. She said, "I have to go!"

"When can I see you again?"

"You best call me," she said, as she slid out on the passenger's side of the truck and ran inside.

After I saw Lena run into her house, I said to myself, "Carl, you blew it. Milbra will never let you take her daughter out again!"

I was partially right! The second, third, and fourth dates were spent well supervised in Milbra's home. As soon as I arrived, she was enticing me with her magnificent apple and peach fried pies. Wow! Could that lady cook! No sooner had the pies settled in my stomach, when Milbra was up popping popcorn. She was a good popcorn popper as well.

It didn't take me long to realize what Milbra was doing. She wanted to keep us where she could watch us. Food was her enticement.

After Milbra regained her trust in me, she started letting me take Lena to the movies again. I'm not sure she ever knew about our dates when we would park at the Lone Pine Church of Christ.

All during our dating years, Milbra switched the porch light on and off as a means of saying, "Lena, get in the house and let Carl go home!" It was always hard for me to understand why she made such a big thing of us sitting in the truck in her front yard. Didn't she realize that if we were going to make out, we'd do that at the Lone Pine Church of Christ parking lot? Little did she know, her front yard was the safest place for her daughter to be?

From stories I've heard from Lena's sisters, Milbra continued to utilize this same routine of the flashing porch light all during their dating years.

Lena and I dated on and off the rest of our high school years. We loved each other but knew getting married would jeopardize our chances of getting a college education.

My senior year at Quitman went well. Once again, I was successful in making the starting lineups in both basketball and baseball. My grades had improved tremendously at Quitman. I was now an A and B student and was on the honor roll. I was focused and ready to look into college.

When I was a senior, several recruiters from different colleges and universities came to recruit students for their respective schools. I visited with the representative from Arkansas State Teachers College in Conway and the recruiter from Arkansas Tech, Russellville, Arkansas. Mr. Paul Fisher was the recruiter from Arkansas Tech University. I liked him right off.

Since my parents were not financially able to pay for any of my college, I had to have a job to help pay for my education. Mr. Fisher headed up the work-study program at Arkansas Tech and offered me a job in the school cafeteria. The work study program would pay for my room and board, but I still had to come up with my tuition and some spending money.

Lena was in the same predicament with her finances. She, too, was able to get a work-study job in the cafeteria at Arkansas State Teachers College in Conway.

During our years at West Side and Quitman, Lena and I were active in the Cleburne County 4-H club. When I was a senior, I served as president of the Cleburne County 4-H Leadership Council. The president's position allowed me an opportunity to develop my leadership skills. I had the opportunity to travel to the University of Arkansas for state 4-H week where I participated in public speaking and parliamentary procedures.

Because of our active participation, Lena and I made applications for Rural Endowment Student loans. With the help of letters of recommendation from Mrs. Myra Turney, Cleburne County Home Demonstration Agent, and Mr. Howard Young, Cleburne County Farm Agent, we both were awarded Rural Endowment loans.

After graduating from high school, I spent the first summer in St. Louis, Missouri, where I was blessed to be able to stay with my brother Willie and his wife, Norma. They lived in an apartment three blocks east of the busy Kings Highway.

After arriving in St. Louis, I applied for several jobs. I was fortunate to find employment with the Gaylord Box Company making four dollars and twenty-five cents an hour. That was pretty good money in 1962 for a boy from the foot hills of the Ozark Mountains.

This was the first time I had ever lived away from home and the first time I had experienced some of the evils of living in a large city like St. Louis. Since I didn't have an automobile to drive to work, I caught a city transit bus three blocks from Willie and Norma's apartment.

One night after work, as I was waiting at the bus stop near the Gaylord Box Company, a stranger pulled up at the bus stop, rolled down his passenger side window, leaned over, and asked, "You want a ride?"

I had always been warned not to get in a car with a stranger, so I stood there for a few seconds and said, "Thanks, but I'm expecting my bus anytime. I appreciate the offer."

The guy threw open the passenger side door and said, "Come on, let's have some fun." He then proceeded to proposition me into engaging in an inappropriate activity with him for money. My heart was pumping faster than I had ever experienced, even when playing basketball at Quitman High School. I finally got up the nerve to slam the passenger door shut and said, "I'm not interested." I was relieved when the stranger speed off down Kings Highway.

That night was the last time I had to catch a bus at night. The next day at work, I was able to find a nice lady who volunteered to give me a ride to my brother's house. It was three blocks out of her way, but she didn't want me to be subjected to the evils of St. Louis again. God again answered my prayer.

While in St. Louis, I received notice that my Rural Endowment loan had been approved. I started making plans to return home to attend Arkansas Tech.

Before I returned home to Arkansas, Willie offered to let me buy his 1955 Ford. He knew I needed a car, and he and Norma had been shopping for a new automobile. During my stay with them, they didn't charge me rent, and I had saved a considerable amount of money. More money than I ever dreamed I'd make in just one summer.

After paying Willie for the car, I still had a good amount of savings that I could fall back on in college. I felt good! I now had my own car, a car I could use to court the love of my life during our college years and to get back and forth from home to Arkansas Tech.

Upon returning home from St. Louis, Pa and I had some serious conversations about my quitting my four-dollars-and-twenty-five-cent an-hour job. He was upset about my decision. He always equated wealth with someone who owned his own farm, had cattle, chickens, hogs, horses, and other things that most farmers acquired.

Pa started off by saying, "Carl, I just don't understand why you quit a good job making four dollars and twenty-five cents an hour to come back here to go to college. How is college going to help you?"

Since no one in my family had previously gone to college, he didn't understand. How was I going to answer his question?

"Pa, I know I've disappointed you by quitting a good job, but I don't want to own a farm. I don't want to pick cotton and strawberries and other fruit all my life. You, of all people, know how incapable I am at plowing behind a horse. I'm just not cut out for farming. I want something different, something I can do that will give me satisfaction. I want a job that I can love, and coaching is what I want to do. I want to use my talents and skills to work with kids. Please try to understand that."

"Well, I guess there's nothing I can do about it. You've made up your mind, I see."

"Yes, I have. I'll be here for about a week before I report to my job at Arkansas Tech. Is there something I can do for you in the meantime?"

"Yes, there is! I need you to drive me to Bald Knob to get a load of watermelons and peaches. The Old Soldiers Reunion in Heber Springs is coming up in a week, and I want to take a load of produce down to the spring park to sell. I always make good money during the week of the reunion," he added.

"I can do that. You tell me the date, and we will go."

CHAPTER 13

Bargers Don't Quit

As part of my work-study program at Arkansas Tech, I had to report one week earlier than the actual starting date for regular students. The cafeteria was responsible for feeding the football jocks, who reported one week earlier as well.

I was assigned to Wilson Hall, one of the largest male dormitories at Tech. It didn't take me long to realize there was only me and one other male student and our dorm mom, Mrs. Helen Hays, residing in Wilson Hall at the time.

It was on the first day at Tech that I met Robert Martindale, the other male occupant of Wilson Hall. He preferred to be called Bob, so Bob it was. We were not roommates but spent a lot of time together that first week working in the cafeteria and getting oriented to Arkansas Tech and the city of Russellville. Bob was from Hot Springs, a much larger town than Quitman. He was playing in the Tech band on a scholarship. Between his band scholarship and work study, his tuition and room and board were covered. Bob was poor, like me, but highly intelligent. He laughed at my imperfect enunciations.

I would say, "all right, hot shot, I want you to pronounce that word?"

Bob and I became very good friends, and, although he presently lives in San Antonio, Texas, we still get together, along with our wives, two to three times a year.

When classes started, I found I was not nearly ready for college work. I didn't possess the study skills I needed. I spent too much time playing tennis, intramural football and basketball, and doing other things instead of doing homework.

Near the end of the first semester, I was summoned to Dean Creigbough's office. Being summoned to the office of Education and Student Affairs was a serious matter, so I was pretty nervous.

"Come in, Carl, and have a seat. How are you doing?"

"Good," I said.

"Well, Carl, I'll get right to the point. At this time in the first semester, I have to bring students in my office and give them a little pep talk. Do you know what I mean?"

"Yes, Sir, I think I do."

"Carl, I've been looking over your current grades, and what I'm seeing doesn't look good. Do you really want to go to school here at Arkansas Tech?"

"Yes, Sir, I do."

"Well, Carl, we'd like to keep you here, but you've got to do better on your grades. You need to start right now studying for your finals. If you don't, you may flunk out."

"Yes, Sir! I must confess, I've been neglecting my studying."

"I can see that, Carl. But now that you know you are in trouble, I expect you will do better, won't you?"

"Yes, Sir, I'll do better!"

"I'm going to count on you, Carl. If you pass your finals, I believe you will be back next semester. Your grades in physical education and history are good. You must be majoring in physical education or history?"

"Yes, Sir! I'm majoring in physical education and minoring in history. Someday, I hope to coach basketball and teach history."

"Well, Carl, do you know anyone who could tutor you a little in math and English?"

"Yes, Sir, I do."

"Well then, it's my recommendation that you get some help in those areas where you are falling behind. Carl, Dr. Billy Burt Baker speaks highly of you. He thinks you have a great personality and wants to see you succeed. He thinks you have potential to be successful in life. Please don't let him down. He's your friend!"

Dean Creigbough had given me my wakeup call. I decided to start using my time wisely by studying. Bob was really good in English, and he agreed to work with me on my grammar and writing. Another friend agreed to help me with math. I stopped all my physical activities and started studying. I really didn't want to flunk out of school. What would my pa say to me if I did that?

The first semester finals came, and I was better prepared than ever before. I waited until all the grades were posted before going home for Christmas. I couldn't stand not knowing if I had flunked out. As I went from building to building checking my final grades, I found I had made Cs in English and math. My prayers were answered! My grade point wasn't anything to brag about, but I had passed. God had given me another chance to succeed at college, providing I wanted to continue to go to college.

On my way home for Christmas break, I found myself getting depressed. Even though I had passed all my courses, I begin to wonder if I was cut out for three and half more years of studying to be a coach and history teacher. For the first time in my life, I was uncertain. I had never been depressed in my life. I questioned whether Pa was right. Maybe I should go back to St. Louis and find a good paying job. Maybe I was not cut out for college work.

After returning home, my depression was still with me. I spent many hours in anguish over the idea of quitting college. How would I tell Ma, who had supported me in my decision to go to college? Pa would probably be happy with my decision since he didn't want me to go to college in the first place.

I waited until after Christmas to make my decision. One day, after finishing dinner, I asked Pa and Ma if I could have a talk with them. We went to the small living room next to the kitchen. My parents sat together on the big couch. I took a seat across from them in Ma's rocking chair.

"There's something I need to tell both of you," I said with trembling lips.

"Oh, Lord, Carl! You've not got Lena pregnant have you?" my mother asked.

I couldn't help laughing. She always feared that one of her girls was going to get pregnant or one of her boys was going to impregnate a girl.

"No, Ma, it's nothing like that!" I quickly responded.

"Well, what is it?" she asked.

"I've decided not to go back to Arkansas Tech. I've decided to go to St. Louis and find a job." I looked at Ma and tears began to run down her cheeks. I could tell she was so disappointed in me.

Pa just looked at me with a puzzled expression on his face, and then he stood up, walked over to me, and started shaking his finger right in my face. "Carl Bargers, don't quit! You are not quitting college. You've started something, and you're going to finish it, you hear?"

I never expected this. What had come over my Pa? I thought he'd be jumping up and down with joy.

"Pa, I thought you'd be happy about my news."

"Well, I'm not! Since you've been going to school, I've had several people come in my store and tell me how proud I must be to have a son at Arkansas Tech. I got to thinking about that. I *am* proud of you, Carl. You have a dream of working with kids, and from what I've found out, a college degree helps people earn more money. I want you to go back to Arkansas Tech and get yourself a good education. You will be the first Barger I know to graduate from college."

Pa's words were the most encouraging he'd ever spoken to me. Right then I gained a lot of respect for my pa.

Ma had merely been sitting there not saying a word. She finally said, "Son, I too am very proud of you. You know how much I want you to stay in school. When you graduate from college, you will have set the example for your sister Leona Faye and your nieces and nephews. Maybe they will choose to do what you have done. You've got to go back, son!"

With that encouragement, how could I not go back to Arkansas Tech? I made my decision right then not to look back but to go forward and work harder to achieve my goals. I would not let my mother or father down. I would return to Arkansas Tech!

I returned to Arkansas Tech with a new attitude toward studying and a new outlook on life. I couldn't play around anymore; I had to study and concentrate on building new skills and applying those skills to my life. I set my goals high and worked consistently to accomplish each goal.

Lena and I continued to work at different jobs during the summer months and continued to apply for and receive student loans. We both continued to work in the college cafeterias at our respective colleges.

My grades improved each semester. It was during my junior year that Lena and I decided we'd get married during the Christmas break. She had gone through college in three years. She would graduate a year before I would. We decided we'd get married on December 19, 1964.

After setting the date for our marriage, Lena and I laughed on several occasions about the possibility of the old ladies in her community gossiping about us getting married in the middle of the year. Normally, when a couple got married suddenly, the old ladies thought the girl must be pregnant. In our case, they would be wrong!

Lena and I were married on a cold, icy afternoon at West Side Baptist Church in Greers Ferry, Arkansas, by our good friend, Rev. Jerry Murphree.

My best man was my best friend, Bob Martindale. Hubert Alexander, my roommate at Tech, was my only groomsman.

Lena's maid of honor was her sister Earlene and her only bridesmaid was her roommate, Annie Joe.

We were too poor for a honeymoon, so we decided to go back to Russellville and spend a couple of nights in the Sands Motel. We enjoyed our meals at the nearby Old South, a popular restaurant in town.

After spending two nights in the Sands Motel, we moved to our new home in the Balkman Apartments, a married couples' complex on the Tech campus.

CHAPTER 14

The Beginning of Graduations and Careers

At the beginning of the second semester, I returned to Arkansas Tech and our apartment to live alone. Lena returned to ASTC, where she would have nine weeks of block courses to prepare her for student teaching.

We saw each other almost every weekend, but our time together was far from perfect as we usually spent that time at my folks's or Lena's mother's house.

After Lena's nine weeks of block courses, she moved to Heber Springs, where she was assigned to do her student teaching.

Lena had asked her high-school home-economics teacher, Mrs. Frances Barrett, for suggestions as to where she might find a room for the nine weeks of student teaching. Mrs. Barrett invited Lena to stay with her, as she was a widow and her house was only two blocks from Heber Springs High School. Since Lena could not drive, this was a real blessing.

Mrs. Barrett had taught Lena home economics from the eighth through twelfth grades at West Side School District. Lena loved Mrs. Barrett, and Mrs. Barrett loved her. They would be good for each other, since Mrs. Barrett had lost her husband and was living by herself in Heber Springs.

Fridays became the most important day of the week for me. I knew if I could just get through the week, I would be able to see Lena on weekends. Every Friday I would jump in my car and head for Cleburne County. Sometimes we would stay at Lena's mother's home in Greers Ferry and sometimes at my parents' home in Pearson. We were so in love that it really didn't matter where we stayed. Our only regret was that neither home afforded us the privacy we longed for.

It was the longest semester of our lives. Finally, in early June, Lena finished her student teaching and joined me at the Balkman Apartments at Arkansas Tech. She later graduated from ASTC in August 1965.

During my last year at Arkansas Tech, Coach Sam Hindsman of the Arkansas Tech Wonder Boys basketball team, asked me to become his team manager. Since I was majoring in physical education and wanted to coach basketball, I jumped at the opportunity. The job paid my tuition. I learned so much under Coach Hindsman. He was one of the kindest and most gifted coaches that I'd ever known. I loved and admired him for his coaching ability, his rapport with the basketball team, and his character. I took several of my physical education courses under him. He and I got to be good friends.

Coach Hindsman ventured out into the remote areas of Arkansas and recruited country boys to play at Arkansas Tech. He said, "Country boys are stronger and better shooters than city boys and, because of the physical work they do on the farm, they jump higher too!" Some of his best players were Kenny Saylors of Bruno Piatt, J. P. Lovelady from Dover, and Billy Burt Baker from Marshall. Some team and individual scoring records have yet to be broken at Arkansas Tech.

During my senior year, I supplemented my income on Saturdays by working as a bookmobile driver for Lena, who was employed as bookmobile librarian for the Yell County Public Library in Dardanelle, Arkansas. She loved her job! Since my job as manager only paid my tuition, Lena's job and my part-time job, came in handy in providing us with extra money. We immediately started a savings account with the Farmers Bank of Russellville for a future home.

During the fall semester of my senior year at Arkansas Tech, I was blessed by doing my student teaching at Dardanelle High School. Dardanelle was only five miles from Balkman Apartments.

In early December, Lena was employed by the Hector Public School System as an English teacher. Hector was a small rural school about seventeen miles to the north of Russellville. After Lena got her first pay check from Hector, we felt that we were in high cotton. The extra money really helped our budget.

By Christmas break, I had completed all my requirements in student teaching at Dardanelle High School. All I needed now was three hours of history to complete the requirements for a Bachelor of Science Degree in Physical Education with a minor in history.

A week before Christmas break, I received a call from Mr. Benny Dosikell, superintendent of the Pottsville Public Schools. Mr. Dosikell had contacted Coach Sam Hindsman to see if he knew a student who wanted to finish out the 1965-66 school year coaching basketball. Coach Hindsman recommended me. Although, I had not yet finished my three hours of history, Pottsville was able to employ me on an emergency certificate.

In less than a year, God had blessed two young people from the foothills of the Ozarks with jobs that gave us more than ample money to live on. We now had two incomes and were "rolling in the dough," you might say! In a period of one year, we went from being poor during the first twenty-one years of our lives to becoming rich—at least we felt rich.

We decided we'd give one tenth of our income to our church as our tithe. The Bible teaches that at least ten percent be given to the church to promote God's work. Lena and I had both accepted Jesus Christ as our savior during our teenage years. I had been saved on Mother's Day in the Church of Christ in Higden, Arkansas, at the age of sixteen.

Lena and I had gone to church all through our childhood and teen years. While at State Teachers College of Arkansas and Arkansas Tech we were involved with the Missionary Baptist Student Fellowship (MBSF). We dedicated ourselves to doing the Lord's work. Our faith in God was real, and because of our serving God, He blessed us abundantly. It pleased me to know that God enabled Lena and me to accomplish our goal of obtaining our college education. We gave God all the credit for our accomplishments. We had lived in poverty all our lives, but now God had allowed us the opportunity to achieve our goals and be able to work with young people. Praise Him! Praise Him!

I shall never forget my graduation at Arkansas Tech. It was in May 1966 that I walked across the stage and received my diploma from Dr. J. W. Hull, president of Arkansas Tech. Those attending my graduation were my older brother, Willie, and his wife, Norma, from St. Louis, Missouri. Other family members were my beautiful wife, Lena; my dear mother, Mamie Ann Totten Barger; and my baby sister, Leona Faye.

I shall never forget how my mother looked on that day. I can't remember a time prior to graduation that I had seen her wearing lipstick and high-heel shoes, but for this historical day and event, she was dressed for the occasion. She looked very nice. She had come to see her youngest boy graduate from a higher institution of learning.

Pa wasn't able to come to my graduation. He ran a small country grocery store and couldn't get away. Although I was somewhat disappointed, I didn't let it bother me. He was never one to go to our school events. All during the years that Willie, Jimmy, Roy, Ella Mae, Faye, and I participated in sports and other school events, Pa never attended. It was Ma who always had been there for us.

CHAPTER 15

Our Careers Blossom

After I graduated Arkansas Tech, Lena and I started looking for teaching positions. We wanted to teach in the same school system if possible. One such offer for an interview was from Scotland Public Schools in Van Buren County. Scotland wasn't far from Greers Ferry and Quitman where our parents lived. Scotland was also a remote area, twelve miles from Clinton, Arkansas.

A few days before our scheduled interviews, we decided to detour from our regular route home to Greers Ferry and drive by the Scotland School System. The road to Clinton had several dangerous curves, like a snake. It was the longest twelve miles I had driven.

As we drove into the school campus, Lena and I looked at each other and smiled. We were both thinking: *no way do we want to come to this little school system.* The largest building on campus was the gymnasium.

We had pretty much decided to call and tell the superintendent, Mr. Othal Thompson, that we had decided not to come for our interviews, but for some reason I just couldn't get Scotland off my mind. God began to prick at my heart as if to say, "Carl, don't pass up this opportunity."

After much discussion, we decided we'd keep our interviews at Scotland. By the time Mr. Thompson got through with us, we were convinced that God wanted us at Scotland. The only problem was that there was no housing available for us to move into. The little town of Scotland had one grocery store and one gas station. The other stores in town were out of business and had been for several years. It was like a ghost town.

Lena and I had saved money from teaching at Pottsville and Hector, so we used some of our savings to purchase a twelve-by-sixty-foot mobile home. Mr. Thompson allowed us to move it north of the gym on campus.

My job included coaching four basketball teams and teaching history. Lena was employed as the English teacher of grades nine through twelve. She also was the high school librarian and algebra 1 teacher.

It didn't take us long to realize that God was already taking care of us by bringing us to Scotland. We were quickly taken under the wings of a wonderful family—the Windsors—who became our family away from home. We spent most of our free time in the home of this great family.

Our year at Scotland was one of the best years of our lives. We moved in during the summer, and I immediately started practicing my basketball teams. I loved working with the kids at Scotland. They were well-mannered children—they had been taught to respect their teachers. The majority of the kids lived on dairy and chicken farms.

During my first week at Scotland, I was having senior boys basketball practice when I turned and saw a nice looking woman in her early forties standing at the double doors leading into the gym's concession stand area. She was watching our boys run up and down the floor when I crossed the court, walked up to her, and asked, "May I help you?"

"Yes, you may! Can you tell me where the coach is?" she asked.

At first, I thought she was kidding me, but I quickly realized she was serious. "I'm Coach Barger," I said, as I reached out my hand to greet her.

She looked at me in a puzzling way and said, "Oh, I'm so sorry! I thought you were one of the boys!"

I shall always remember that moment. Although I looked like one of the boys, I was treated with respect from both my basketball teams and the patrons of the Scotland School District.

The woman was Mrs. Mavis McNabb, the mother of my star basketball player, Paul McNabb. She later became one of my biggest supporters.

Our year in Scotland Public Schools was a tremendous asset to Lena and me. We learned to give and take and to show empathy to students in need. The students who attended the Scotland School System reminded us of how we had grown up in the remote community of Westside in Cleburne County.

Scotland was located in the western-most part of Van Buren County. The community was made up of poor-to-average income families who had to travel great distances to get to their jobs. Some students were bused as far as forty miles away.

In the spring of 1967, my superintendent, Jessie Huffman, who had taken Mr. Thompson's place as superintendent, came to the gym and asked if he could talk with me? We went into my office and closed the door.

He said, "Coach, I got a call today from Mr. Gibert Depner, superintendent of the Southside Bee Branch School District. He wanted my permission to visit with you in regard to hiring you as their basketball coach and high school principal for the 1967–68 school year. I don't want to lose you, but I gave him permission to visit with you."

"Mr. Huffman, I don't know what to say."

"I don't know how to guide you. I do know it pays more, and the school board is willing to pay for your administrative hours to get an endorsement to become a principal. That's a pretty good offer, I'd say."

"I don't know whether I'd like being a principal," I said.

"He's going to call you this afternoon. I just wanted you to have a heads up when he calls."

"Thanks, Mr. Huffman. I appreciate the heads up."

I couldn't focus any longer on my coaching that day. I just couldn't get Mr. Huffman's information out of my head. What was I going to say to Mr. Depner when he called? Should I say, "I'm not interested, but thanks"? Or should I say, "I will come and visit with you about the job"?

Between classes, I ran to the high school to get Lena's thoughts on the matter. After visiting with her, she looked at me and said, "Sounds like a golden opportunity to me."

"You really think so?" I asked.

"Yes, Carl, I really mean it. I think it's an honor for you to be contacted about the job. You do what your heart leads you to do."

Lena had always been one who encouraged me to do what I thought was right for me and her. There have been times I wished she would have just said, "You need to do this!"

The call from Mr. Depner came. I told him I would come and visit with him. An interview time was set, and I drove to Bee Branch to visit with Mr. Depner.

The offer was too good to turn down. Mr. Depner offered me the job, and I accepted. During my first year at South Side Bee Branch, I coached all four basketball teams and was high school principal. Besides a good salary, the school board voted to pay for twelve hours of graduate level hours at the University of Central Arkansas in Conway, Arkansas. The twelve hours gave me a principal's endorsement and motivated me to get my Master's Degree. I was stepping out on faith because the school had nothing to offer Lena who had a degree in English and library science.

Mr. Depner agreed to let me move our mobile home onto the school's property, which would be an asset to me and my coaching. The new job meant no summer break for me. That didn't upset me much, because I felt the sizeable raise and paying for my principal's endorsement outweighed a few months off from school.

Since Southside had no position for Lena, she applied for an English position at Greenbrier Public Schools and got the job. The only problem with her job was that she couldn't drive. We were faced with the issue of how to get her to and from Greenbrier once school started.

I had given Lena a few driving lessons in our Chevrolet Corvair, which had a standard transmission. Getting started without killing the motor was a major problem for her. Backing up was not a problem, though. So one afternoon while I was at basketball practice, Lena got in the car, backed it up to the baseball field and started driving. For some reason, someone had mowed around the baseline. With no one to criticize and nothing to run into, Lena got all the practice she needed.

One day when I came home from summer school, she met me at the door and said, “Don’t sit down. Let’s take a drive.”

“Where are we going?” I asked.

“It’s a surprise,” she said.

“Where are the keys to the car,” I asked.

“I got them right here,” she said while dangling them before my eyes.

I had no idea what this girl was doing. I felt she was up to something, but what? When we got to the car, I started to get in the driver’s side when she grabbed me by the arm and said, “You go to the passenger side. I’ll handle the driving.”

I did as I was instructed, thinking that I would be setting close to her to help her should she run into trouble. I had worked with her earlier on, but that was a disaster. I had made her nervous, so she made me nervous, and I just gave up.

The car was a stick shift, making things a little harder for a beginning driver. Lena started the car and off we went as smooth as silk. I couldn’t believe it!

There was a gravel road running in front of our trailer house that led out into the country. She turned on the gravel road, picked up some speed, shifted to second gear, and later to third gear, without grinding the gear shift. She shifted when necessary, holding the car on the road and doing an outstanding job of driving.

“What’s going on here?” I asked.

“I told you it was a surprise,” she said with a big smile on her face and excitement in her voice.

“I’m really surprised! When did you learn to drive?”

“I’ve been practicing almost every day on the baseball field, and for the last few days I’ve been driving on this gravel road. What do you think?”

“Honey, I’m really proud of you!” I said with joy in my voice, my heart beating faster and faster.

She turned into a drive-way, backed up, and headed back to our house.

“When can I take my driver’s test?”

“Have you been studying a manual,” I asked.

"Yes, I think I can pass," she said with excitement.

"I don't have to go to class on Friday. We can go to Clinton and you can take your driver's test then," I said.

Oh, what a surprise! My wonderful and beautiful wife had resolved my main worry of getting her back and forth to Greenbrier.

On that day, I knew my lovely wife was capable of accomplishing about anything she set her mind to. Oh, how fortunate I am to have her as my soulmate, and, by the way, she scored 100 percent on the written test!

My first year at Southside Bee Branch was very successful. It was a rebuilding year for both senior girls and boys. The principal's job turned out to be enjoyable as well. I didn't like to paddle, but during that time period, that was the main way of disciplining students for certain infractions.

I don't think I could have handled both the principal's role and coaching if it hadn't been for my secretary, Linda Pennington. She was a real joy to work with, and she kept me well informed. She did most of my principal's reports, which freed me up to handle student problems and work with the staff. If someone had asked me what I would be doing at age twenty-three, I certainly wouldn't have guessed that I would be performing the duties of a high school principal.

During my second year at Southside, Lena joined me at the high school as librarian. Her year as English teacher at Greenbrier was rewarding, but the drive wasn't always pleasant.

In February 1967, while driving on patches of ice on Highway 65 to Greenbrier, Lena lost control of our car. She went up an embankment, spun completely around, and headed back to Southside. It's a miracle that she didn't flip the car. After seeing the tire marks on the steep road bank, I realized that God had been with her every second. I'm convinced it was He who was riding with Lena and keeping her safe, but after that accident, we made sure she didn't drive on icy roads again.

On September 6, 1968, Pa died in the Heber Springs Hospital. I was able to be with him when he died. I had seen only one other person die before: Grandmother Mary Elizabeth

Heiple Barger. I can still remember seeing Pa take his last breath. So many memories flashed before my eyes as I sat there in that hospital room watching him struggle with his breathing. I knew it wasn't going to be long. My brother Roy and I had given our mother a break, and she was in the waiting room with other family members when he died.

I owe so much to Pa. If it hadn't have been for his strong objection to my dropping out of college, I wouldn't be where I am today. He actually paved the way to what success I've experienced over the years. He was my friend, one that I'd miss in days to come. I shall never forget that day in their home at Quitman when he pointed his finger in my face and said, "Carl, Bargers, don't quit!"

We had a good year in basketball. My senior boys won the Van Buren County Tournament, and we went to the semi-finals of the district tournament held at Central Baptist College in Conway, Arkansas. My oldest brother, Harvey, moved to Bee Branch so that his two sons could play basketball for me. That was truly a blessing for the senior boys team and me.

My nephew Kent was one of the best shooting guards in Arkansas. He and Bennie Fuller from the Arkansas School for the Deaf, literally shot the lights out in two games they played against each other. Kent was a natural guard. No one was going to take the basketball from him. He could dribble behind his back and make passes you wouldn't believe. He was my top scorer and he and his younger brother, Terry, were certainly a big part of the success of my basketball team.

The sad thing about basketball coaching is that you never know when some political aspect will enter in and you won't have a job the next year. That's what happened to me. Southside had the reputation of turning a coach over every two to three years. I thought, with the success we had during the season, I was safe from being fired. I was wrong! Due to the political and powerful influence of the same old ruling class, I was asked to resign and move on. Needless to say, that broke my heart. I hated it, because my brother had moved his sons from Quitman so they could play for me. Kent had one more year and Terry had two years left.

God, again, came into the picture for Lena and me. I received a call from two good friends in McNeil, Arkansas. Wylie and James Staggs were graduates of McNeil and knew all of the school board members. There was a coaching job available for all four basketball teams. They encouraged me to apply for it. Wylie was presently coaching in the Willisville School District about fifteen miles from McNeil. The McNeil School District also had an English teacher position open. Lena and I applied for the jobs and were both hired in late May 1969.

During our two years at Southside Bee Branch, we experienced several blessings. One such blessing was completing my Master's Degree from the University of Central Arkansas in Conway. Part of my Master's Degree included the principal's endorsement. I didn't know it at the time, but the endorsement would later play a major role in my future as a school administrator.

On July 1, 1969, the movers came to Southside, hooked up to our mobile home, and moved it to Magnolia, Arkansas. Magnolia is located five miles south of McNeil and had the only nearby mobile home park.

CHAPTER 16

McNeil and Forced Integration

On August 19, 1969, the first semester of school opened with much excitement in the little town of McNeil in Columbia County, Arkansas.

During the summer before school started in August, a federal court judge handed down a forced integration order for McNeil to integrate its white and black schools. The court order stated, "The McNeil Board of Education shall at the beginning of the 1969–70 school year completely integrate the ninth through twelve black students at South Side High School with the seventh through twelve grades at North Side High School." The federal court also ordered that all grade levels be integrated at the beginning of the 1970–71 school year.

The court order made North Side High School the junior and senior high school, which would house grades seven through twelve, while South Side would become the elementary school and house grades one through six.

On the first day of school, the black students refused to go to classes at the white school. Instead, they, along with their parents, marched and demonstrated in front of North Side High School. They were bound and determined to defy the court order. By way of local, state, and national media, they put out the word they wanted the court's ruling to be reversed and let them continue to attend their school on the south side of McNeil.

The McNeil School Board consisted of an all-white board: Charles Cross, Clyde Gunnels, Franklin Gunter, Perry Polk, and George Kyle. The white school board governed the affairs of both the black and white schools. The blacks blamed the school board for promoting the federal court order to integrate the two schools.

The majority of the black community joined the black students in protest, and they marched daily during the first week of school. They were joined by the NAACP, which made state and national television. The news media was at McNeil every day filming the demonstration and interviewing parents, students, school administration, and school board members.

I went about doing my job as basketball coach. Every day, after teaching my history classes at North Side High School, I slowly made my way through the big crowd of black protesters, who had blocked the street between the gym and high school. Each day, I would say, "Excuse me please," as I cautiously made a path though the large protesting crowd. For some reason, I was never afraid of those protesting.

The black patrons and students always treated me with respect. It was only later I realized that my three black basketball players, who had been attending North Side on a "Freedom of Choice" agreement prior to the federal court order, had put out the word that I was a cool guy.

I will always appreciate those young men for helping me. The three black students were John Smith—I called him Big John, because he was six-foot-seven and had hands like Goliath—Vandon Warren, and William Glasper, three of the nicest young men I have ever coached. They were polite and worked hard to improve their game.

After the first week, it was rumored that government officials had held a meeting with the black community over the weekend and told them if they didn't send their children to school they would be held in contempt of the federal court order and would either be jailed or fined for their actions.

On Monday of the second week, the black students in grades ninth through twelve entered North Side High School without incident. They were instructed to go to the auditorium where they were given their class schedules and a quick tour of the high school.

All during the second week, tensions were high, but there were no fights or incidents worthy of mentioning. The teachers stood in the halls during the changing of classes, and bathroom breaks were taken only during break times or when an emergency occurred.

By the third week, I thought everything was going well. I was in the gym coaching my senior boys when Mr. John Dunsworth, the new superintendent, came to the gym to see me. He asked if we could go to my office and have a talk. To be honest, I thought I might be in trouble about something. We went to my office, and I sat down behind my desk and offered him a chair across from me.

"What can I do for you, Mr. Dunsworth?"

"Coach Barger, I would like you to meet with me and the school board tomorrow at noon in the science room."

My heart began to race faster and faster. I just didn't understand what was going on. All I could think about was whether I had done something wrong.

"Mr. Dunsworth, am I in trouble or something?"

"Oh, no, Coach. You're not in trouble at all. I hope I didn't lead you to think that."

"What's going on?"

"Coach, as you know, I have two teenage children I'm raising by myself. My wife died last year, and I'm their only living parent. My children are scared to death here. My daughter is being harassed in the hallway. There have been times her hair has been pulled. My son is under a great deal of pressure. They call him names. Our house has been rocked several times at night since school started. I've got to get my kids out of here."

I felt sorry for Mr. Dunsworth. I could see tears in his eyes as he shared these things with me. "How can I help?" I asked.

"We're having a special board meeting tomorrow at twelve o'clock. I'm going to resign my position, and I want to recommend you to take my place."

"Mr. Dunsworth, I appreciate your thinking about me, but I wouldn't know where to start as a superintendent. The only administrative work I've done has been as a high school principal. I don't think I could do a superintendent's job?"

"Coach, you can do it. I've already talked with Mr. Gilbert Depner, your former superintendent at Southside Bee Branch, and he's assured me you have the ability to do the job."

"He's somewhat prejudice because he likes me," I said.

"I think he's right about you. I've been watching you. You have a unique way of dealing with these children and their parents. Your personality speaks very highly of you. I don't know anyone around here that dislikes you. Will you please come to the meeting?"

"Mr. Dunsworth, let's just say I'm willing to take the job. What's going to happen to my basketball teams? I want to coach them."

"I can understand that, Coach. But doing two jobs would be extremely tough on you. How old are you?"

"I'm twenty-five years old."

"If you decide to take the job, there would be ample money for you to hire a replacement to coach your basketball teams."

"That's just it, I'm not sure I want to give them up."

"Coach Barger, I've got to go. Can I depend on your coming to meet with me and the school board tomorrow?"

"Yes, I'll be there. What time should I come?"

"I need to spend about fifteen minutes with them, prior to your coming in. You be there around twelve fifteen. How's that sound?"

"I'll be there!" *Oh, what have I done?* I thought. What have I done to deserve this? What if they really want me to take this job? I only want to coach. Oh, dear Lord, what do you want me to do? I really need your help!

I wasn't worth my salt for the rest of the day. I might as well have gone home. I dismissed my boys, mopped the gym floor, checked the bathroom commodes (all a part of my job description), picked Lena up, and headed to our mobile home in Magnolia.

On the way home, I was very quiet. All I could focus on was the meeting with Mr. Dunsworth. Lena knew something was wrong and began to question why I was so quiet. I had never kept anything from her, and I wasn't going to start now. I related to her my meeting with Mr. Dunsworth and then asked her what she thought?

"Carl, I think you need to do it," she said excitedly.

I looked at her like, what's come over you, girl!

She smiled and said, "I think it's a golden opportunity for you. Go for it. I know you can do it!"

"I'm going to have some of the best basketball teams I've ever coached. I don't want to give up my coaching at this time."

"I know you love your kids, and I know how much it means to you to coach, but Carl, think about your future and our future. Being a superintendent pays a lot more money than a coach's salary," she said.

"I know money is important, but a peace of mind, to me, is more important. I want you to pray with me about this. Who knows, the school board might not ask me to take the job. Let's just pray about this."

Lena assured me she would certainly pray with me. I tossed and turned all night long. I was keeping Lena awake, so I decided to get up and sleep on the couch. I don't remember just when I finally fell asleep, although I do remember looking at the wall clock at two fifteen in the morning.

Lena prepared a nice breakfast for us. She knew I loved sausage, eggs, biscuits, strawberry jelly, and cold milk. I liked white gravy as well, but Lena really didn't like to make white gravy except on Saturdays. She always said, "It's too messy!"

As we sat down to eat, she looked at me and said, "I'm so sorry you didn't sleep well. What have you decided?"

"I've decided if the school board offers me the job, I'll take it, providing they let me coach all four basketball teams."

Lena laughed and said, "How did I know you were going to say that very thing?"

"I know, you think I'm crazy!"

"No, I don't think you're crazy. I just know you, my love!"

"Maybe the board will think I'm crazy as well, and thank me for my time, and say they will find someone else."

"Well, I don't want you to worry anymore about this today. You go to school, teach your American history and civics classes, and get this off your mind."

"That's going to be easier said than done, you know!"

The time seemed to past so slowly. I couldn't do what Lena wanted me to do. My classes suffered badly. I was not my enthusiastic self! I loved civics and American history and prided myself in thinking I was a really good teacher.

Finally, twelve fifteen arrived, and I went to the science room, knocked on the door, and Mr. Dunsworth invited me into the room. The school board was sitting at a large table, big enough for six people.

"Coach Barger, I think you've previously met all members of the school board have you not?" Mr. Dunsworth asked.

"Good evening, gentleman," I said.

"Good evening back," they responded.

"Coach Barger, I've submitted my resignation to the board, and they have accepted it. I've also explained to them why I think you need to be employed to take my place as superintendent. I believe our school board president, Mr. Perry Polk, has a few questions he would like to ask you."

"Mr. Barger, would you rather be addressed as Coach Barger or Mr. Barger?"

"It really doesn't matter, Mr. Polk, I'll respond either way," I said.

Mr. Polk owned a big store in McNeil and was the pillar of the little town. Everyone loved him and admired him for his Christian beliefs and values.

"May I ask how old you are, Coach Barger?"

"I'm twenty-five years old, Sir!"

"You are in the prime of your life, young man," he said.

"We've heard good things about you. Mr. Dunsworth says you're well respected among our students, staff, and in the community. We're going to need someone like you to get things settled down around here. We need to start having school. We've got a lot of catching up to do.

"Mr. Dunsworth tells us that he's talked to you about the possibility of taking the superintendent's position."

"Yes, Sir, that's correct."

"How do you feel about that?"

"Well, Sir, I consider it an honor to be considered, but to tell you the truth, I've had no prior experience at being a superintendent."

"Mr. Barger, I've visited with Columbia County School Supervisor Lila Smith. She's assured me that, if you are hired as the superintendent, she will help you with the financial end of running the school. She may know more than most superintendents in Arkansas about school finances. She's more than willing to help you."

"I am sure I would need her help. It's my understanding that managing the school budget is, perhaps, the most important part of a superintendent's job description."

Mr. Polk looked around to the other school board members and asked if they had any questions.

Mr. Franklin Gunter, the vice-president of the school board, asked, "If we offered you the job, Coach Barger, would you take it?"

"Gentleman, I've prayed about this more than I've prayed about anything. I know if I take this job, my life and career are going to change forever. I believe this morning, God made it clear to me what I need to do."

"Coach Barger, what would that answer be?" Mr. Polk asked.

"If the school board will allow me to coach my four basketball teams, I'll accept your offer, if that's still what you want!"

I tried to read their faces. They looked at each other and smiled. Mr. Dunsworth must have told them I was reluctant to consider the superintendent's job because of my basketball teams.

"Coach Barger, I know you are young, but do you realize how much work and time you will be committing yourself too?" Mr. Polk asked.

"Yes, Sir, I have considered that, but I believe I can handle it. I don't mind work. I've worked hard all my life. My dear mama always said to us, "Hard work never killed anyone!" I believe that!

"Coach Barger, I'm going to ask you to wait in the hall for a few minutes while we deliberate on what we need to do as a board. This shouldn't take long!"

"Yes, Sir," I said as I turned and closed the door quietly behind me.

The school board deliberated about five minutes and called me back to the science room.

"Coach Barger, the school board has unanimously voted to hire you as our new superintendent."

"Congratulations!" Mr. Polk said.

"Thanks! I guess!"

That statement created a big laugh from everyone.

"Coach Barger, the school board has agreed to pay you the salary that Mr. Dunsworth was making, plus utilities, insurance, and reimbursement for all administrative expenses. We also decided that since you are doing two jobs, we want to pay you a stipend for coaching all four basketball teams," Mr. Polk said.

I thanked the school board and said, "Gentlemen, I prefer letting the coaching stipend go back into the school's operating budget."

Mr. Dunsworth had shared with me how close the finances were for that current school year. It was my understanding the previous superintendent, David Scott, had projected an ending balance of only two-hundred-fifty-nine dollars, which was cutting it pretty close!

If I accepted the stipend, I was afraid I might not be able to finish the school year in the black. I certainly didn't want my first year to be labeled as a superintendent who didn't know how to manage school funds.

The school board accepted my wishes in regard to the stipend. Mr. Polk said, "Someday young man, this board will make it up to you."

"Coach Barger, I've asked my granddaughter, Mrs. Jo Woods, to come in and be your secretary. She's not a bookkeeper, but she can write and record checks for you, answer the phone, and organize your appointments. I believe you will like Jo," he said.

"If she's related to you, I'm sure I will," I said as I shook his hand.

"By the way, Coach Barger, you will need to start next week. Mr. Dunsworth will be here through Friday. He will be sharing with you all he can before leaving," Mr. Polk said.

I left the science room feeling like a hundred pounds of cotton had been lifted from my shoulders.

The Magnolia Banner-News carried a big article on my being named as the new superintendent of McNeil. Mr. Dunsworth spent as much time with me as possible before he officially gave up his position as superintendent. Because of his several years of being a superintendent, his knowledge of school budgets and reports was beneficial. He emphasized to me the importance of getting reports to the State Department of Education in a timely manner.

Jo Wood was able to spend a day with us while Mr. Dunsworth was still aboard. During that day, Mr. Dunsworth showed her how to record and write checks. Jo wrote things down in sequential order, and I was given a copy. Between Mrs. Lila Smith, Jo, and me, we should be able to keep a set of financial books and balance it monthly.

Jo was not an experienced secretary or bookkeeper, but she was a fast learner. She was taking a leave of absent from working for her father, James Polk, who owned and operated a big furniture store in Magnolia. She was more or less doing this as a favor to her grandfather, Mr. Perry Polk. I really appreciated her for stepping in and helping me. She was up front with me in the beginning. She said, "Mr. Barger, I will do the best I can, but you will need to be on the lookout for someone permanent for the next school year."

CHAPTER 17

The Leather Strap

On the first day of my tenure as superintendent, I felt compelled to have an assembly for grades seven through twelve. I wanted both my staff and students to get to know me and know what I expected of each of them in their role as student or teacher. I wanted to challenge each one to use those talents that God had blessed them with to promote McNeil's school and make it one of the best in Columbia County.

One of my immediate goals was to appoint a student bi-racial committee as well as a community bi-racial committee. My purpose was to use both committees to help head off or resolve any racial problems, grievances, or other problems that might come up unexpectedly during the school year.

The idea of appointing a bi-racial committee was not my own. I had heard about other schools, which had received a federal court order, being successful in bringing about calm through a bi-racial committee. I believed it was the right thing to do, and if we handled things correctly, we could concentrate on having school and not spending valuable teaching time putting out fires.

My goal in involving students and the community was to create an atmosphere of partnership. I've always felt that involvement promotes a feeling of ownership. Ownership promotes pride, and pride creates a willingness to work for achievement. Those areas were necessary to accomplish the goals I'd set for the McNeil School District.

I appointed a student bi-racial committee and met with them weekly for lunch and discussion. I was excited about what was happening in the McNeil Public Schools. We had no incidents after I took over. The students were talking to each other, working together on class projects, riding buses together (which had been unheard of in the past), and they were volunteering their time to school projects.

The same thing was happening with the bi-racial community committee. We were getting help from ACTAP, an organization out of Ouachita Baptist University. It was a federally sponsored organization created to help schools that had been forced to integrate.

The best thing that happened with the community bi-racial committee was a sponsored, weekend retreat on the campus of Ouachita Baptist University. This was the first time we had spent two days and two nights together planning what was best for our community and giving every committee member an opportunity to voice their concerns. This retreat was needed and was successful in building friendships and trust! The federal court order was set in play, and we were now educating kids.

There were several weaknesses that had to be resolved before the 1970–71 school year. One such weakness was not having a principal at the South Side School, which was not integrated, and still had attending students in grades one through eight.

The best I could do was to name James Boyd, a black male and social studies teacher, to the position as head teacher. I relieved him of some of his teaching load so he could be free to help other teachers, especially with discipline problems.

I was fortunate to have Mrs. Pat Ward, the business teacher, to assist me with discipline at North Side. She was a hometown girl who knew just about every white family and most of the black families in McNeil. She was a tremendous help to me.

I went back and forth to the black school to check on things with Mr. Boyd. I went around noon so I could eat in the school cafeteria. By eating in the cafeteria, I got to know the staff as well as the kids. I also got to eat the food cooked by some of the best cooks in the world. The head cook was Mrs. Belle. She had been at the black school for thirty years. She made the best cinnamon rolls I have ever eaten. I gained ten pounds the first year in McNeil.

I didn't know it at the time, but that first year was going to be the biggest challenge of my life. Although it was a major undertaking, I was determined I could do it. There were no breaks for me at school. When I was not in the superintendent's office performing my duties, I was in the gym coaching. I was back and forth across the street doing two jobs.

Dr. Frank Irvin, who taught administrative courses at Southern Arkansas University in Magnolia, often used me as an example in his school administration classes. He would say, "Ya'll, I visited Coach Barger at McNeil the other day. When I arrived at the superintendent's office, I was informed he was in the gym working with his boys basketball team. In a few minutes Coach Barger shows up in his office with his coaching shorts on and says, "Welcome, Dr. Irvin. I hope you've not had to wait too long. I'm wearing several hats around here as you can see!"

Dr. Irvin always enjoyed poking fun at me. He liked me and went out of his way to help me. I believe he felt sorry for me since I was going back to school, working at being a superintendent, coaching four basketball teams, driving a school bus to some basketball games, and keeping the gym nice and clean. I knew from the way he graded my papers that he felt sorry for the load I was carrying. He became one of my best friends. Oh, by the way, my grades were good.

My staff seemed to realize my need for help. They knew I was putting my heart and soul into trying to provide a quality education for the kids. They also knew that I supported them and appreciated all they did for the school. They were a group of dedicated teachers. I really enjoyed being around them.

I shall never forget my first encounter with the way the black teachers punished or disciplined the black children. One day I visited the black school unannounced. As I entered into the hallway, I could hear Mr. Boyd talking loudly to someone in the principal's office. As I entered the office, I saw Mr. Boyd whipping one of the boys across the back with a leather strap.

The strap was about three inches wide and about twelve inches long. Mr. Boyd quit hitting the young boy when he saw me come into the room. He dismissed both boys and told them to return to their classes.

"What were you doing with those children?" I asked.

"Mr. Barger, that's how we punish our black children."

"Mr. Boyd, that's cruel punishment!"

"Mr. Barger, that's the only type of punishment our children understand. They choose whether they want to be whipped in the palm of their hands or across the back with a strap."

"Mr. Boyd, never again will you use the strap on any student in this school system."

Mr. Boyd seemed to be very surprised that I thought this was cruel punishment. I realize some people used the strap at home, but the strap would never again be used in my school.

"Mr. Boyd, I will get you a paddle made. From now on if a child needs corporal punishment, you will use the paddle and not the strap."

"You're the boss, Mr. Barger."

During my first year at McNeil, I found that several inequities existed in the black school. It didn't take me long to see why the black children didn't do very well in their academics. I found that the white students had up-to-date textbooks and the black students had the outdated textbooks. The black students had fewer supplies and mostly hand-me-down furniture.

What I found really disturbed me. I had grown up poor, was one of eleven children in the family, and was a migrant worker until I was seventeen years old. I could identify with these poor black children. I couldn't believe what I was seeing! After discovering the textbook issue, I immediately went about correcting the problem. It wasn't long before the black students received the same basal textbooks that were being used by the white students. There were so many inequities I will not attempt to write them all in this book. All I will say is that, under my administration, a lot of the inequities stopped.

The 1969–70 school year was a great learning experience for me. Not only was I the superintendent and basketball coach, but I also got to do some custodial work, bus driving, and nursing. Since I didn't have a qualified bookkeeper, I learned school finances from Columbia County Supervisor Lila Smith.

During what little spare time I had, I was in Mrs. Smith's office learning bookkeeping and doing Social Security and Teacher Retirement monthly reports. After the first of the year, I learned how to do W-2 forms for income tax purposes. I was three cents off on my report for several days before I found the mistake. I almost went crazy! I had to balance to the penny before I could send my employee W-2 forms out. What an experience that was!

I soon realized I had taken on a tremendous task being superintendent and the coach of four basketball teams. I found myself in the superintendent's office many nights until ten o'clock working on bookkeeping or reports. It was tiring, but I was twenty five, and God had blessed me with good health and a lot of energy.

At the end of the 1969–70 fiscal school year, my operational balance was $10,569.00. Needless to say, I was excited! I had come out in the black. The money I turned back into the operational account from my coaching salary really helped pull me through the school year.

When I agreed to take the superintendent's position, I also had agreed to go back to graduate school to get my school superintendent's certification.

I started my course work during the 1969–70 school year. The school administration courses were offered on Wednesday night, which was good because our basketball games were played on Tuesday and Friday nights.

Bobby Smithson, the superintendent from Gurdon Public Schools was seeking his superintendent's certification as well. We shared rides to the Little Rock Graduate School on Wednesday nights. It was nice to have Bobby as a companion. The trip to Little Rock from McNeil was a long one. I would get home at midnight most Wednesday nights and have to get up and be at school around seven forty the next morning.

As I prepared the budget for the 1970–71 fiscal year, I recommended that we hire two full-time principals and a basketball coach. By adding these additional employees, I would be able to give my superintendent's position the attention it deserved. I really needed more time since I was taking administrative courses during the school year.

CHAPTER 18

A Baby Girl

During the summer, Lena and I moved our mobile home to McNeil. We also moved our church membership from Calvary Missionary Baptist Church in Magnolia to the First Baptist Church in McNeil.

It was during the fall that Lena and I decided God was telling us that adoption was His way of giving us a family. For the past few years, we had tried everything we knew to get pregnant. We underwent several medical tests to find out that both of us had some physical problems, and most likely we'd never be able to have children of our own.

Due to the results of the medical tests, Lena and I decided to go to the Arkansas Department of Social Services office in Magnolia. There we met with Mr. Bryan Cordell, who helped us with our application for a baby through the Social Service Department in Little Rock, Arkansas.

In November, we received a call from Mr. Cordell informing us that our application had been approved, and Social Service was looking for a baby for us to adopt. We didn't specify the sex, because we were told that if we specified a sex, it would take longer to find a baby for us. We didn't really care whether our first baby was a boy or girl.

Early in December, after our application had been approved, someone who knew Mr. Cordell told us that a rumor around the social services office was we would get our baby by Christmas.

We were so excited, though unprepared. We bought a crib and a few baby things. Lena and I painted the small room in our trailer for a nursery. We painted it yellow and decorated it with animals. Since we didn't know if the baby would be a girl or a boy, we thought it would be appropriate to decorate with animal decals.

As Christmas approached, we anxiously awaited a call from Mr. Cordell. A few days before Christmas, we called his office and left the phone numbers of our mothers' homes, and then sadly drove there to spend Christmas with them. Day after day, as the awaited call didn't come, we became more and more dejected. I don't remember one single gift given or received that Christmas.

After Christmas, we started back to school. Lena's replacement had already been hired to take over as soon as we got our baby. The days were long, and we made many calls to Mr. Cordell, to which we always received the same response: "Be patient. These things take time."

After school on the afternoon of Friday, February 5, 1971, my telephone in the outer office rang. Pat Ward, my high school principal and dearest friend, answered the phone.

"Mr. Barger, I think you will want to take this call."

"Who is it?" I asked.

"Mr. Bryan Cordell."

"Yes, I do want to take Mr. Cordell's call."

As luck, or divine intervention, would have it, Lena walked into my outer office as Pat said, "It's Bryan Cordell."

By the time I had the phone to my ear, Lena was standing by my desk with a look of excited anticipation on her face. I moved the phone so she could hear the conversation just as Mr. Cordell said, "Mr. Barger, this is Bryan Cordell."

"How are you, Mr. Cordell?"

"Mr. Barger, I am doing really well, and I've got some good news for you and Lena. We have a baby girl for you. She was born yesterday at four-fifty-one in the morning at St. Vincent's Hospital in Little Rock. She's a healthy baby. You and Lena can go to Little Rock and pick her up on February eighth.

We were elated! We could hardly believe what we were hearing. After all these years, we were finally going to be parents.

After his short description of the birth, I informed Mr. Cordell that Lena was standing behind me and was equally excited about his news. In a louder tone he said, "Lena, congratulations!"

She raised her voice in excitement and said, "Thank you, Mr. Cordell. You have made this the happiest day of my life." Again, he said congratulations to both of us and informed us he would get back with us with further details.

I immediately got up out of my chair, turned around, and looked at Lena. I wish everyone could have seen her expression and her reaction. She put her hands to her lips and began to cry. She looked at me and said, "Is it really true? We're not dreaming are we?"

"Yes, it's really true," I said as I took her in my arms and held her.

The word soon spread throughout the school and the community. Everyone was so happy for us. People began to plan baby showers. This, too, was welcome news, because we had not purchased anything, not knowing the date of birth or sex of the baby. The people of McNeil were just wonderful!

Since we were to get our baby in Little Rock on Monday, we decided to go to our folks's homes in Quitman and Greers Ferry so we could be closer to Little Rock. As we were in Greers Ferry, bad weather moved in. We decided to go on to Little Rock on Sunday afternoon. By growing up in the Ozark Mountains, we knew very well what ice and snow did to country roads. We didn't want to take a chance by waiting and not being able to pick up our baby girl.

We checked in at the old Lafayette Hotel in downtown Little Rock. The Lafayette Hotel was not far from the Social Services Department where we were to go to pick up our baby girl. About midnight, I looked out the window and saw snow and sleet falling. The streets looked slick.

I didn't tell Lena, who was already asleep. She goes to sleep very easily, a gift that I don't possess. I am a late-night person, and I guess the thrill of the next day was keeping me awake. The next six hours seemed like an eternity. Morning finally came, and I told Lena about the weather. She looked out the window and said, “What are we going to do, Carl?” I encouraged her not to panic. I didn’t say it, but I knew in my heart that God had gotten us this far, and he wasn’t going to let us down. We would be able to get our baby girl.

I assured Lena that at the right time I would call Mrs. Sue Noble, the director of the Social Service Adoption Department. She would know if there were any changes to picking up our baby. We went downstairs to the restaurant and ate breakfast.

About nine o’clock in the morning, I made my call to Mrs. Noble. “Yes, Mr. Barger,” she said, “the plans are still on, but the location has changed. The hills to the Social Services Department are too slick for an automobile to climb, so we are taking the baby to the Arkansas Department of Welfare complex. You can pick up your baby there.”

At ten o’clock in the morning, we were at the Arkansas Department of Welfare, not far from the Arkansas State Capitol. We had not been there long when Mrs. Noble came to meet us and escorted us into a conference room for final instructions.

We heard a baby crying in the next room, and every time we heard a cry, Lena and I looked at each other and smiled. She grabbed my arm and dug her fingernails into it. We could hardly wait until we could hold her in our arms! Actually, we were on pins and needles, as the saying goes.

At one time, we were seated on a couch in a room with about twelve young women sitting at their desks. From the looks on their faces, we must have been an odd-looking couple. We carried a diaper bag packed with enough diapers and clothes for a month, a baby carrier, and blankets. It was cold outside, and we didn’t want our baby to catch cold on her first day with us.

From time to time, we heard that baby cry, and, assuming it was ours, Lena would grab my hands and squeeze them so hard I thought she would cut off the circulation. As I looked around the room, every girl in the office broke into laughter. We must have been some sight!

We were finally called into a small office where Mrs. Noble gave us last minute instructions. I don’t think her information really registered with Lena and me. All we wanted at this time was to get our hands on our baby.

Mrs. Noble knew we were ready and went to the door and asked that the baby be brought in. A nurse brought our baby through the door and handed her to Lena. When I looked at her, I knew this baby was God's gift to us. Lena and I had already decided we'd name her Carla Lynn Barger.

Carla was the baby Lena had longed for all the years of our married life. This baby would bring many joyful minutes into our lives. Our lives would never be the same, and that didn't bother me in the least.

As Lena stood holding Carla, I could feel God's presence. I knew without a doubt that God had made Lena to be a mother. Although, she didn't carry Carla in her body, she was going to be a great mother.

Mrs. Noble left us alone with the baby for about thirty minutes. We held her, passed her back and forth, cried, and laughed some. Our hearts were so full of joy we could hardly speak.

After about thirty minutes, Mrs. Noble came back in and said, "Well, do you want her?"

That was the stupidest question we had ever been asked. In fact, I would have liked to have seen her try to take that baby away from us. She asked what we planned to name her. We told her Carla Lynn, and she wrote it down. We wrote her a check for ten dollars to pay for the pink, one-piece suit Carla was wearing, and she told us we could take her home.

On our trip home from Little Rock, Carla opened her eyes off and on. She didn't cry a minute and was so good. She seemed to sense security in Lena's arms, and she certainly would fill that empty space in our hearts for a child.

Lena didn't go back to work. She began her daily routine as the mother to our Carla. God had blessed me by helping me find someone to teach English in the middle of the school term. Lena called me every day to relate something that Carla had done that we'd not seen her do before. The mother-daughter relationship had begun. Lena was such a good mother. She provided for Carla's every need.

Since I worked during the day, Lena took on the responsibility of getting up with Carla and feeding her during the night. It wasn't long after we got Carla that she started sleeping all night long. She was really an unusual baby. It didn't take Carla long to have me wrapped around her little finger. Lena told me that was an understatement! For the first time in my career in education, I was managing to get home before six o'clock.

Lena was so complimentary toward Carla. Since she took care of her most of the time, she saw things in Carla that no one else would see. She kept telling me that Carla was a perfect baby. I know there is no such thing, but she was as close as any baby ever came. She was pleasant and almost never cried, except during sponge baths. We had been told by our pediatrician to give her a sponge bath till her navel cord came off.

Lena had a wonderful book entitled, *Better Homes and Gardens Baby Book.* It contained much valuable information like step-by-step instructions on making formula, sterilizing bottles and nipples, and bathing a baby. We relied heavy on that book.

The day finally came for the first tub bath. Much to our surprise, Carla loved the tub bath. She didn't cry and loved the water.

Carla started sucking her thumb when she was seven days old. I thought that was the sweetest thing I'd ever seen. There was no need for a pacifier, which could be dropped on floors or tied around her neck on a ribbon.

Our love grew for her each passing day. We had a family, and I was certainly enjoying what we were experiencing. We loved to take Carla to church and out to eat with us. We went to the Town House Restaurant in Magnolia every Sunday for lunch. Lena would first feed Carla, and then Carla would sit in her high chair and chew on a hard crust of bread. She loved bread! Everyone who came by made comments about how beautiful she was. Naturally, we enjoyed every compliment!

In a way, the first six months after Carla came to us seemed like a long time. We were told that the biological mother had a right to change her mind about giving Carla up for adoption. We lived with the fear that this just might happen, but we prayed that God would let Carla remain with us.

The six-month waiting period was finally up. Our lawyer, Mike Kinard of Magnolia, was hired to do the legal work for us to adopt Carla. The day came for the court hearing for the birth certificate to be changed to our names as parents of Carla Lynn Barger. We were so excited and took Carla with us to court.

When Mr. Kinard was reading the information to the judge, he mistakenly called out Carla's given name, "Susan Ann Gates," a name, I would never forget! We were not supposed to have heard the name. It would be twenty six years later that I would understand why Mike Kinard called out the name of Susan Ann Gates. It was all in God's plan!

The judge's degree was handed down, and we were awarded Carla as our legal and wonderful daughter. After the hearing, Mr. Kinard came back and congratulated us on being the legal, adoptive parents of Carla Lynn Barger. We felt a sense of security knowing that it was over. No one could take our beautiful daughter away from us. We were her parents and would always be her parents.

CHAPTER 19

Bobo the Cat

Three months after we brought Carla home with us from Little Rock, she developed allergies. From the allergies she developed a runny nose, which caused her to develop a horrible cough and wheezing. At the age of four months, she spent a week in the Magnolia hospital with pneumonia. Soon after she was free from pneumonia, she developed ear infections.

It broke our hearts to see our little baby girl go through this type of suffering. For the first year of her life, Carla coughed and wheezed so badly that many nights Lena sat propped up on the couch holding her upright on her chest. In that position, she coughed less and could sleep.

Since the allergies were causing so many problems, I convinced myself that part of Carla's problems might be Bobo, our live-in cat. All during the time I was growing up, I heard Ma and her friends discuss cats. One such story went like this: One morning a lady went out to milk her cow. When she returned to the house she found her baby dead in its crib. As she entered the room, she saw the family's large yellow cat jump from the crib and run past her into the hallway. She was convinced that the cat had lain across her baby and smothered it to death. Needless, to say, her husband killed the cat. Other tales were similar to my way of thinking that the dust or dander from cats contributes to certain types of allergies.

Ma would never let any of us have a house cat. She would tolerate them in the barn to kill rats but wouldn't let them come into our house.

When Lena and I were living at Balkman apartments on the Arkansas Tech campus, I brought home to Lena the prettiest little white cat I'd ever seen. The cat had one blue eye and one gold eye. We named him Bobo.

Lena previously had owned a male cat by the name of Sugarfoot. One day he got out of the apartment and mysteriously came up missing. We never knew what happened to him, but my guess was that he ended up in a science lab being dissected for a science grade.

Lena immediately had fallen in love with Bobo. At times, I thought she loved him more than she loved me, but I didn't let her know that. I might have been a little jealous of Bobo.

It was partly my and a friends's fault that Bobo became a mean cat. We played rough with him to see him get mad and fight back. He had a violent temper, and after he'd had enough of our roughness, he would lunge at us with all his might and tear into us. He never bit us, but he wanted to.

Bobo had been with us since our Arkansas Tech days. He was with us when we moved to Scotland. Later he moved with us to Southside, Bee Branch, and on to McNeil. I guess you could say he was our one and only child. Lena really loved that cat!

One day I stayed at home with Carla while Lena went into Magnolia to get groceries. After hearing Carla cough and wheeze I decided that Bobo had to go. I loaded him and Carla in the car and took off down a country road, not knowing what I was going to do with this beautiful but mean cat. I didn't want Bobo to starve to death. If I released him in an unknown area without food or water, he might die. I could never live with myself if I did that.

After driving for about two miles, I saw this nice clean yard with a white house on it. I knew someone had to live there. I drove past the house to a point that I felt was safe for me to release Bobo. I took him in my arms and said, "Bobo, after I leave, you go over to that house. I'm sure someone will give you water and food. I'm sorry for doing this to you, but under the circumstances, Carla comes first. Please forgive me for doing this to you." Then I gently released him to an unknown world. As soon as I released him, he just stood there and looked at me and meowed. I was so ashamed. This cat had always been a house cat. He had been neutered for several years. Oh, what had I done? That was the cruelest thing I had ever done in my life. I wondered if I could ever forgive myself. My only hope was that whoever lived in that white house would look after him and give him a decent home.

Carla and I got home before Lena returned from Magnolia. Everything was "cool" for several hours. Nightfall came around nine o'clock and Lena began to look for Bobo. I heard her go outside and call him several times. I was watching television, and pretended nothing was wrong. She came into the living room and said, "Carl, I'm getting really worried about Bobo. He normally is in the house by this time."

I told her maybe he was enjoying being outside tonight and not to worry about him.

By ten thirty, Lena was really upset. She was crying by this time. She looked at me with tears streaming down her cheeks and asked, "Carl, where could Bobo be? I just know something awful has happened to him!"

I was feeling really bad. What was I to do? If I told her, she would want to go out in the country and try to find him. "Honey, let's don't worry anymore about Bobo tonight. I'm sure when we get up in the morning, he'll be at the front door wanting in." Did I ever feel like a liar, which I was! This was certainly not like me at all!

Lena finally went to bed. She cried off and on all night. I lay there regretting what I had done, but I knew if I told her, it would be worse. The next morning came, and Lena was up checking for Bobo. He was nowhere to be found. I heard her going all around our trailer house calling his name. She came inside and said, "Carl, I know something bad has happened to Bobo. What are we going to do?"

"Lena," I said, "you know that male cats stray off sometimes and stay gone a few days. Let's don't panic right now." That was a stupid statement, and Lena knew it. We'd had Bobo neutered several years before, and Lena knew Bobo wasn't capable of responding like an alley cat. She gave me that crazy look, and I knew not to say another word.

I went to my office to start my day's work. Lena called my office in mid-morning and told me she had called the radio station and offered a reward for anyone who might have information about Bobo. I really didn't know how to respond. Although, I knew my conscience would not let me bear my secret much longer. I couldn't continue to put my wife through this torture. "Honey, when I get home today, we'll get in the car and drive the roads around our place and see if we can find Bobo." I knew exactly where I dropped him off, and if he were nearby, we would find him.

"Oh, thank you, Carl!" she said.

I began to feel like a low-down, good-for-nothing human being. God was surely chastising me for my actions!

About three o'clock Lena called my office and said, "Carl, a lady has just called in response to my radio appeal for Bobo. She said a cat that answers that description is under her house."

"That's great news!" I said.

She asked me if I could come home and go with her to check to see if this cat could be Bobo.

"Yes," I replied. "I'll be there shortly!" This was it! Maybe this was my way out of this problem. If this was Bobo, I would reveal to Lena what I had done, even though it would create a disastrous strain on our marriage.

I picked Lena and Carla up at our house and off we drove down that dusty country road which I had taken to drop off Bobo. The lady had given Lena directions to get to her house. Sure enough, we were heading in the same directions where I had dropped him off. When we arrived at the lady's house, Lena knocked on the door, and a nice looking, older, gray-haired woman greeted her at the door.

Lena introduced herself and explained that she was the one who earlier had visited with her by phone about the white cat. "The cat is under the house, I think, or he was earlier," the woman said.

As Lena began to call for Bobo, we immediately heard that familiar cat's meow and out came Bobo. He was so happy to see Lena! Lena picked him up, hugged him, and told him how much she loved him, and all that good stuff.

We returned to the house with Bobo and things got back to normal. Everything appeared to be all right with Lena and Carla, but my guilt feelings were still much alive in my heart and mind. Two weeks passed and I couldn't stand it any longer. I had to get this thing off my chest. It was driving me crazy.

I went home one day early from school and asked Lena if I could visit with her on the couch in our trailer. She immediately asked, "What's going on? Has something happened at school?"

"No, nothing has happened at school."

"What is it?" she asked with a strange look on her face.

"I have a confession to make to you."

"What kind of confession," she asked.

I spilled my guts to her about Bobo's mysterious departure. I explained the motive behind my actions. I shall never forget the look on Lena's face. She looked straight into my eyes and said, "I can't believe you would do that, Carl. How could you do such a thing?"

I felt awful again! She began to cry.

"I know now that I did the wrong thing, and I promise you I will never do that kind of thing again. I didn't do it to hurt you, I hope you know that." I put my arms around her and told her I was sorry and I loved her.

She just lay in my arms for a minute crying, and then she pulled away from me and said, "Carl, it's going to take me a while to get over this. I hope you know that."

"Yes, I know it," I said.

Things weren't good for the next two weeks. I found myself sleeping on the living room couch for the first time ever. However, after two weeks, Lena found it in her heart to forgive me for my crazy loss of judgment. I asked God to help me not to make that kind of mistake again.

As time passed Carla grew out of her allergy problems and became a very healthy and happy young lady. She was, and still is, my sweet baby.

CHAPTER 20

A New Son

Lena and I waited one year after the adoption of Carla and decided it was time to adopt another child. This time we asked for a boy. Knowing how long it took to adopt a child, we felt we needed to get the procedure started.

I called our good friend, Bryan Cordell, and shared with him our desire to adopt another child. I asked him what he thought our chances were in asking for a boy.

"First of all, I compliment you and Lena for wanting to adopt another child. You have proven yourselves to be good parents. I think you have a good chance. Although, keep in mind, it may take longer to find a child since you're specifying a boy. The sooner we get started on the application, the better. When can you and Lena come in to see me?"

After meeting with Mr. Cordell and filling out the necessary paper work, he shared with us that we had filed our application in a timely manner. The Arkansas State Social Service Department had voted to limit adoptive parents to one child. The new mandate would go into effect at the beginning of the next month. We had gotten our application in just under the deadline.

He informed us that several things had occurred to limit adoptive parents to one child. He said fewer and fewer babies were being given up for adoption, and more and more abortions were being approved.

Lena and I felt God's love and kindness was shining upon us once again. I am still amazed by how God loves us so much. Although we don't deserve the abundance of blessings, His acts of love keep on coming. What a loving and merciful God, He is!

It was on August 1, 1973, that we received another historical call from Bryan Cordell. This time it was Lena who answered the phone. She immediately pushed the speaker button so both of us could hear and make comments to Mr. Cordell.

Mr. Cordell asked if both of us were present.

"We are," Lena answered.

"Lena and Carl, we have a boy for you!"

"Oh, thank you, Mr. Cordell," Lena said with great gratitude and respect for Mr. Cordell, who had worked so hard for us.

"You can go to Little Rock and pick him up on Friday." We immediately let him know that Friday was a good time for us.

Our baby boy was four and half months old when we received Mr. Cordell's call. He had been living in a foster home recuperating from pneumonia. The doctors wanted to be sure that he was going to be okay before leaving Little Rock. We later learned that the birth mother had had a hard time deciding to sign the papers.

My heart felt it was going to burst with joy. Then it completely stopped when Mr. Cordell said, "There is a little problem I need to tell y'all."

I looked at Lena as she turned to look at me. I knew then that Lena's heart must be pounding with apprehension as mine was.

"Oh, what is it?" Lena asked.

"The baby has a condition called Pectus Excavatum," he said. "That's a slight indention in his chest caused from a curved sternum."

Much relieved, Lena exclaimed, "That's okay! I have the same thing." It wouldn't have mattered if he had told us the baby was blue-and-white striped. What mattered was that he was going to be our son, and he was, from the first moment we received the call from Mr. Cordell.

We scheduled an appointment for later that day in Mr. Cordell's office in Magnolia. At the meeting Mr. Cordell showed us a picture of the baby. The picture of the baby was taken in the home of the foster parent. He was propped in the corner of a brown chair. He was smiling and was the most beautiful little boy we had ever seen. Lena couldn't wait to get her hands on him.

Mr. Cordell shared some background information with us.

Our baby boy was born on March 15, 1973, at the Baptist Hospital in Little Rock. At birth he weighed eight pounds and five ounces and was twenty-one inches long. The current health information now shows he weighed thirteen pounds and five ounces. He had brown eyes, two teeth, and no hair.

The birth mother was sixteen years old. She was musically talented and athletic and had brown hair and brown eyes. The maternal grandmother was a school administrator.

Mr. Cordell said we were to pick him up at the Child Service Center in Little Rock at two o'clock in the afternoon on Friday, August 3, 1973.

Carla was two and half, but she knew she was getting a baby brother. As soon as we told her, she went to her room and returned with a large alphabet block and a blanket. Since she had a security blanket, she thought her baby brother should have one, too.

Mr. Cordell had told us the baby's favorite toy was a Fisher Price bluebird crib toy. We decided to go to Wal-Mart and buy the bluebird. We wanted something familiar for his homecoming. I was a little concerned, since he was already four and a half months old, that he might be overwhelmed by a houseful of strangers. His room had been ready since we moved from the mobile home to the superintendent's newly refurbished home in the middle of town.

Carla had graduated to a twin bed with a room full of new furniture. She was a big girl, not a baby anymore.

We had already decided we would call our new son Jeffrey, but had not yet selected a middle name for him. As we were traveling through Prescott, Arkansas, Lena saw a sign that read Christopher Real Estate Co. She had always liked the name Christopher.

"Carl, look at that sign. Let's call him Jeffrey Christopher. Since it has Christ as part of the name, I don't see how we can go wrong," Lena said.

I was in full agreement with her and right there in Prescott, Arkansas, we gave our son his name: Jeffrey Christopher Barger.

We arrived at the social services office around mid-morning and met with Mrs. Sue Noble, who went over the last-minute instructions with us. A woman came out of an adjoining room with our son. She brought him over and stood by Lena.

"Would you like to hold him?" she asked.

"Oh! Yes!" Lena answered as she reached for our baby boy.

Jeffrey reached out to Lena and jumped into her hands. I've never seen such excitement on this little boy's face, which broke into the widest smile, and then he popped his thumb in his mouth. That thrilled Lena, because Carla had been a thumb sucker too. Jeffrey was dressed in a blue-and-white-striped, one-piece outfit with little blue tennis shoes.

I walked over to Lena and the baby, and Lena asked if I wanted to hold him. I said, "Yes, let me hold him." He came to me willingly. I thought, *What a boy!* Here I was, a total stranger, and yet he came to me as if he knew I was his father. He was smiling with his thumb in his mouth. We had been blessed in so many ways! God saw fit to give us a second child. It was at that time I felt that our family was complete. Little did I know that seven years later God would have something else in store for Lena and Carl!

Before we left, we were asked what his name would be, and we said, "Jeffrey Christopher Barger." We were told about his feeding schedule, his breakfast time was six-thirty in the morning. He was being fed from an infant feeder in which all of his food was mixed. We were told he would rather play than eat.

Lena told me, as we were driving back to McNeil, about what happened to her when Jeffrey reached for her and she held him for the first time.

She said, "Carl, I can't rightly explain what happened inside my heart today. That little boy gripped my heart today, and I think it's always going to be that a-way. I know right now that we formed a bond today, one that will have a firm grip on our lives as long as we both shall live."

Over the years, I've observed Lena and Jeffrey's strong mother/son relationship.

All the way home, Jeffrey slept and woke up periodically. He'd open his eyes, look at Lena, and smile.

When we got home, Ann Coleman, a dear friend and our pastor's wife, had dinner prepared for us. We fed Jeffrey first, and then went to their house to eat. All through our meal, Jeffrey lay on a quilt in the den, slept some, smiled, and cooed the rest of the time. Ann remarked sometime during the evening, "That child is going to charm his way through life." She was right; he was a delightfully charming child and grew into a charming young man.

Carla and Jeff were asleep by eight o'clock, and both slept all night. Lena was up with Jeff's breakfast of cereal and fruit ready at six-thirty in the morning. She didn't want to make him wait on his first morning. He slept till eight thirty, so from then on he had breakfast at eight-thirty. Carla had slept till eight-thirty since she was a few weeks old.

We found out quickly that the woman in Little Rock had been right: he would rather play than eat. For several weeks, Lena had to clear the room when feeding him. If anyone else was present, he would "talk" and bounce around but would not eat. Soon, though, he grew out of that and could be fed with Carla. Both were good eaters. They would eat anything but liver.

For the next few days our house was like Grand Central Station. All our friends wanted to come see our new son and bring gifts. While visiting they would go on and on about how cute he was. He certainly got a lot of attention. We knew then that he could be a politician. He soon had everyone eating out of his hands.

We began to take him to the Town House Restaurant in Magnolia after church just as we had with Carla when she was little. He, too, loved to sit in his high chair and watch people as they went by. If they got close to him, he would kick at them and laugh.

Lena would take Carla and Jeffrey grocery shopping with her. She would let Jeffrey sit in the grocery cart, and Carla would walk along by her side. When he got old enough to talk, he would say to people, “Hi, what’s your name? You got any gum?” Everyone thought that was just precious! He was certainly an active child.

Jeff started walking when he was eight months old. He jumped out of his baby crib when he was fifteen months old. We had to put him in a regular bed at fifteen months for fear he might hurt himself by jumping over the rails of the crib. After he started sleeping in a regular bed, he would get up numerous times every night and come into our room. Lena or I would carry him back to bed. This went on for months. We would get up at night and go check on him for fear that he might get outside some way.

We installed locks high on the doors where Jeffrey couldn’t reach them. One night, Lena went to check on Jeff, and he was missing. We looked all over the house, and we were about to panic when I looked behind the couch. I don’t know how he got behind the couch, but there he was asleep on the flour!

I pushed the couch away from the wall and reached down to pick him up. He was so stiff. At first I thought he was dead. *Oh, God, don't let him be dead!* As I touched him, I felt the warmth of his body, and I saw he was breathing. I was so relieved! I called to Lena to inform her that I had found him. I picked him up and carried him back to his bedroom. As I lay him in his bed, he woke up and said, “Hi, Daddy!”

“Hi, Jeff. Are you okay?”

He smiled, closed his eyes, and went back to sleep.

Lena and I never knew what caused Jeff to sleep walk or be stiff as a board when we found him stretched out somewhere in the house. We just treasured the times he paid us visits in our bedroom in the wee hours of the night.

For three years after Jeff arrived in our family, we continued to experience happiness and contentment. I don’t think I could have been any happier anywhere else as a superintendent. I was blessed with an excellent school board, good staff, and some of the best kids in Arkansas. They were awesome!

CHAPTER 21

Coaching Changes

It was the beginning of my fourth year as superintendent at McNeil that our basketball coach, Phil Easley, resigned to return to his home school at Genoa Central near Texarkana, Arkansas. Coach Easley had been coaching all four basketball teams, as I had during my first year at McNeil.

The coach I wanted to hire for the boys was none other than Coach Ronald Jones of Quitman High School, Quitman, Arkansas. There was one problem. I had heard that Coach Jones would not be interested in coaching girls basketball! I decided to give him a call and discuss the possibility of his coming and coaching for us at McNeil. I explained my situation to him and said, “I’d like for you to come down here and win us a state championship.”

“Mr. Barger, I feel honored by your offer, but I have to refuse it because I will not coach girls.”

“What if I offered you the boys coaching job only? Would you accept it?”

He said, “Now we’re getting somewhere!”

Ronald Jones was one of the most popular boy’s coaches in Arkansas and had picked up the nickname of “Hoss Jones.” He was a builder of boys basketball programs. He was a great disciplinarian, and his coaching techniques, knowledge of basketball, and personality were respected by coaches throughout Arkansas.

There wasn’t enough money in the school budget to employ two coaches. Therefore, with the school board’s permission, I was given the opportunity to coach the girls. I felt good about my decision. If I could coach four teams back in 1969–70 when I became superintendent, surely I could handle two girls teams.

To make a long story short, the school board approved my recommendation to employ Coach "Hoss" Ronald Jones as our new boys basketball coach and approved my coaching the girls.

At the end of Coach Jones's first year, his junior high boys and senior boys won the regional tournament and went on to be successful in McNeil's first appearance in a state basketball tournament. Although he didn't win the championship game, he managed to get the senior boys in the semi-finals of the state tournament before they were defeated.

As for as the girls program, my junior girls won the district tournament, and my senior girls went on to the state tournament, where they were defeated by one point in the semi-final game by a powerhouse girls program from Guy-Perkins School.

After Coach Jones's first year at McNeil, his father became ill. He resigned his position as boys coach and returned to Hoxie, Arkansas, to take care of his father. His leaving left me without a boys coach. Our school budget had grown in revenues, and I was able to employ both a boys and girls coach.

I replaced Coach Jones with Jimmy Allen, who became a good friend. For our girls, I employed Nelda Smith from Emerson. I always felt I had hired the cream of the crop when it came to coaches.

During my fifth year at McNeil, there was a lot of talk about small school districts having to consolidate with larger school districts. I feared that if I stayed at McNeil, we would be consolidated with the Magnolia or Waldo Public Schools. I knew consolidation wasn't going to sit well with the people of McNeil. They loved their school and would fight to keep it.

I decided it was time for me to look around for a larger school system. Ironically enough, the Emerson Public School System's superintendent's job came open. Emerson was located in Columbia County and was about twelve miles south of Magnolia.

Lena and I decided that Emerson would be a good place to work. I applied for the superintendent's position and was hired in March 1974. The Emerson Public Schools system was larger than McNeil, and the pay was better. Emerson also provided a house on the school campus for the superintendent.

It was hard leaving McNeil, because the people there were so good to us, but I had decided if I wanted a career as a superintendent, it would be best for me to "climb the ladder," so to speak! McNeil will always hold a special place in my and Lena's hearts. It was at McNeil that God blessed us with two beautiful children. These babies brought joy and happiness to our hearts.

It was at McNeil that God blessed me with my first superintendent's job, one that prepared me for a bright future in public school administration. It was at McNeil that we made lifelong friendships: Pat Ward, Terry Teutsch, Jane Gunnels, Jo Polk, Curtis and Ann Coleman, Betty and James Pace, Franklin and Martha Jean Gunter and family, James and Wiley Staggs, Dale and Janie Mitchell, Cheri Gist, Hurlon Cross, Allen Cranford, James Crain, Jimmy Allen, Perry Polk, James and Janis Polk, and too many others to mention.

CHAPTER 22

Time for a Change

It was at Emerson that Carla started her formal education. She appeared in several little plays and Halloween contests. During kindergarten she was named Fall Halloween Queen in her class. I had the privilege of crowning her at a school assembly. I must confess that thrilled my heart!

I can still remember an incident that occurred when Carla was a kindergarten student in Emerson. My office was located in the Elementary School. Each morning two kindergarten students were sent to my office to get snacks for their morning break. Carla and another student did this for one week. During the week. Carla was responsible for coming to pick up the snacks, and she would come into my office and give me a hug and kiss. I was usually reading my newspaper and drinking coffee.

One day I was visiting her class and the teacher took time out to introduce me to the class. She then asked the class if anyone knew what the superintendent did. Carla immediately raised her hand. "Carla, do you want to tell us what the superintendent does?"

Carla's reply was, "He reads the newspaper and drinks coffee." I thought I was going to die from laughing. The teacher also cracked up. She finally got her composure and said, "Carla, that's right. Mr. Barger reads his paper to keep up with all the things that are happening in the world."

Art Linkletter, a popular television personality, once had a TV show called, *Kids Say the Darndest Things*! After Carla's answer, I decided I'd better watch my step from then on out.

It appears that kindergarten children can be very observant. Carla's teacher never let me live down the newspaper and coffee thing.

Like McNeil, we made several lifelong friends at Emerson. I was surrounded by some top-notch administrators in the state of Arkansas. They were experienced and very knowledgeable in their particular grade levels. Mrs. Evelyn Fitzpatrick, my elementary principal, was a hometown girl. She and her husband, Everett, adopted us, so to speak, while we were in Emerson. They were several years older than Lena and me, but that didn't seem to matter. They were young at heart and very sociable.

Evelyn loved to cook, and she'd cook dinner for us regularly. We attended the same Baptist church as they did. Evelyn and Everett became some of our closest friends in Emerson and remained close to us for the remainder of their lives.

Glen Turner was my high school principal. After I was hired as superintendent, I interviewed him for the high school principal's job. He had been at Emerson once before and was unhappy with the move he'd made. He jumped at the opportunity to come back to Emerson. His experience was much noticed upon his return. Between Evelyn and Glen, I had two of the best principals in Arkansas. They were good Christian people, whom I could trust, and they kept me well informed.

I've always heard that behind a successful superintendent was his secretary/bookkeeper. I can certainly attest to that. My secretary/bookkeeper was Peggy Maloch. She too was a hometown girl who had spent her entire life in a community west of Emerson. She and her husband, Elwin, owned and operated a large cattle farm. Peggy and Elwin were blessed with three of the smartest students in the Emerson Public School System. One of their sons, Bruce Maloch, is currently a State Senator in Arkansas.

Peggy actually made my job easy. Her financial experience as a bookkeeper was a great asset to me. When I needed to know something about our finances, she quickly had me an answer. Her personality was tops. She never met a stranger. She knew something about everyone who entered the front door of my office. If they were angry, she would have them settled down by the time they came into my office. She took care of me and kept me well informed.

When Mr. Turner left to take a superintendent's job in the Locksburg Public Schools, I was able to replace him with my senior high basketball coach, Arthur Pharr. Arthur's family lived next door to us in Emerson, and we had gotten to know each other well. Arthur and his wife, Nelda, had three children: two daughters and one son. Like the Turners and Fitzpatricks, they too were members of First Baptist Church of Emerson.

After I left Emerson to take the Nashville superintendent's position, Arthur was elevated to my position as superintendent.

While we were in Emerson, Lena continued her role as wife and mother. We decided early on, before we adopted, that she would not teach again until our children got to be school age. She continued to enjoy her role looking after our beautiful children.

After moving to Emerson, Lena decided Carla and Jeff needed to take dance lessons. She had read that dance and music played a positive role in one's academic achievement. The dance recitals became a big part of our life with the kids.

Jeff, at first, didn't enjoy taking dance, but after he got the hang of it, he enjoyed it. One of my primary responsibilities was to video tape all the recitals that Carla and Jeff participated in. It wasn't a problem because I was use to videotaping everything they did.

The four years we spent at Emerson were some of the happiest years of our lives. I had a wonderful job that paid me a good salary, a wonderful staff, a great little church, and several close friends we loved and with whom we enjoyed doing things.

The son of our basketball coach was old enough to attend kindergarten, but was immature. His parents, Ted and Barbara Waller, decided they wanted to hold him back a year, giving him an opportunity to mature. They asked Lena if she would babysit Trey. Since they lived next door, Lena felt this was a good idea as Trey and Jeff were already friends. It would be good for them to be playmates during the day.

Trey and Jeff became big buddies. There was little idle time for either boy. Our backyard was enclosed with a chain link fence. We locked the fence gates and let the boys play outside as much as they wanted to. Our German Shepard, Lady-K, became our babysitter in the backyard. If anyone came close to the fence or tried to come into the yard, she would lunge at them as if to tear them up. I think she felt the boys were her responsibility.

One day Ted came to my office to visit with me about a basketball problem. On his way back to the gym he looked toward our house and saw Jeff and Trey on the roof. He went to the back door of our house and called Lena.

"Lena, do you know where our boys are?"

"Yes, they are in the backyard," she replied.

Ted laughed. "You better come and look at this," he said. "Does that look like Trey and Jeff up there?" he asked, pointing and laughing at the same time.

"How did you get on top of our house?" she asked the boys.

Jeff pointed to a ladder, which I had left leaning against the house.

Ted and Lena went to the ladder and instructed the boys to climb down. When they were both on the ground, he looked at Lena and said, "You take care of yours, and I will take care of mine." Needless to say, both boys got spankings!

It was at Emerson that I first played golf. Ted was an excellent golfer. He played every time he got an opportunity. He invited me to play with him several times before I decided to take him up on his offer.

Ted played golf in Haynesville, Louisiana, a small town about six miles south of Emerson. He was a good teacher with lots of patience, which were needed when it came to teaching me the skills of golfing. I was awful! The first thing I had to learn was not to try to kill the golf ball. I also had to overcome my baseball swing when hitting the golf ball.

After accomplishing the correct stance and swing, his next challenge was teaching me the correct way to chip a golf ball. My chipping technique was just awful! In all my golfing time since playing with Ted and others, I still have very poor chipping skills. To make a long story short, Ted was an amazing teacher, one that I'll always love and respect.

In March 1974, I received a call from a good friend, Eddie Talley, from Nashville, Arkansas. He said, "Carl, my man, I've got a job for you!"

"I've got a job!" I replied.

"Yes, I know that, but I want you to apply for the Nashville School District Superintendent's position."

"I didn't know it was open," I said.

"It just came open."

Eddie went on to share with me that Dwight Jones, who had been superintendent at Nashville for what seemed to be an eternity, decided to retire. Eddie told me he had already put my name in the hat. He said it was wide open. No one within the system was being considered.

I asked myself if I was ready to move from a six-hundred and-fifty student enrollment to a school that had some nineteen hundred students. Eddie gave me Mr. Neely Cassidy's phone number. Mr. Cassidy was president of the school board. The search was on, according to Eddie.

After praying about it and consulting with Lena, I decided to apply for the job. Mr. Cassidy called me a few days later and invited me to come to Nashville and visit with him and the school board. I accepted, and I was hired to take the reins as superintendent beginning on July 1, 1978.

CHAPTER 23

Great Things in Nashville

Lena was more excited about this move than she was about Emerson. Nashville was a larger town, and Immanuel Baptist Church, where we were planning to attend, had a big GMA girls program. While we lived in McNeil and Emerson, Lena was heavily involved with GMAs.

The move to Nashville gave us an opportunity to purchase our first home. During the past nine years at McNeil and Emerson, a house and utilities had been furnished as a fringe benefit to the superintendent.

With a higher salary, I was able to buy our first home and start accumulating equity in it. It gave me a feeling of ownership for the first time since I had become a superintendent. It has always been my belief that a well-groomed yard complemented a house and made it more appealing should one have to sell it. I looked forward to working in my yard and making improvements to what was already there.

Lena and I quickly learned that shopping for a home was not as easy as we thought. We looked at several homes before deciding to relocate to a three-bedroom, two-bath, brick home, located on the corner of Oak and Ash Streets, in the west part of Nashville. The home was close to my office at the high school and the primary school, where Carla and Jeff would go.

The 1978–79 school year got off to a good start. Carla was in the second grade and Jeff started Kindergarten. Carla adapted to the second grade really well. She loved school and always looked forward to getting up and going to school.

Since Jeff was always a very active boy, we worried he would give his teacher fits when he started school. However, our worries were in vain. Jeff turned out to be a good student. His teacher, Mrs. Charlotte Hill, was always bragging about how well behaved he was and how smart he was. I asked myself several times, is this the same Jeff I have living in my household? Lena and I were so proud that he was a good student and that he wasn't giving his teacher fits. We felt at ease after hearing his teacher was bragging on him.

It was my responsibility to get Carla and Jeff to school each morning. I really enjoyed this time with them.

During the summer I purchased a green Vega station wagon. The color could be seen from far off. It was the type of color that everyone stopped and took a look at. In a few weeks, I was known around town as the superintendent that drove the green Vega.

Every morning as Carla and Jeff got in the Vega, we played a game. I would say, "Vega, say good morning to Carla and Jeffrey." I would disguise my voice and say, "Good morning, Carla and Jeff, how are both of you on this nice day?" They would laugh! I would then say to Carla and Jeff, "Say good morning to Vega."

They would say, "Good morning, Vega!" Vega played a major part in their lives each morning. It was my way of getting them ready for school and getting a few laughs along the way. I'm sure they thought Dad was crazy, but they were smart enough to play along with me. I think they got as much enjoyment out of being silly as I did. Carla has reminded me on several occasions about Vega. Vega for six years played a major role in Carla's, Jeff's, and my life. We had lots of fun laughing and being silly.

It became part of my responsibility also to help the kids get ready for school. I remember the song I sang to Carla and Jeffrey every morning while they brushed their teeth. I would ask, "Are you ready? Get set! Go!"

When they started brushing their teeth, I would begin my song. It went like this, "Brush those teeth! Brush those teeth!

Brush them up, brush them down, and brush them around and around! Get 'em clean! Get 'em clean! Brush, brush, brush!"

After brushing their teeth, I would ask them to open their mouths to let me see if their teeth were clean. Every now and then I would say, "Carla, you didn't pass, brush those teeth again." I did this so they would become conscious of doing a good job brushing their teeth.

Carla's teeth were crooked, but Jeff's were almost perfectly straight. I dreaded the day we'd be spending large amounts of money for braces on Carla's teeth. But, at the same time, I knew she was worth every penny we would spend.

I found challenges in Nashville that I hadn't had in McNeil and Emerson. Nashville High School was in pretty good shape, as far as looks and functional aspects of classroom use go, but the junior high school was awful. We were using the old high school downtown as a junior high school. It was outdated and had asbestos problems, along with several other weaknesses in the physical plant.

We were faced with getting our school patrons to support a bond issue to build a new junior high school, a new agriculture building, and make some needed repairs to the elementary schools.

This was my first experience selling a bond issue to the community. I found myself hosting community meetings and speaking at events at the local Rotary Club, Lions Club, and basically anywhere I could find a captive audience. I didn't do it by myself; I had a good local mileage committee who dedicated themselves to helping sell the community on a tax increase.

On September 18, 1979, we were at the Howard County Courthouse waiting for the results. When the county clerk announced the numbers, we were elated to learn that we had won by a two to one margin. Needless to say, it was a glorious night in the town of Nashville, Arkansas.

The passing of the mileage increase presented a new experience for me. I was now faced with learning to work with the bonding company we had retained, as well as the school architect.

While I was working on my school-administration degree, I had the privilege of taking several courses under Dr. Glen Cochran from the University of Arkansas. One such course was School Plant Planning, a course which thoroughly taught me the proper procedures to use when going into a new building program. Because of Dr. Cochran's teachings, I was able to lead my school board in the right direction in making decisions about our building program, which was a good experience for me. What I learned in Nashville would help me in future building programs in school systems where I would serve.

The beginning of the 1979-80 school year brought another huge change to our family. With both children in school, Lena felt it was time for her to go back to work. When the high school librarian's position opened at Nashville High School she applied for and got the job. Going back to work after being at home for eight years was a big adjustment for Lena—and for me as well. To make things easier for her, I took on some housework chores. I became a very good hand with the vacuum cleaner, if I do say so myself.

In late October, Lena was suffering from extreme fatigue. I thought it might have been brought on by her unhappiness with a job outside the home.

One day in early November, she became dizzy and lay down in the teacher's lounge where Kathy Ellis, the secretary, found her. When Lena told Kathy about her fatigue and dizzy spells, Kathy said, "Lena, have you ever considered that you might be pregnant?"

Lena said, "No, but since I'm thirty-five, it may be menopause." Lena decided to go home. She needed to lie down for a while. Bill Dawson, our high school principal, agreed and told her to go home. He would get someone to fill in for her at the library.

The more Lena thought about what Kathy said to her, the more she got excited. On her way home she went by the local drug store and bought a pregnancy test kit. The next day, she still wasn't feeling well and decided to stay home and rest. After we all left the house, Lena performed the pregnancy test.

That morning, I had been at the new junior high site with the school's architect, and then had gone to the local Rotary Club meeting. When Lena's pregnancy test showed positive, she called Jo Jo Reed, my secretary. She called several times to see if I had come back from Rotary. When I returned to my office, Jo Jo said, "Mr. Barger, Lena is trying to get in touch with you. She told me to tell you to come straight home and not to stop anywhere along the way."

That message really alarmed me. *What could be wrong?* I thought?

I jumped into my Vega and off I went, speeding to my house to check on Lena. If there had been a policeman on my route, I'm sure I would have been delayed by having to sign a speeding ticket.

When I rushed into the living room of our home, I saw Lena sitting on the couch in her robe. "Honey, what's wrong?" I said.

"Carl, come over here and sit down by me." She was smiling from ear to ear. Those beautiful brown eyes were beaming out at me like they had never done before.

When I sat down next to her, she looked at me with the sweetest smile on her face and said, "Carl, what if I told you I was pregnant?"

I jumped to my feet and said, "What?" Surely she was joking!

She said, "Yes, come with me." She took me by the hand and pulled me to the bathroom and showed me the test. It showed a blue plus sign.

"What does this mean?" I asked.

"Look at the picture on the box. If it looks like this picture, I'm pregnant," she said with an excitement I'd never seen in her.

I looked at the picture, and then I looked at the pregnancy test. They looked the same. "Honey, it looks like you are pregnant!" I shouted.

"I do believe I am," she very calmly said.

I hugged her and said, "This is just too good to be true!"

"I agree, but I think it's true," she said.

"You must go to the doctor right away and get this confirmed," I said.

We called Dr. Peebles, our local family doctor in Nashville, and shared with him the positive results of the pregnancy test. He said, "Lena, I want to be up front with you. I make it a practice to refer women who are having their first baby at your age to Dr. Jack McCubbin in Texarkana. He's the best doctor I can refer you to."

A few days later, we went to Texarkana, Texas, to see Dr. Jack McCubbin, who was to become not only Lena's doctor but also a good friend. Lena's pregnancy was confirmed by Dr. McCubbin on the Monday before Thanksgiving in 1979. The projected due date was June 28, 1980.

On Thanksgiving Day, Lena's mother and all her sisters came to Nashville to celebrate Thanksgiving Day with us. We had not yet told any of them the good news. This would be a total surprise for all of them.

Lena's youngest sister, Patsy Fife, was pregnant and expecting in February. After we sat down to eat our Thanksgiving meal and before the blessing was said, I told everyone we had an announcement. After getting everyone's attention, I said, "Y'all, Lena and I have some sweet news to share with you. I'm going to let her tell you what it is." Almost immediately everyone turned their attention on Lena.

"Carl and I have just found out that I'm pregnant." No sooner had Lena got the words out of her mouth when her mother said, "I knew it would happen someday. I just knew it!" Everyone was clapping and paying congratulations from all directions. They were all so happy for us. That day would go down in history as one of our fondest memories.

After reading Dr. McCubbin's full medical report, Earlene, Lena's younger sister, laid the paper down and said, "I wonder why it took fifteen years for this to happen!"

Lena replied, "I know why. God intended for us to adopt Carla and Jeff, and if this had happened when we first got married, someone else would have them." God's timetable and plans are so much better than ours.

CHAPTER 24

Pregnancy and Birth

Our first visit to Texarkana to see Dr. Jack McCubbin was interesting, to say the least. While visiting with Dr. McCubbin, he informed us that we needed to decide by our next monthly visit whether we wanted to have an amniocentesis done. He explained the risk of the test and also the urgency. He explained that, should the test reveal any abnormality, such as downs syndrome, that the time-limit to have an abortion was rapidly passing. We listened carefully, but neither of us said anything.

As we were driving home, we both remained quiet for about twenty minutes, and then Lena said, "Carl, I don't want to have that test done."

"Why?" I asked.

"I won't have an abortion regardless of the results."

"That's how I feel too, but I needed to hear you say it first."

We continued to discuss our feelings. We both felt that God had a special purpose for the child Lena was carrying, and we would just put our faith in Him and trust He knew what was best for our family.

On our second visit with Dr. McCubbin, we shared our decision and explained why we didn't want the amnio test. Dr. McCubbin leaned back in his chair and smiled. He said, "I'm glad you made that decision. Now I want to share something with you both." He told us that he was an only child and his mother was forty-two when she gave birth to him. He said, "Look at me. I turned out pretty good, didn't I?" Then he said, "We are going to do everything we can to see that this is a healthy baby."

Carla and Jeff had always known they were adopted but didn't understand fully what that meant until they saw Lena pregnant with our biological child.

As the baby started to move, Lena let Carla and Jeff feel her stomach and the movement of the baby. It was at this time that Jeff began to ask questions. Carla seldom asked a question. She was, by nature, an introspective child, while Jeff was very open and expressive. If Jeff thought something, it came out of his mouth. So Jeff had lots of questions about his "Birth Mother," as he called her. He wanted to know what she looked like, where she lived, how old she was, why she gave him up, and a thousand other questions. Lena and I always answered his questions as honestly as we could with the information we had been given from the Arkansas Social Service Department. Carla always listened to our answers to Jeff.

We always told Carla and Jeff that we didn't know who their birth mothers were or where they lived but we knew their birth mothers loved them very much.

Jeff's response to that answer was, "If she loved me so much, why did she give me away?"

Our answer to that question was, "She loved you so much she wanted you to have two parents to love you and a home that she wasn't able to give you when you were born."

We always told them that God gave them to us and that we are so thankful for them. We told them they are special!

As time went on, Lena became more beautiful by the day. She never had morning sickness like some women. She continued to be active with our family activities and looked forward to that special day when we would go to Wadley Hospital in Texarkana to give birth to our boy or girl. We chose not to take any test to learn which sex the baby would be.

The summer of 1980 was hot and dry. The temperature was over one hundred degrees for fourteen days in a row. My beautiful yard burned up. I tried to save my grass and flowers by watering daily, but it didn't help.

A week before Lena's due date, I was working in my yard when I injured my back. The pain was so bad I couldn't straighten up. I could hardly walk, and when I did, I walked stooped over. I walked around like an old man. I could barely motivate myself to put one foot in front of the other. My back injury couldn't have come at a worse time. Lena was already a few days past her due date.

Dr. McCubbin had previously scheduled Lena for a stress test on July 7. He wanted to see if everything was still all right.

We got up early in the morning, and I could barely straighten up my back hurt so bad! I managed to take grandpa steps to the car. I was hurting but didn't want Lena to know how bad. I wasn't about to let her go to the hospital without me.

We arrived at Wadley Hospital around nine o'clock in the morning. After checking in, the lab technician took Lena and me back to the lab where he performed the stress test. The stress test was to induce false labor to see how much stress was on the baby's heart. I'm not sure what all it measured, but it had to do with determining if the child's life was in danger.

At times, I felt I too was in labor because of my back pain. The test turned out good, and Dr. McCubbin told us to return to Nashville. He said, "It's just not time for the baby to come yet." We returned to Nashville and settled in for the rest of the day.

I left at six-thirty in the afternoon for my monthly school board meeting. The school board agenda was full, and the meeting lasted until around ten o'clock. Upon arriving home, Lena informed me that she had started having some tightening in her abdomen area. At first she thought it was just effects from the stress test that had been done earlier in the day. The contractions had started around seven o'clock and had become stronger and more regular, but were still several minutes apart. I immediately decided it was best for us to leave for Texarkana, since the hospital was fifty-five miles from Nashville. Our neighbors, Mr. and Mrs. Glenn Powers, came over to stay with Carla and Jeff, who both were already asleep.

Upon arriving at Wadley, Lena was placed in the waiting ward where expectant mothers were kept until they were ready to be wheeled to the delivery room. There were several women waiting to have babies. Some were young women, and some were older.

All around us I could hear ladies screaming and crying, "Oh, Lord, help me!" Some cried out for their mothers. They would scream, "Mama, help me." It was nerve racking! I never dreamed a woman went through so much pain giving birth to a child. I had never experienced this, and it certainly was not an encounter I was enjoying.

My back was hurting so bad, and by this time I had taken the pain pills and muscle relaxers prescribed by the doctor. I thought to myself, *Could my back pain be anything like what these ladies are experiencing?* I thought not!

I was so proud of Lena. While other ladies were screaming and crying and calling out for help, Lena did not scream out one time. What a tough and courageous wife I had! Lena had always been tough! She tolerated pain much better than I did, in fact. I always want a shot or some strong pain medicine when I feel pain. I'm a big baby when it comes to pain!

The waiting seemed to go on and on. The screams and crying went on and on. Lena would look at me and smile. At times I could see her grit her teeth, and I knew she wanted to scream out, but she didn't.

The nurse checked Lena from time to time to see how much she had dilated. The nurse would say, "Lena, just hang in there. It want be long!"

Gosh, I thought, *what does dilation have to do with it? Let's get this over!* With my back hurting as it was, I didn't have any patience. About 11:00 a.m. on July 8, the nurse said to Lena, "Lena, it's time to go." Lena just nodded her head in agreement.

Dr. Holland, the doctor on call, explained to Lena that he was going to do a spinal block because the baby was turned backward. The nurses had tried unsuccessfully to turn him several times.

Lena looked at Dr. Holland and said, "Just don't knock me out. I want to be awake when my baby is born."

Before Lena was wheeled into the delivery room, Dr. Holland looked at me and said, "Mr. Barger, you can come with us to the delivery room if you would like."

"Thanks, Dr. Holland," I said, "I believe I'll stay in the waiting room."

Dr. Holland looked at me and smiled. I think he was aware I was in pain. I knew if I went, I would have to stand, and standing was killing my back.

I gave Lena a kiss as they wheeled her into the delivery room. I wasn't prepared for child birth. We had not been to any child-birthing classes, so I wouldn't have known what to do anyway. As I look back on those crucial moments before the birth of our son, I now believe I was a down right coward.

The wait seemed like an eternity. I wondered how long it took to give birth to a baby. The only time I'd seen anything give birth was when I was a child back on my pa's farm in Higden, Arkansas. I saw one of our old sows give birth to several piglets. It didn't seem to be too difficult for her.

I tried reading, but that didn't work. My back continued to hurt. I tried standing, I tried sitting, and I tried about every position one could get in, but no relief came.

About 11:15 a.m., the nurse came out of the delivery room and said, "Mr. Barger, you have a son."

"Did I hear you right? I have a son?" My speech and body language must have been funny to the nurse, because she laughed.

"Yes, you have a son. Do you want to see him now or wait until we get him cleaned up?"

"I'd like to see him now, if that's possible," I said. For some reason, I didn't feel any back pain during my conversation with the nurse. My boy was big! I can't remember ever seeing a baby as big as he was. I immediately asked, "Is he okay?"

The nurse smiled and said, "Mr. Barger, yes, he is okay. He's a healthy baby."

I said, "Thank you." I felt such a relief. I was worried because he was so big. I thought something might be wrong with him. I had seen other new born babies, but nothing could compare in size to my boy. His chest was huge! The head was supposed to be the largest part of a baby's body, but our baby's chest was larger. He weighed nine pounds and eight and a half ounces. Lena and I had done well. With the help of God, we had created something very special!

Another nurse took me to the recovery area and told me I could wait there until they were finished with Lena. While waiting to see Lena, I started calling as many of our relatives as possible. The first person I called was my mother.

"Ma, we have a healthy baby boy, and he is huge!"

"Carl, I am happy for you. Give Lena my congratulations, and tell her I love her and look forward to seeing my new grandson soon."

"Ma, I can't believe how big he is. He's a monster!"

She laughed! I then called Lena's mother, who volunteered to call Lena's sisters. I was glad she offered to call, because I had used all my quarters at the telephone booth.

After completing my calls, I quickly went to the nursery to see our baby boy. I couldn't believe my eyes. The nurse had put my son in the middle of about eight other babies, and he made all of them look like baby dolls. When people came up to the window to look at the babies, I could hear them say, "Look at that baby. He is so big!"

I could not stand it any longer. My father's pride got the best of me and I said, "That's my son!"

I then went to see my lovely wife. As I entered her room she was just waking up. When she opened her eyes and looked at me, she said, "Carl, isn't he beautiful?"

I said, "You bet your life he is!"

Actually, I thought he was the ugliest baby I had ever seen before the nurses cleaned him up. He was now beautiful! We rejoiced together and praised the Lord for our new son. We named him Jonathan Curtis Barger.

CHAPTER 25

A Hot and Dry Summer

Three days passed, and it came time for us to take our son home to Nashville. Earlene had already arrived at our home in Nashville to help look after Carla, Jeff, and Curt until Lena got back on her feet. As we arrived home, we immediately discovered the air compressor in the main air conditioner of the house had gone out. It was extremely hot, too hot for a newborn baby. Fortunately, we had a den that had been added onto the main part of the house, and it had a window air conditioning unit. We moved Curt and his cradle into the den where it was cool.

I called my friend who owned the local Western Auto Store and pleaded for his help in repairing—or replacing—the main air conditioner. Because of our friendship and due to the nature of my emergency plea, he placed us at the top of his priority list. I was thankful to hear that it was the compressor that had gone out and not the entire unit. In a matter of few hours, his men had our air conditioner up and running. We were so thankful to again enjoy the pleasure of feeling cool air coming from the air conditioning vents.

Carla and Jeff couldn't keep their hands off Curt. They were having a hard time calling him Jonathan so we told them to call him Curt. It was Curt from that day on.

The lack of rain brought on the worst drought that Southwest Arkansas had ever known. The grass was dead, and it crackled when we walked on it.

Our beautiful German Shepard, Lady K, died of a heart attack or a heat stroke. She had been in the family for ten years.

We all loved her. I found Lady dead underneath a shrub. I didn't want the kids to see her dead. I went into the house, told Lena and Earlene the news, and asked them not to let Carla and Jeff come outside for a while. Lady's death was like losing a member of the family. She had been a great babysitter over the years with Carla and Jeff. We never worried about the kids being outside in the back yard when Lady was there with them. She was so protective.

I took Lady to the country and buried her on a friend's farm. I wished there had been an animal cemetery to bury her in. I thought about burying her in the back yard where the garden was, but there were city restrictions that prevented anyone from burying animals on city property.

After I arrived back at the house, I informed Lena and Earlene that I needed to tell Carla and Jeff about Lady's death. Lena and Earlene followed me to the den where I had asked Carla and Jeff to meet me. I sat down in front of them and told them I had something to tell them.

"What is it, Dad?" Carla immediately asked.

"I'm afraid I have some bad news for you."

They just looked at me with question marks written all over their faces. I decided I would just be honest with them and tell them what happened.

"I'm sorry to tell you this, but Lady died today. I didn't want you to see her dead so I carried her to the country and buried her."

"Lady's dead?" Carla cried.

"I'm afraid so," I said.

"Daddy, how did she die?" Carla asked.

"I'm not sure, but I believe the heat was too much for her. You know how hot it is out there."

"We should have brought her inside," Carla said.

They began to cry. Lena came over and helped me comfort them. They loved Lady so much. For several days there were moments of sadness in our house.

I was thankful Curt was born during this time. He was a new toy, so to speak, for Carla and Jeff. They loved him and played with him at every opportunity they could. Curt was the stabilizing factor in helping all of us get through the grieving process of losing of our family pet.

Earlene was a life-savor during this time. She loved Carla and Jeff like her own and was so good with them. I don't know what we would have done without her.

The drought we were experiencing continued on into August. According to historical weather records, August 1980 would go down in history as being the hottest and driest month in Arkansas's history. During the latter part of August, we had a few showers that cooled things down, but the showers came too late to bring back the grass.

The farmers in the area were forced to sell a big portion of their cattle herds. The cattle market was flooded and the farmers took a tremendous loss because of low selling prices. It would take several years for the farmers to recover their losses.

When school started in the middle of August, Lena stayed home with Curt. I guess one could say we were old fashion in believing that the mother should stay home with her babies. Anyway, we had done that with Carla and Jeffrey, and we'd do that with Curt.

The next three years at Nashville were pretty uneventful. We had settled in as a family of five and were enjoying our church and participating in community events. We had made several friends, mostly from Immanuel Baptist Church.

During the six years that I served Nashville as its superintendent, we brought the high school and junior high into the North Central Accreditation, which put us up with the very best accredited schools in the nation. Our football program, under Coach Gary Segrest, was one of the strongest football programs in 4-A classifications in Arkansas. Everything was going smoothly.

It was during Christmas break in 1983 that I received a call from a good friend in Northwest Arkansas. He told me that Marvin Higginbottom, superintendent of the Bentonville Public Schools, had just announced his retirement beginning at the end of the school year. He went on to say that the school board was taking applications for his replacement.

For the last few years, I had become interested in the Bentonville Public Schools and decided, when Marvin Higginbottom retired, I would apply for his position.

I knew Marvin Higginbottom well through our Arkansas School Administrators Association. He was a nice man who was respected among the superintendents in Arkansas. He was perceived as being one of the top leaders in school administration in our state. Over the years, he shared some interesting things about his school system. The job opening came as a surprise to me because the last time I visited with Marvin, he indicated he would probably stay on for at least two more years.

My years in Nashville had prepared me for another challenge in my life. I believed the Bentonville School System, which was the fastest growing system in Arkansas, would offer me another challenge. In size, the Bentonville School System ranked in the top ten.

After visiting with Lena, I decided I'd submit an application to the Bentonville School Board. When the Bentonville School Board closed their application process, I was told that there were forty-eight superintendents vying for the position, of which twenty-three had their doctorate degree in education administration. Since I didn't have my doctorate, I felt I had a slim to none chance of getting an interview.

In early March, I received a call from Bentonville School Board President Charles Burke. He asked me if I was still available for an interview. I immediately said, "yes, Sir, I'm available."

The drive from Nashville to Bentonville was a long one. I was tired when we arrived in Bentonville for my interview. The school board arranged for me and my family to stay at the Ramada Inn in Bentonville for two nights. The Ramada Inn was located close to Ken's Pizza, where my family voted to eat dinner. We all loved pizza and frequent the Pizza Hut in Nashville quite often.

My family accompanied me to the administration building where I introduced them to members of the Bentonville School Board. I was impressed by how well my kids reacted to the board members' greetings. After introductions were made, Lena and the kids went to a nearby conference room where they stayed until my interview was over.

That was the first time I had interviewed before an eight-member board. After finishing my interview, I was convinced it had been a good one. The school board asked many questions about which I had some knowledge. I had spent a lot of time studying important facts about the school district, including finances, growth patterns, building needs, and curriculum needs. If I remember correctly, every school board member asked me questions.

I believe my previous experiences in McNeil, Emerson, and Nashville had prepared me well for my interview. For some reason, I was completely relaxed during the interview. I felt right at home with all eight of the school-board members.

On the second day, I had the privilege to ride around with two school board members to each school in the system. At each school, I was introduced to the principal who escorted me and the two school board members through the school. Meeting the principals gave me an idea of who I might be working with and what I could expect if I became their next superintendent.

On our way back to Nashville, my family and I discussed what they liked or disliked about Bentonville and the school system. My kids had the opportunity to see where they would be going to school should I be offered the job. They were all excited!

I really wanted the Bentonville Superintendent's job. I was confident that, if God wanted me to have the job, He would make it happen. I told myself I had to wait and be patient.

Two weeks passed before I received a call from Mr. Charlie Burke, the president, of the Bentonville School Board.

Jo Jo buzzed me in my office and informed me that Mr. Burke was calling. She asked, "Do you want me to put him through?"

"Yes, put him through!"

"Mr. Barger, our board has reached a decision, and you've been selected as one of the two finalists for the Bentonville Superintendent's job. Are you still interested?"

"Yes, sir, I am very interested," I said.

"Mr. Barger, do you have any objections to our board visiting your school? We will want to visit with your principals and some of your teachers."

"I have no objections at all," I said.

"There will be eight of us flying down from Bentonville. Some will be visiting downtown and some will visit the schools," he said.

I invited all eight of the school board members to have lunch with us in our cafeteria. Our cafeteria was serving fried chicken and peach cobbler for dessert on that particular day. Our cooks made the best peach cobbler in Arkansas. I knew I wouldn't be disappointed in their cooking.

After lunch, the school board met with me in our board room at the high school. They were very complimentary about how the citizens of Nashville and my teachers felt about my leadership role as superintendent. Mr. Burke even went so far as to get a haircut from Dale Reed, my personal barber.

"Did you find any faults in me from Dale?" I asked.

"I wish my barber had as many good things to say about me as your barber did about you. Do you tip him a lot?"

I laughed and said, "Dale's a good man!"

For some reason, I was nervous. I told myself to be calm and not show my nervousness. I really don't know why I was nervous. I wasn't nervous at all during my interview process in Bentonville.

It was three days later when Mr. Burke called me on the phone. To be perfect honest, I was a little hesitant about taking the call. I had been on pins and needles since their visit. I was afraid he was calling to let me know the board had gone with the other applicant because he had a doctorate degree.

When Jo Jo, put Mr. Burke's call through to me, I said, "Hello!"

"Mr. Barger, this is Charles Burke. How are you doing this morning?"

"Everything is good with me, Mr. Burke," I said.

"That's good, Mr. Barger. I have some good news for you."

I can't express to anyone how I felt when he mentioned good news. Just maybe, just maybe, he meant I got the job.

"Mr. Barger, the Bentonville School Board met this morning and voted unanimously to offer to you the position of superintendent of the Bentonville School System. Will you accept the offer?"

"Yes, Sir, I will accept!" I said.

I was glad he wasn't able to see me when he announced the school board's decision. I was so excited I was bouncing all over my office. My body was making movements I'd never made before!

"We would like you to come to Bentonville on Thursday, March 20, to sign your contract and to attend a press conference," he said.

"I will be there," I said.

On Thursday, March 20, 1984, I officially signed my three-year contract. I would begin my tenure as the new superintendent on July 1. My prayers had been answered. *Hallelujah!*

We were successful selling our Nashville home, and on June 15, 1984, we moved to Bentonville. It was hard to leave our friends behind. Carla took it the hardest. She had finished the seventh grade and was at an insecure age. She didn't make friends easily. She just knew she would never have friends again.

Leaving our first home in Nashville had been one of the hardest things Lena and I had encountered. For six years we had enjoyed the comfort of our first home and making friends with several families in Nashville. It was in that home that Lena and I conceived our son, Curt. It was in that home that Curt spent the first four years of his life. It was in that home that we realized our family was complete.

The Nashville Public School System afforded me the opportunity to grow in leadership roles. As superintendent, I became active in both community and state activities. While in Nashville, I served one year as president of our local Rotary Club. My leadership role in Rotary gave me an opportunity to get to know the business people. It was through Rotary Club and my church affiliation at Immanuel Baptist Church that I acquired a good grasp of community affairs. I served on several state legislative committees as well and lobbied for educational bills in several of the state legislative sessions during my tenure as superintendent. It was also here that I first met and became friends with Bill Clinton, governor of Arkansas and later two-term President of the United States of America.

Governor Bill Clinton was a big supporter of education in Arkansas. While serving as superintendent, Governor Clinton was our keynote speaker at two of Nashville High School School's graduation ceremonies.

I was active in both Governor Clinton's gubernatorial races as well as his campaign for President of the United States of America. One of Bill Clinton's qualities as a person was his ability to remember a person's name. Once he met you, he'd call you by your first name.

I can still remember sitting in a large meeting room at the Arkansas State Capitol when Mr. Clinton was addressing a group of legislators and superintendents. Mr. Clinton looked over to his left where I was sitting and asked, "Carl, what are your feelings?" I can't even remember what we were discussing at the time. However, I do believe he liked my answer. The thing I do remember was that my ego got a big boost that day. I was honored to be asked my opinion by the governor of Arkansas.

During Governor Clinton's terms as governor, he continued to be a peoples' governor and was well respected by the majority of the voters of Arkansas. In my opinion, he was one of the best governors we've ever had in Arkansas. It was during his terms as governor that our teachers received the largest raises ever given in Arkansas.

The balancing of the United States budget was a major accomplishment during Clinton's presidency, an accomplishment that hasn't been achieved again by any president since.

It was hard to leave good friends like Tom and Shirley Garney. Tom served on my school board, and we both attended Immanuel Baptist Church.

Jo Jo Reed, who had been my secretary for six years at Nashville who I came to love and respect, really took good care of me as superintendent.

I had always heard that there were two people in a school system who could make or break a superintendent: the superintendent's secretary and his bookkeeper. I was fortunate in both cases with Jo Jo as my secretary and Mrs. Maxine Branch as my bookkeeper.

The last people I want to mention here are Neely and Nina Cassidy, who became two of our closest friends in Nashville. He served as president of my school board when I was hired as superintendent, and we served on the deacon board together while attending Immanuel Baptist.

Mr. Cassidy ran for state senator from Howard County and portions of other counties in Southwest Arkansas and easily won. He served several years in the Arkansas State Senate before retiring.

It was an honor for me to help with his first race as state senator. He is one of the sharpest business people I've ever known. He has done well in his life and has contributed much to the economy of Nashville. He and Nina reside in Nashville and continue to give God the credit for all they have.

CHAPTER 26

The Challenges in Bentonville

It was always easy for me to adjust in new places, but I found that not to be the case for Lena and Carla. As we moved around from place to place, Lena described me as a person who can rip up my roots at any time and leave nothing of myself behind, whereas she is totally the opposite. She puts deep roots in a house and community, and when we move, she pulls them up, one by one, and replants them in the same manner. Therefore, transition takes longer for her.

One of the first things we did after moving to Bentonville was to change our church membership from Immanuel Baptist Church to Bentonville Baptist Church. First Baptist was a large church in the middle of town. Its pastor was Brother Tom Smith. We immediately fell in love with Tom and his family. It didn't take me long to see that Tom and I had lots in common, mostly sports. He loved playing basketball, and so did I. For exercise, we battled it out time and time again on the basketball court playing one-on-one. He, like me, was a competitor. He didn't like to lose. Neither did I.

Lena and I have always been in agreement that one of the main criteria in selecting a church is its youth program. We wanted a church that had a good youth program so our kids would be involved in Christian activities with Christian friends. First Baptist had one of the best youth programs of any church in Bentonville.

After a few weeks at First Baptist Church, our family returned to being normal again. The kids were happy and loved the church and their new friends.

My assistant superintendent, David Green, and his lovely wife, Nanci, became two of our best friends. David and Nanci had a daughter, Ricci, who was in the same grade as Carla. Ricci and Carla became good friends and, on the first day Carla attended Bentonville Junior High, Ricci was right by her side. Ricci introduced Carla to several of her friends, and it wasn't long before Carla had adjusted to her new school.

Jeff was enrolled in Old High Elementary School, the formal Bentonville High School. It didn't take Jeff long to make new friends either. He came home the first day of school announcing that his new best friend was also named Jeff. He and Jeff Wagner remained friends all through high school and even shared an apartment when they both attended college at the University of Central Arkansas in Conway.

We enrolled Curt in the Building Place Pre-school, a school which taught Christian principles. Curt was unhappy from day one. He cried every day when Lena dropped him off and every day when she picked him up. Since we had paid for two weeks of child care, I insisted he stick it out, thinking he might adjust and start to enjoy it before the two weeks were up. He didn't, so he became a school-drop out at age four.

My first year at Bentonville was truly an interesting one. After taking the job, I was informed by the school board that we were in great need of a building program. The school had not had a mileage increase in eighteen years. The past administration had been blessed with property growth assessment so they could use second-lien bonds to keep up with the building needs. Things quickly changed, however. Bentonville School System was growing so fast that the school board could no longer rely on second-lien bonds. The district badly needed a new mileage in order to keep up with the school district's building needs and to employ additional new teachers.

There was one big obstacle standing in our way of getting a new mileage rate passed: convincing the community of Bella Vista to support a tax increase. Bella Vista was a retirement resort of over eight thousand people who came to the area to escape high taxes where they had been living before, mostly from the northern part of the United States.

As superintendent, I was given the responsibility to convince them to support the school mileage. To accomplish this, I spent many days speaking at professional clubs, such as Rotary, Kiwanis, Lions, and women's social groups. By the time the school mileage came up for a vote, I had pretty much convinced those in Bella Vista to support it. On the third Tuesday in September, our mileage passed by a 3-1 ratio in Bella Vista. I felt good. It was a momentous task to educate the community of our educational needs, but the Bentonville school district voters came through with flying colors.

During the next four years, the school district of Bentonville doubled its enrollment. We again had to go back to the voters for a mileage increase. I followed the same plan I had used during the first mileage campaign, and again it worked. We were successful for the second time in getting the mileage passed.

Carla, Jeff, and Curt all became active in their schools. Carla made the starting lineup on the junior high basketball team. It was at Walton Junior High that Carla began to come out of her shyness. She became involved in Drama Club and landed a starring role as Peppermint Patty in "Snoopy." She was great in the role! She became popular in school and involved herself in many clubs and organizations. She ended up being one of the top graduates in her senior class.

Jeff was an all-around athlete. By the time he was in the ninth grade he was starting on the basketball team and shared the quarterback role with his friend Scotty Redman as co-quarterback of the Bentonville Tiger Cubs football team. He loved football—and girls! Yes, I did say girls! Jeff attracted older girls. That was something Lena and I had to monitor during his sophomore year.

One of the worst things that happened to Carla during her five years in Bentonville was a motorcycle wreck. When Carla was in the eleventh grade, she and her friend Rhonda Abram had a motorcycle wreck on a country road near our home. Rhonda was the only one wearing a helmet. Carla was riding behind Rhonda. As Rhonda rounded a curve in the road, she applied her brakes, got in some loose gravel, and lost control of her cycle. Carla was thrown from the cycle face down onto the road. Rhonda was thrown onto the shoulder of the road. The cycle ended up in a ditch.

I was working in my front yard when neighbor Ann Burkes drove up. She said, "Carl, Carla and Rhonda, have had a wreck between my house and here. They don't seem to be hurt badly, but you need to go down there."

I immediately jumped into my car and went to the wreck. As I approached the wreck site, I saw blood flowing from Carla's mouth and dripping all over her shirt.

"My Lord, let her not be hurt bad," I prayed. As I approached her, she began to cry, and I said, "Sugar, are you hurt?"

She looked at me and pointed at her mouth. She was bleeding badly. I was thankful I had a clean handkerchief in my pocket. I immediately handed the handkerchief to Carla and instructed her to apply pressure to our mouth with the handkerchief. As I pulled the handkerchief from her lips, I saw she had completely torn her lower lip away from her gum area. It was awful! I told her to hold my handkerchief tight to her mouth and for her and Rhonda to get into my car.

Rhonda was holding her arm. It wasn't broken, but badly bruised and scratched. I rushed both of them to the emergency room at Bates Memorial Hospital about two miles from where the wreck occurred. Upon arrival, the nurse took one look at Carla and called the doctor. Carla was escorted to a waiting room. Rhonda's parents were called, and she was taken to the x-ray room.

As we waited for the doctor, I took a close look at Carla's mouth. I knew she had really messed up her lower lip. I knew it was going to take a lot of stitches. The doctor was going to have to numb her lip, and Carla was going to have a fit. She hated shots.

The doctor entered the room, took one look, and said, "Young lady, you sure did it up right!" He explained to Carla that he was going to have to clean her lip before starting the stitching.

Carla screamed, "No, I don't want a shot! Dad, please don't let him give me a shot!"

"Carla, the doctor knows what he's doing. He's going to have to give you a shot. The shot will numb your mouth so he can clean your lip. You have lots of foreign objects he's going to have to remove before he can stitch your lip. I'll be right here holding your hand. Trust me, it's going to be all right," I said as I held her hand.

Carla didn't like it much and cried when the doctor was injecting her with the needle. I knew it had to be hurting from the way she was flinching. It took several minutes to remove the gravel in her lip and remove the excess skin she had torn loose. The doctor put thirty-two stitches in her lip, a major undertaking. She also had to have three stitches above her upper lip. After the doctor finished, she looked awful! I followed the doctor outside and asked him if the lip would grow back to its original position.

"Mr. Barger, I'm concerned about the damage Carla's done to her lower lip, but I do think it will look normal after it completely heals. I've done the best I can and will monitor the healing process carefully for the next few weeks. It will take five to six weeks before she will be completely healed. She needs to drink only liquids for a while."

Rhonda was waiting in the waiting room with her parents when Carla and I came out of the doctor's office. After being assured that Rhonda was going to be all right, I took Carla home. When we arrived back at the house, Lena had returned from her teaching job at Oakdale Junior High School in Rogers. I had previously called her and told her about the accident. I told her to stay at home, because I had everything under control, and we'd be home shortly.

Lena met us at the door and immediately started crying when she saw Carla. It really upset her to see Carla in such a mess. She and Carla just stood with arms around each other and cried. Carla had not yet seen herself in a mirror. I really dreaded that moment. She was not going to like how she looked. Lena and I took her back to her room and she looked in the mirror. She began to cry again, and once more I told her she would be okay. I tried to reassure her by telling her the doctor said, after she healed, she would look normal. By now her lip had swollen to three times its normal size. I informed Carla that she could stay home for a few days until the swelling went down.

The next morning came and we heard Carla up in her bedroom moving around. Her bedroom was above ours. Lena went upstairs to see why she was up moving around. When she entered Carla's room, Carla was getting ready for school.

"Carla, what are you doing?"

"I'm getting ready for school."

"Carla, I don't think you need to go to school."

"Mom, I can't miss school. I've got these tests coming up and yearbook assignments that have to be completed."

"Carla, are you sure you are up to this?"

"Mom, I know I look awful, but, yes, I'm up to going to school."

Although we felt it would be better for Carla not to go to school, we decided it was her choice and supported her in her decision. I admired her so much. She looked pretty terrible, but all of her friends were so nice to her at school. They were all happy she had not been hurt any worse than she was.

She made it through her first day without any problems and never missed a day of school because of the wreck. She was a brave young lady, and I respected her for her courageous attitude. She, like her dad, was not a quitter!

After five weeks, Carla's lip looked normal. Although her lip had healed, she developed a habit of picking her lower lip. I thought maybe the doctor didn't get all the fine gravel out and that it bothered her. At times she would pick her skin enough to make her lip bleed, but after a few months, she stopped picking her lip.

When she was a senior, Carla survived a car accident with two of her friends. She was riding around on a country road with Dwayne Webb and Jeremy Axe, both friends from our church.

Dewayne was driving and lost control of his Bronco and flipped three times before coming to a stop. None of the three was seriously hurt. Carla had a bump on her forehead but nothing serious. We were thankful that none was seriously hurt.

Lena and I did a lot of praying that God would help us get through these teenage years without losing a child.

Carla's senior year was very busy. She and her friend Ginger Brown were yearbook editors. Carla was also active in several clubs and organizations. She graduated with honors from Bentonville High School. I was very proud of her!

It gave me a real sense of pride and achievement to be able to present my first child with her high school diploma. The baby God gave us some eighteen years earlier was now a beautiful young lady who had accomplished the task of graduating Bentonville High School. She was graduating with honors, which she had worked hard to achieve. She would be going to the University of Central Arkansas in Conway in the fall.

As Carla started across the platform to receive her high-school diploma, I thought to myself, *Do I just shake her hand and say, "congratulations," or do I hug her?* I didn't have to do anything. My daughter put her arms around my neck and gave me a big hug and said, "Thanks, Dad!"

"Congratulations, Carla," I replied.

She smiled and walked off the platform. That was a very touching moment in my life. My little girl would soon leave her nest and become part of this big world. I asked myself if we had prepared her for what lay ahead.

CHAPTER 27

Ma's Death

It was one o'clock in the morning, July 10, 1988, that I was awakened by a phone call that brought grief and sorrow to my soul. The phone call was from my niece Cindy Leslie, who lived nearby and taught school in the Roger's School District.

As I reached for the phone, next to my bed, the strangest feeling came over me. "Hello," I said.

"Uncle Carl, this is Cindy. Has anyone called you about Grandma?"

"No one's called. What's wrong, Cindy?"

"Dad called me a few minutes ago and said Grandma died."

My mind just froze! My train of thought was blank. Lena touched me on the chest and said, "What is it, Carl?" I certainly wasn't ready to hear this type of news at one o'clock in the morning. Finally, I got my composure back and told Lena what had happened.

"Cindy, did Jim say when this happened or how she died?"

"Dad said Grandma passed away around eleven thirty last night. He asked me to call you. I think Faye and Bob went with the ambulance to Heber Springs. That's probably the reason Faye hasn't called you."

"Cindy, Ma was doing well last weekend when I was there."

"Dad said she had a heart attack. She went peacefully."

"Thanks for calling, Cindy. I'm going to try to call Faye to find out more information."

I sat on the edge of our bed and started crying. Lena got up and came over and embraced me. She stood there with her comforting arms wrapped around me. She knew how badly I was hurting. Other than Lena, mother was my best friend. In a matter of minutes, my whole life flashed before me in regard to her. As a kid, I would think that if Ma died, I'd want to die too. I wouldn't want to go on living without her. Time and distance has helped over the years to prepare me for the day God would take her soul to be with Him in Heaven.

The last weekend I spent with her, she showed no signs that anything was abnormal with her heart or sleeping habits. She was joyful and happy all weekend. I would miss her so very much. She brought me into this world. She nursed me and cuddled me when I was a baby. She rocked me when I was sick. She fed and clothed me, doctored me, worked hard to provide for my needs. She was my adviser, my encourager, and, in so many other ways, she was my mentor.

The news of her death quickly left a hollow place in my mind and heart. I kept asking myself what it was going to be like without Ma. She had been an asset to so many of my brothers, sisters, and me. She practically raised all of my nieces and nephews before she became handicapped by her stroke.

Ma had suffered a stroke four years earlier, and it had left her paralyzed on her left side. She could walk with a cane, but mainly remained in her big rocking chair most of the day. She didn't want to leave her home to go to a rehab center. We agreed, as a family, not to put her in a rehab center, but decided to employ someone to come in to her house and give her physical therapy.

That worked pretty well, but the type of stroke she had suffered destroyed the part of the brain that controlled her left side and, regardless of how much rehab she had, it wasn't going to make her better.

The family pitched in financially and hired a full-time caregiver to stay during the week and family members stayed on weekends. It wasn't possible for any of us to stay during the week because of our full time jobs. Ma did well with these arrangements. Her thinking skills were not damaged by the stroke, and she was able to communicate with us very well. We were thankful God provided us an opportunity to be with her during her last four years of life.

I was finally able to make contact with my baby-sister, Faye, who lived next door to Ma. Faye and her husband, Bob, had just returned from the Olmstead Funeral Home in Heber Springs. Faye apologized for not letting me know. She had been through so much that the only people she informed were those siblings living nearby.

When I asked her for details she said, "Edna, Mother's caregiver, came to our house around ten thirty. She was frightened. She said, 'Faye you need to come quick. Miss Mamie is having breathing problems.' I called Bob and we both ran over to Mother's house. When we arrived, we went immediately to her bedside. She was breathing hard and gasping for breath. Bob and I were able to get her up and put her in her wheel chair. I looked down at her and told her we were taking her to the hospital. She looked up at me and smiled, and then dropped her head. That was it. She died so peacefully. It was so quick."

"So she didn't have to suffer long?"

"No, she went quickly. The doctor said she died of congestive heart failure."

"Faye, I'm so sorry. I'll be coming down tomorrow. Can you think of anything I need to do?"

"No, Mother had a paid-up funeral, and all arrangements have been made with the Olmstead Funeral Home. Since you are the only one who lives away, we thought we'd have the funeral two days from now. That will be Thursday, if that's all right with you?"

"That's fine with me. We will come down tomorrow. I love you, Faye. Thanks for all you've done for our mother."

The funeral was held at Ma's church in Quitman, Arkansas. She was a member of the Church of Christ. She had many family members and friends who completely packed the little church. Several people who couldn't get in remained outside. After the service, the funeral directors let those who had waited outside come in to view Ma's body and pay their final respects to one of the finest women who ever walked this great earth.

Ma was buried in the Shiloh Cemetery at Shiloh, Arkansas, next to my father, Edward Barger, who preceded her in death on September 6, 1968.

CHAPTER 28

Time to Move On

After my mother's death, I started assessing and analyzing my life and my job at Bentonville. Since coming to Bentonville as superintendent, I had averaged fifteen hours a day on the job. The superintendent's position was the most demanding job I'd had in my career as a superintendent. The school district was the fastest growing school district in Arkansas, and it was a tremendous challenge. There were several constrains of serving as superintendent in the Bentonville School District, and one of those was not having enough time with my family.

I've always believed that, next to God, family is the most important ingredient in my life, and I certainly wasn't coming close in those two areas of my life. The long hours I spent as superintendent left Lena as the chief provider of transportation and getting the kids to their many activities. This was hard on her since she was holding down a full-time English teaching position at Oakdale Junior High in Rogers, Arkansas. After much prayer and thought, I decided to resign my position at Bentonville Public Schools.

After I tendered my resignation and before I left, the Bentonville Rotary Club roasted me. As a part of the roasting, a chronological film clip was put together of different interviews I had been in over the past five-years. The clips came from five different television stations, all covering Northwest Arkansas during my five-year tenure. There were two channels from Fayetteville and three from Joplin, Missouri.

As I sat there watching the television clips, I couldn't believe my eyes at how much I had changed in appearance over those five years. The most obvious change was in my hair color. I went from being black haired to gray haired in five years. I knew right then that I had made the right decision to leave.

I've always heard that stress is a silent killer. After viewing the clips, I was convinced that stress was one of the worst things about my job. Although I learned a lot from being superintendent at Bentonville, I counted my blessings that God gave me an opportunity to take a job in Warren, Arkansas.

Just as at other schools in which I served as superintendent, Bentonville had its strong points as well. The Arkansas Department of Education always ranked us as one of the top academic school systems in the state. We paid our teachers well and were able to get good ones. Plus, I had a great administrative staff.

When I went to Bentonville, I brought my high school principal, Bill Dawson from Nashville, with me. Bill became the assistant principal at Bentonville High School under Bruce Jones. Between the two of them, the high school worked like a charm. Both were great principals and disciplinarians. I didn't have to worry about anything at the high school.

It was a privilege to get to know Sam Walton, his wife, Helen, and their son, Jim. The Waltons was big supporters of the Bentonville Public School System. Mrs. Walton was a lover of the arts. She would come to my office on different occasions and say, "Mr. Barger, I want our kids here in the Bentonville School System to be exposed to the finer arts. There are lots of art shows we can bring here for the kid's enjoyment. I'm willing to pay to have art programs brought here for their pleasure. There is only one thing I would ask of you. I don't want any recognition, do you understand?" Mrs. Helen would write personal checks to be deposited in our school's operational account to pay for the art shows brought to the campuses.

Mr. Sam and Mrs. Helen made several of our open house events. They kept up with what was going on in our schools. Some of Jim's and Rob's children were attending our schools. Jim Walton had a daughter attending the R. E. Baker Elementary

School. She and my son, Curt, were in the same grade. During the time they attended R. E. Baker, we became friends.

Jim also was generous with his personal money. Like his mother, Jim came to my office and wrote out a personal check to fund three, economic-education aides, plus supplies for economics to be offered in the elementary schools. Jim was a big supporter, and still is, of teaching economics in our public schools in Arkansas. He, too, didn't want any recognition for his donations.

On some mornings, I would go to school early enough to swing by Howard Sands Donut Shop which was located in town. It was owned and operated by Howard Sands, one of my eight school board members.

It was at Howard's Donut Shop that Sam Walton could be found most mornings. He would drive his old pickup truck, park it in the parking lot, go in and order the same thing each morning. He would get his donuts and coffee and go to a corner table where he would enjoy them while reading the newspaper from front to back. It was just understood that the table in the corner was his table, and everyone else should avoid sitting there. I'm not saying that someone else couldn't sit at Mr. Walton's table, because that would be far from the facts. Mr. Walton didn't put on airs. He was the same every time you saw him. He was a people-person and everyone loved and respected him.

The Walton Family put Bentonville on the map. Anyone who travels can see Wal-Mart trucks on the interstates. What started out as a five and dime store in Bentonville has grown into a global business that is worth billions. It is one of the largest family-controlled businesses in the United States.

CHAPTER 29

Twelve Years in Warren

Before moving to Warren, Lena and I bought a large tri-level house on Central Street near the Bradley County Hospital, which was only a rock's throw from our driveway.

The move to Warren was really hard on Jeff. It was a sad time for him. He was leaving behind some good friends he thought he'd never see again. Regardless of what we said or did, the move to Warren was an emotional strain on him. I didn't realize it would have such a traumatic impact on him.

During our second day in Warren, things begin to look a lot better. Jeff and I were out in the front yard playing catch with his football. We noticed a church van, with "First Baptist Church" written on the side, pass our house twice. The van was full of young people.

After the van passed the second time, it went down to the next street, turned around, and came back. This time the van pulled into our driveway. As soon as it stopped, several kids got out and came up to Jeff and me. One of the young people was the youth director from First Baptist. He and some of his youth group members came to welcome us to Warren and to First Baptist Church. The youth director was a friendly person with a likeable personality. He introduced himself and members of his youth group. Jeff and I introduced ourselves to the group. It wasn't long before members of the group invited Jeff to go to the Sonic with them to get a coke. Jeff looked at me and asked, "May I, Dad?"

The youth minister said, "Mr. Barger, I assure you, I'll have Jeff back in about an hour."

I gave him permission to go with the group and the rest is history. The First Baptist Youth Group was the best thing that could have ever happened to Jeff. After they left, I said, "Thank you, God!" I was hoping that would be just the thing to get Jeff through his depressed mood. After that day, he never looked back. He easily made friends and became happy at Warren.

Carla didn't make the move to Warren. She had a summer job with Wal-Mart. She stayed behind with our good friends, Richard and Anne Wells, who had two girls, Joyce and Marni, close in age to Carla. They were good friends, and we knew we could trust Richard and Anne to take good care of Carla.

After Carla's summer job at Wal-Mart ended, it was time for her to report to the University of Central Arkansas in Conway. Her close friend, Ginger Brown from Bentonville, was her roommate.

When school started, Jeff started playing football. He was backup quarterback to Bubba Smith, a senior. Jeff later played basketball for the Warren Lumberjacks. During Jeff's senior year, he achieved his goal of becoming quarterback of the Warren Lumberjacks, who finished the regular football season with a record of 8-3. Jeff went on to lead the Lumberjacks to the quarter-finals of the Class AAAA State Football playoffs.

Jeff was an all-around student in school. He was popular and everyone liked him. He was self-motivated and showed an interest in acting. He landed the top role in both the junior and senior plays. Because of his leadership skills, he became president of our local Beta Club and later ran for state Beta Club president. He didn't win, but he came in second.

Curt, like Jeff, had an outgoing personality and made friends easily. He attended Brunson Elementary School on the west side of Warren. His close friends were Sam Wisener, Joseph Calloway, Chase Ellis, Patrick Ellis, Curt and Bart Goodwin, and Chad Wharton.

Bradley County was a paradise for hunters. People from surrounding states and all over Arkansas came to Bradley County for the annual deer and duck hunting seasons. Bradley County had one of the largest deer populations in Arkansas.

Deer hunting was so popular that we built "Deer Day" into our school calendars. Deer Day is the first day of regular gun season each year.

It didn't take Jeff and Curt long to get exposed to deer hunting. Almost all of their friends went deer hunting and were members of their dads' deer camps. Both Jeff and Curt turned out to be successful deer hunters. We always had deer meat in our freezer. They also loved fishing. The Saline River ran within two miles of Warren. Both Jeff and Curt spent lots of time fishing either in the Saline River or in big stock ponds belonging to some of their friends' parents.

It didn't take Lena long to get adjusted to Warren. All she needed was a good church for our family to worship in. While we were in Warren, she took a teaching role in an elderly lady Sunday School Class. She loved those ladies and they loved her. She would visit them when they were sick and dedicated herself to ministering to their needs. She also loved her English teaching job at Monticello Junior High, seventeen miles from Warren. She didn't mind the drive each day. If fact, she said, "The drive gives me time to relax and reflect upon my day."

After Carla's freshman year at University of Central Arkansas in Conway, she moved in with us. She enrolled in the University of Arkansas at Monticello, majoring in Early Childhood Education. After graduation, she was employed by the Rogers Public School System as a kindergarten teacher. While working there, Carla dated Brent Phillips, the son of some of our dearest friends, Boyd and Marty Shelton. After Brent graduated from Dartmouth University in New Hampshire, she and Brent were married on June 22, 1996. After their honeymoon in Hawaii, they moved to Boise, Idaho, where Brent was employed with Hewlett Packard, and Carla took a job with the Star Elementary School as a school safety aide.

Jeff's two years as a Warren Lumberjack were two of his best years. He did well in his academic studies and graduated in the top 10 percent of his class. When he graduated from Warren High School, I was proud to award him his high school diploma. As he walked across the stage, I was prepared to just shake his hand and say "Congratulations, Son," but when he approached me, he reached out, shook my hand, hugged my neck, and said, "Dad, I love you!"

I said, "I love you, too, Son!"

Jeff finished his degree in biology at the University of Central Arkansas in Conway in December 1996. In the fall of that year, he went to Seattle, Washington, where he was employed with a government agency that places people on commercial fishing boats in Alaska. Jeff's responsibility was to monitor the type of fish caught and regulate the number of fish caught in the Baring Sea. He loved it, but admitted it got really cold on the boat.

After Jeff returned to Arkansas, he shared with Lena and me that if he had slipped and fallen into the ocean, he would have frozen to death within six minutes.

Lena said, "Jeff, I'm so glad you waited until now to tell us that. I would have worried myself sick if I had known that."

Jeff took a job with the Arkansas Nature Conservancy in Little Rock in 1997. We were so relieved to have him back in Arkansas.

CHAPTER 30

The Search Begins in Warren

While I was in Warren, I developed a keen interest in genealogy. I had always been interested in knowing more about my ancestors, but never had time to do any research because of my job as superintendent of schools. While in Warren, I became friends with Baker Peebles, a local pharmacist, who headed up the Bradley County Historical Society.

My interest in genealogy grew rapidly. One might describe me as becoming obsessed in my quest to find out more about my Barger and Heiple ancestors.

During the spring break of March 16–19, 1997, Chester and Willie, my older brothers, accompanied me to Missouri where I did extensive genealogy research at the Historical Archives in Kansas City and at courthouses located in Ray and Lafayette Counties.

Before I went to Missouri, I found that my Barger and Heiple ancestors came from the Black Forrest area of Baden-Württemberg, Germany. They came to America by way of Philadelphia, Pennsylvania, and then to North Carolina, Tennessee, Missouri, and finally to Arkansas. Before coming to Arkansas from Missouri, they lived in Ripley, Reynolds, Coal, Moniteau, Ray, and Lafayette Counties.

Chester and Willie were good companions. They, too, wanted to see areas where our father had been born and raised before coming to Arkansas.

Pa was born in Orrick, Missouri, located in Ray County. He later lived in Higginsville and Bates City, both in Lafayette County, before coming to Higden, Arkansas.

A week after I returned to Warren, Carla flew home from Boise, Idaho, to spend her spring break with us. We had not seen her since Christmas. While she was visiting with us in Warren, I shared with her my research findings in Missouri.

Carla looked at me with her beautiful hazel eyes and said, "Now, Dad, you can understand why I would like to know who my biological parents are."

It hit me like a bullet! Genealogy research had made me realize the importance of knowing about one's biological parents: who they were, where they lived, and what they did as an occupation. When Carla said that to me, I realized it was time for me to attempt to fulfill a promise I had made to her several years earlier during her senior year of high school: I had told her that, after she turned twenty-one, if she still wanted to know who her biological parents were, I would do my best to find them.

It was during this time that I had been appointed to serve on two legislative committees that met weekly in Little Rock. I asked Carla if she'd like to go with me. She said, "Yes, I'd love to go." Carla always enjoyed going places with me, and I enjoyed her company. She met people well, and it certainly didn't hurt my reputation to be seen with a beautiful blonde.

The night before leaving for Little Rock, I shared with Lena what Carla had said to me about wanting to know who her biological parents were. Lena said, "Carl, maybe it's time you stopped looking for dead ancestors and start searching for Carla's biological parents." I was glad to hear that Lena was in agreement with me. I didn't want to do anything without her knowledge and approval.

Before leaving for Little Rock on Wednesday, I pulled the information I had on Carla, which we received at the time of her adoption. On Carla's maternal side of the family, we had her given name: Susan Ann Gates. Her name was called out by mistake in court by our lawyer at the time the adoption was finalized. The other data I had was that Carla's mother was nineteen years old when she gave birth to Carla at St. Vincent's Hospital in Little Rock, Arkansas, on February 4, 1971.

We had some additional information that I felt would be helpful. First, Carla's biological mother had a terrible auto accident when she was sixteen years old. She received eight broken ribs, one girl was killed in the accident, a boy had a broken hip and third-degree burns, and another girl had received a concussion.

Carla's maternal grandmother was a math teacher in a private academy. Carla's maternal grandfather had two years of college and owned and operated a general hardware and furniture store. Carla's mother had a brother who was sixteen years old in 1971 and attended the private school where his mother taught math.

Second, the information revealed that Carla's biological father was twenty-five years old in 1971. He had one year of college and was working as a construction manager. According to the information, Carla's paternal grandfather was a state senator; the grandmother worked in a department store as head of the cosmetics department. The biological father had two sisters, ages twenty-three and twenty-one in 1971. Both had two years of college. Carla's biological father had a twin brother who was killed in 1967 and a younger brother still living at home.

On the way to Little Rock, I told Carla that I had been thinking about what she said to me concerning wanting to know about her biological parents. I told her that my genealogy research had made me aware of how important it is to know about one's background. I said if she wanted to, we would try to do a little research on her adoption while we were in Little Rock. I could tell immediately that this really interested her. I told her we would go by the Arkansas History Commission to see if we could find any information on adoptions in Arkansas to get us headed in the right direction.

I didn't have a clue about a starting place. We arrived at the History Commission about nine o'clock in the morning. We first visited with Russell Baker, who was the head librarian of the historical archives. I had gotten to know Russell well when I started doing my genealogy research at the archives. If anyone could help us, he could.

After arriving at the archives, we sat down with Russell and I shared with him why we were there. He asked me if it was an Arkansas or an out-of-state adoption.

"It's an Arkansas adoption," I said.

"Carl, I don't think we have anything that will help you," he said.

"Not anything at all?" I asked.

"Are you aware of the adoption laws of Arkansas?" he asked.

"I know there is a confidentiality thing involved, but that's about all I know."

"If you adopt a child in Arkansas, all records are sealed. It is almost impossible for adopted children to find their biological parents, or for the biological parents to find the child they gave up for adoption. The state of Arkansas is very clear on the law.

"It's my understanding that there is a registry at the Department of Social Services which allows the biological mother and the adopted child an opportunity to sign a registry and fill out an application. The application consists of certain information that might be useful in linking two people together. This procedure isn't very effective unless both parties participate in signing the registry. To be truthful with you, I don't know how successful that program has been."

We thanked Mr. Baker for his time, and Carla and I left the archives disappointed.

Our next stop was St. Vincent's Hospital where Carla had been born. We started at the office of records and inquired about records for Susan Ann Gates. This was the name our lawyer called out in court on the day the birth certificate was changed from Susan Ann Gates to Carla Lynn Barger.

The lady at the receptionist's desk picked up the phone and called another lady about the record on Susan Ann Gates. In a few minutes, the lady came to the front office and introduced herself to Carla and me. After we introduced ourselves to her, she asked, "Are you the adoptive father, Mr. Barger?"

"Yes, I am," I answered, "and this is Carla, my daughter."

"Mr. Barger, I can't discuss any of the contents of this file with you without a court order from a judge," she told me.

"Carla's original name was Susan Ann Gates. Can you not discuss any of the file with her? She is now twenty-six years old."

"Arkansas law is very precise in telling us what we can do and cannot do. I'm sorry, but I can't help you."

"Do you know anyone who might be able to help us?" I asked.

She wrote down a name on a piece of paper and handed it to me. The name was Allen Pettinger, Registry Coordinator with the Department of Social Services, Little Rock, Arkansas. I asked the woman where I could find Mr. Pettinger, and she said, "He's in the Donughey Building in Little Rock."

"I know where that is," I said. I thanked her and left. Carla was very disappointed, but I told her at least the name Susan Ann Gates appears to be the biological name.

On the way to Mr. Pettinger's office, I decided to call him first. It was getting close to noon, and I was afraid he might have left for lunch. I called, and his secretary informed me that, yes, that was the case. I told her I wanted to make an appointment. I gave her my name and she said, "Mr. Barger, I have put you down for a one-thirty appointment."

Carla and I had a few minutes to spare before I had to go to my twelve o'clock committee meeting. I decided to run by the Little Rock City Library to look at their card catalog of newspapers. We knew the state newspapers printed births from Little Rock hospitals. We thought if we searched the birth announcements, we might find a Gates baby born on February 4, 1971, and maybe the parent's name.

In 1971, Arkansas had two state papers: the *Arkansas Gazette* and the *Arkansas Democrat*. Arriving at the library, we told the young man at the desk what we wanted. We also told him we were in a hurry, and asked him if he could help us find the February 1971 editions of the *Gazette* and *Democrat*. He told us they were all on microfilm. He took us to the microfilm section and pulled the film for February 1971.

Carla took the *Arkansas Democra*t, and I took the *Arkansas Gazette*. We searched the birth records from February 2–7 in case the newspaper was slow about getting the births in the newspaper. There was no baby girl Gates listed in either paper.

The Arkansas Social Services Department had done an excellent job of keeping adoption files closed to the public. At this point, it appeared they had thought of everything! We found out later that adopted babies' births were not reported to newspapers.

Our next stop was my committee meeting briefing, which was held at the new Arkansas Teacher Retirement Complex on East Markham Street. Carla and I stayed at the meeting until about one fifteen in the afternoon before leaving for my appointment with Mr. Pettinger at Arkansas Social Services Department. As we entered his office, his secretary greeted us and asked if she could help us.

"Yes, I am Carl Barger from Warren, Arkansas. I called this morning about an appointment with Mr. Pettinger."

"Let me see if Mr. Pettinger is ready to see you," she said. She called Mr. Pettinger, who came out of his office to greet us. He was a young man in his mid-thirties. He was dressed in blue jeans and a casual shirt.

After we introduced ourselves, he said, "Come on back to my office."

After arriving at his office, I said, "I am the adoptive father of Carla. We have always told Carla when she was twenty-one we would try to help her find her biological parents. We are here today to try to find how we might locate them."

"Carla, have you filled out the Arkansas Registry Application?" he asked.

"Yes, I did about two years ago," she replied.

He explained in detail what the Arkansas Registry does. In summary, if the adopted child and the biological mother, father, or grandparents were to fill out applications, then the Arkansas Social Service Department would conduct a study of both parties, and if there were similar items that were considered a match, they would be able to link the two together. The adopted person had to be at least twenty-one years old before he or she could sign the registry.

Mr. Pettinger went on to say, "Other than the registry service there is very little that I can help you with." He explained how strong the Arkansas adoption laws were. He said, "There is one other method one might use, but I don't know anyone personally who has ever used it. In some cases, if the judge within the county where the adoption took place issued a court order to open the adoption files, the files can be opened." Mr. Pettinger was very nice but his hands were tied because of the strict Arkansas adoption law.

"Carla, if you would like to update your file, I can give you the forms, and you can return them to me when you finish," he said.

"Yes, please." Carla said.

After Mr. Pettinger gave Carla the forms, we left.

Carla was so dejected! "Dad," she said sadly, "why wasn't he more understanding and sympathetic?"

I reminded her that his hands were tied because of the Arkansas adoption laws. I told her he could lose his job if he gave out information that was protected. She was still very disappointed as we got into the car.

We had not eaten anything for lunch, so we went to Bennigan's on University Avenue for lunch. At Bennigan's, Carla and I visited several minutes regarding to the stumbling blocks we'd already faced and other pitfalls that still stood in our way.

Carla returned to Boise, Idaho, on Saturday, March 29, 1997. It was hard to see her go. I knew how disappointed she was about not finding out anything about her biological parents.

As Lena and I returned to Warren from taking Carla to the airport, I told Lena I planned to pursue the search for Carla's biological parents. I also decided I'd not let her know I was continuing the search. I didn't want her to be hurt if I kept coming up short.

We decided that if I were successful in finding either parent, we first wanted to know if either would be receptive to meeting Carla. If not, everything would be dropped at that point. If either was, I would set up a meeting for them and Carla to meet. I had heard stories about adopted children finding their biological family members and how it had wrecked their lives. I certainly didn't want this to happen to Carla.

CHAPTER 31

Many Dead Ends

After Carla returned to Boise, Idaho, I laid out a plan of action. I knew the maternal grandmother was a teacher in a private academy. I knew the Arkansas Teacher Retirement System would have a record on every teacher who paid into teacher retirement.

On April 2, 1997, I called my good friend, Bill Sharon, director of the Arkansas Teacher Retirement System. He agreed to help me by compiling a list of current and retired teachers who carried the last name of Gates.

Two days after talking to Bill Sharon, he called and told me the computer found someone that might be a match. The woman was still teaching and was employed with the El Dorado School system in El Dorado, Arkansas. She was now sixty-nine years old.

I knew the superintendent of the El Dorado School System, Mr. Bob Watson, well enough to call him and tell him what I was doing. I called and explained that I was looking for Carla's biological mother and grandmother. I gave him all the information I had given teacher retirement.

"Carl, I know the woman you are talking about," Bob quickly replied. "She teaches special education at the high school. She has two daughters working for us in the El Dorado School System also. One of the daughters might be the right age to be Carla's mother." Bob was very interested in helping me and volunteered to try to find out more about the family and get back with me.

I told Bob I wanted to be very careful about all of this because I wanted to make sure I had the right family before approaching them.

"I certainly understand where you are coming from. I'll call you back when I have something."

Bob called me back in about one hour. "Carl, I don't think this is your family," he said. "The grandmother does have two daughters, but one is too old to be the biological mother and the other is the right age, but, according to my source, she has never had a baby. The source said she's known this family since the girls were small, and she would have known it if the younger daughter had ever been pregnant and given up a child for adoption."

"Bob, I really appreciate your help. Thanks so much!"

Needless to say, I was disappointed again!

What was I to do next? I decided to call Bill Sharon again and ask if the Gateses in El Dorado were the only ones on file who fit the background information.

"They were the only Gateses that showed up on our current status report," he replied.

"Do you have a drop file?" I asked.

"Yes, we do."

"Will you have someone check the drop file to see if a Gates could have taught at one time in the State of Arkansas and moved to another state? The drop files would have this type of information."

Bill called back later and informed me there was no one by the name of Gates in the system.

I thanked him for all of his help. I felt really dejected! I had struck out, and now I didn't know what to do.

I then decided to research the paternal side of the family. The adoption information listed the biological father's father as a state senator. I thought maybe this was the direction I needed to take. I knew there were only thirty-five state senators in Arkansas. How hard could it be to find a senator who had the family background I was looking for? I reviewed in my mind everything I knew about the biological father and his family. I hoped if I could find the biological father, I could find the biological mother through him. Little did I know it was going to be more difficult than I thought!

I went to Little Rock to the office of Mr. Bill Lancaster, director of the Senate Legislative Affairs Office. His secretary called him, and he agreed to see me.

As I walked through his door, Mr. Lancaster greeted me. "Mr. Barger, I'm Bill Lancaster, what can I do for you?"

"Mr. Lancaster, I am here on a personal mission. I am in a search for my adopted daughter's biological grandfather, whom, I believe, may have been in the Arkansas Senate in 1971."

"Do you have a name?" he asked.

"Unfortunately, I don't, but I do have some background information."

I explained to Mr. Lancaster about the Arkansas Adoption laws and the difficulty in finding out anything from the Social Services Department. After visiting about the state senator's background, Mr. Lancaster said, "Let me make a call to a friend of mine." He called Mr. Trent Treat, who worked in the Arkansas Legislative Research Department. "I believe you need to go talk with Mr. Treat. I'll take you to his office," he said.

Upon arriving at Mr. Treat's office, Mr. Lancaster introduced me to him, wished me luck, and left.

"Mr. Barger, how may I help you?" Mr. Treat asked.

I explained my mission and gave Mr. Treat all the background information I had on the senator's family.

"Mr. Barger, I've been here for almost thirty-five years. If anyone can help you, I think I can," Mr. Treat said.

"I will welcome all the help I can get!" I said.

Mr. Treat laughed and called his secretary to bring in a box of old blue books containing information on senators and representatives serving in the State Legislature from 1967–76. We explored the blue books from front to back. Mr. Treat seemed to know something about each person in the books. He was right! If anyone could help me, it would certainly be him.

There was only one state senator who seemed to have the right age and family background that I was looking for. His name was John Fletcher. Senator Fletcher had been deceased for about ten years, but his son and wife still lived in Little Rock.

Mr. Treat thought Mrs. Fletcher once worked in a department store. The son, Bill Fletcher, was now a lawyer in Little Rock.

My heart began to pump faster. Could I have found the right state senator? Would this Bill Fletcher be Carla's biological father? Now I needed a plan to find out! I left Mr. Treat's office at the Arkansas State Capitol and returned to Warren. After arriving home, I went through the blue book again and the information that I found on John Fletcher convinced me that I needed to talk with his son, Bill Fletcher. I had to decide how I would approach him with this sensitive issue.

In a couple of days, I returned to North Little Rock at the Riverfront Hilton Inn to attend a two-day workshop on math crusades. I had decided to try to make contact with Bill Fletcher while I was in Little Rock. I checked into my room and attended the morning sessions. After lunch, I went back to my room and checked the Little Rock telephone directory for a Bill Fletcher.

After finding an address, I decided to get in my car and drive to the location to check out the house and neighborhood. Bill Fletcher lived on a street right off the Rodney Parham Road. As I drove by his house, I noticed he had a basketball goal up in his front driveway. This told me he had children. If this was Carla's biological father, he may not have told his wife about having a daughter, and, then again, he may not have known he had a daughter. Anyway, if he is the biological father, I knew he has kids or grandkids.

I returned to the Riverfront Hilton just in time to take in one afternoon session. The night before I called Bill Fletcher, I called a dear friend of mine, Ann Coleman. I shared with Ann what I was doing, and she thought it was one of the greatest things I could do for Carla. While visiting with Ann, I asked her if she knew Bill Fletcher.

"I don't know Mr. Fletcher, but I am a close friend to Dan Buford who goes to my church. Dan is a lawyer and should know Mr. Fletcher."

"So you know Dan Buford?"

"Yes, do you know him?" She replied.

"Yes, Dan and I have worked together. He handled a school law suit for me in Nashville, Arkansas."

"I'll call Dan to see if he knows Bill Fletcher," she said.

In about thirty minutes, Ann called me. "Carl, Dan does know Bill Fletcher. He told me to tell you to call him and he'd be glad to visit with you about Mr. Fletcher."

"Ann, you are a jewel! Thanks, I'll keep you informed on how this goes."

"Please do," she said.

I called Dan at his home, and we visited about thirty minutes about Bill Fletcher. "Carl, he is a nice guy," Dan said.

I asked him if he thought I could approach him about this sensitive issue.

"Yes, I think Bill will be very receptive to you. If you will come by my office in the morning, I might have some more information I can share with you. We can talk over a hot cup of coffee," he said.

The night before going to see Mr. Fletcher was the longest night of my life. I couldn't sleep for thinking about how I would approach him with this sensitive issue. How would I lead into my story about the adoption? How would I ask him if he could be the biological father? These questions went on and on in my mind all night long! I don't remember when I went to sleep, but what sleep I got wasn't nearly enough. Maybe Dan's hot coffee would wake me up.

After arriving at Dan's office, he told me that this was interesting stuff, and he admired me for trying to find Carla's biological parents. "Carl, I must say, it's unusual for an adoptive father to do something like you are doing for his adopted child," he said.

"What I'm doing, Dan, is carrying through on a promise I made to Carla years ago. Carla needs to know who her biological parents are. The way I look at this is that God has allowed us to have Carla for twenty-six years. During those twenty-six years she has brought joy and happiness to our lives. Now, maybe it is time for her to bring joy and happiness to her biological parents."

"I truly admire you for what you are doing, Carl."

After visiting for about thirty minutes over coffee, he said, "Would you like me to call Bill's office to see if he is in?"

"If you don't mind, I would appreciate that."

Dan called Bill Fletcher's office and the receptionist put him through to Mr. Fletcher.

"Good morning, Dan Buford. To what do I owe the honor of a call from my good friend?"

"I have a good friend in my office who would like to come by and visit with you. Are you extremely busy this morning?"

"No, I think I can work him in. Who is he, and do I know him?"

"His name is Carl Barger. He's from Warren, Arkansas. I've done some work for Mr. Barger in the past. I believe you will like him."

"Is it possible for him to come now?"

"Yes, he says he can come right now."

"Good, send him over."

"Dan, I owe you one. Thanks for helping with this," I said as I prepared to leave.

"Carl, let me know how this all plays out. As I've said, this is all so interesting."

After arriving at Mr. Fletcher's office, his secretary asked if I would like a cup of freshly made coffee. I said, "I'd love some!" She returned with my coffee and informed me that Mr. Fletcher would see me in a few minutes. He was on the phone with a client.

As I sat there in a comfortable chair, I started shaking all over. I don't know what came over me. I was so scared! I said to myself, "Carl, get it together! You can't go into someone's office in this kind of condition."

I heard Mr. Fletcher secretary's phone buzz. She picked it up and looked at me and said, "Mr. Barger, Mr. Fletcher is ready to see you. If you will follow me, I'll show you to his office."

I had finally regained my composure and was ready to visit with Mr. Bill Fletcher. As I entered his office, he got up from his desk and came around, shook my hand, greeted me, and offered me a seat. Mr. Fletcher was a nice looking, bald-headed guy who looked like he might be in his forties.

"Hello, Mr. Fletcher, I appreciate your seeing me this morning on such short notice," I said.

"What can I do for you?"

I explained that I was trying to find my adoptive daughters' biological parents. At first Mr. Fletcher thought I wanted him to represent me in some way about the adoption. But, as I went on explaining what I was doing, Mr. Fletcher looked at me and said, "I am not the father of your daughter, Carla. Although I am not your man, I wouldn't mind being the father of a daughter who is as beautiful as yours." He continued by saying, "When Carla was born, I would have been seventeen years old. My mother never worked in a department store. She always stayed home with me and my sisters while my dad, Senator John Fletcher, worked at the local Channel 7 television station and served in the Arkansas State Legislature."

I explained to him that I was only checking out a lead, and now I realized that he wasn't Carla's biological father. I apologized to him for causing any inconvenience.

"No apologies are necessary," he said. "I think it is just great what you are trying to do for your daughter. I hope you will be successful in finding her biological mother and father." He asked me if I had attempted to get the adoption files opened by going through a judge within the county in which we adopted Carla.

I told him I had checked with my lawyer, Mike Kinard of Magnolia, and he advised me against trying. Mr. Kinard said, "Before a judge would issue a court order, he would have to consider it life-threatening, and in your case it isn't life-threatening."

Mr. Fletcher got up from his chair to walk out with me. He shook my hand and said, "I hope your search will turn out to be successful for you and your daughter."

I thanked him again for seeing me and left his office feeling somewhat ashamed that I had ever presented this situation to him.

I had struck out again! At this point, I really didn't know what to do. I felt like quitting! I just couldn't see any hope ahead. I told myself, "Carl, maybe it's the Lord's will that you don't find Carla's biological mother and father."

The longer I thought about it, I knew that wasn't what God was saying to me. I thought He was saying, "Carl, just be patient. Time will take care of the problem."

CHAPTER 32

Good Advice

I returned to Little Rock on March 31, 1997, for an Arkansas State Systemic Initiative Conference. A friend of mine in Little Rock knew someone who might be of help to me. He told me that this person had helped other adoptive parents find their children's biological parents. My friend introduced me to his friend, Mr. Blakely. I related my story to him and told him I was totally confused. I told him I had spent about one month searching in Arkansas and had accomplished nothing. He said, "Leave me the paper work you brought with you and come see me on Wednesday. By Wednesday, I should know something."

I was so optimistic, at last! I could tell this man wanted to help me. After my friend and I left the man's office, my friend said to me, "He likes you. He doesn't help everyone. He helps only those who he feels are sincere in what they are doing. I think he will have something for you on Wednesday." My friend dropped me off at the Riverfront Hilton Inn where I attended my conference meetings.

The conference ended after a luncheon on Wednesday. I immediately left the Riverfront Hilton Inn and drove to Mr. Blakely's office. As I entered his office, his secretary looked up at me and asked, "May I help you?"

"I'm here to see Mr. Blakely. My name is Carl Barger."

"Let me see if Mr. Blakely can see you, Mr. Barger."

Mr. Blakely's secretary returned and said, "You can go in, Mr. Barger."

"Thanks!" I said.

As I entered his office, he got up from his desk and met me with a warm handshake.

"I appreciate your seeing me today," I said.

"Mr. Barger, before we start talking, I want to say something to you. I think it's wonderful what you are trying to do for your daughter. A lot of fathers wouldn't have the courage to find their child's biological parents. They would fear that once their child was reunited with the biological parents, they would end up losing them."

"Mr. Blakely, that isn't the case with Lena and me. We have never once feared we'd lose Carla's love should she get to know her biological parents."

"I really admire you for what you are doing. Now, I have some good news for you!"

"I'm ready!"

"Carla's biological parents don't live in Arkansas."

Needless to say, his news was exciting, but alarming at the same time. "What state?" I asked.

"I promised my source that I would not give you the state, but I decided, on my own, to give you a clue."

"I'll welcome any clue you can give me."

"All right, let's try something." He looked straight at me and asked, "Mr. Barger, where would you go to gamble?"

"Las Vegas, I guess," I replied.

He smiled and said, "No, Mr. Barger, where would you go to gamble that is closer to Arkansas?"

"Tunica, Mississippi, I guess."

He smiled at me and said, "Mr. Barger, if I were you, I'd go gamble in Tunica."

I knew what he was doing. The clue was enough, and it was given without betraying his source's confidentiality.

"Thank you so much!" I said excitedly.

He got up from his desk, walked over, shook my hand, and said, "Good luck to you when you go gambling in Tunica."

I left the office of my new friend feeling the best I had felt in over a month. I had run into all kinds of road blocks. Now, I knew where to go. With God's help, I felt more confident than ever before.

After returning to Warren, I shared my good news with Lena. She hugged me, looked into my eyes, and said, "Carl, you need to go to Tunica and gamble."

It just happened that my school board was meeting the next night. I needed to share this information with them and get their approval to be gone for a few days to do my research in Mississippi. I had several personal leave days I could use. All I wanted was the school board's blessings.

My school board consisted of a group of fine Christian people. They were excited about what I was doing and wished me well. The path had been cleared. All I needed to do was go to Tunica, use my investigative skills, and pray for God's guidance.

CHAPTER 33

"Gambling" in Tunica

On Thursday, April 3, I left Warren for Tunica, Mississippi. I instructed Beverly Fellows, my secretary, that I could be contacted through my cell phone should she need to call me. I arrived in Tunica at about four-thirty in the afternoon. I was hoping to get there in time to go to the city library. After driving to the library, I saw two ladies coming out the back door. One lady was locking the door. I thought to myself, *Gee, I'm too late*. I pulled up to the sidewalk and said, "Am I too late to do some research today?"

The lady locking the door said, "Yes, we close at four-thirty, but if you can come back in the morning, we will be open at nine o'clock."

"May I ask you one question before you go?"

"Yes, you may."

"Do you have county newspapers dating back to 1967 in your library?"

"No, Sir. Those newspapers are located in the Tunica County Court House. They are bound in several big red books with the year lettered on the front of the book."

"Do you know when they open?"

"I think they open at eight o'clock in the morning and close at four-thirty."

As I was driving on the main street of Tunica, I noticed most of the stores were closed. There was only one store that appeared to be open and that was an antique clock shop. I parked my car in front of the shop and went inside. As I entered the shop, the owner was visiting with two ladies who had purchased a clock.

While I waited, I browsed around the shop. Finally, the ladies left the shop, and I went up to the counter to speak to the owner. As I approached the counter, he asked, "What can I do for you?"

"I am Carl Barger, superintendent of the Warren Public Schools in Warren, Arkansas," I said as I handed him one of my business cards.

"My name is Bobby Papasan. I am a retired superintendent of the Tunica Mississippi Public Schools. What brings you to Tunica?" he asked.

"I am here doing some family genealogy research."

Mr. Papasan had only one good eye and had to look at me a certain way to focus. "Where is Warren, Arkansas?" he asked.

"Warren is forty five-miles south of Pine Bluff and seventeen miles west of Monticello, Arkansas."

"I've been through Monticello. Don't they have a college there?" he asked.

"Yes, it's a branch of the University of Arkansas. Most people refer to it as UAM."

"I went to school at Ole Miss University with a Pat Ward, superintendent of the McNeil Public Schools. Do you know her?"

"Mr. Papsan, it's a small world," I said. "Pat Ward and I are good friends. I was superintendent of McNeil from 1969–1974. While I was there, Pat Ward was my high school principal. When I left, she took my place as superintendent."

"Pat Ward is a fine lady," he said.

"Other than my wife, she is one of the finest ladies I know."

"What kind of research are you doing in Tunica?" he asked.

I told him I was on a personal mission trying to locate the biological family of my adopted daughter. I related my story to him about a friend who told me I should come to Tunica to do research. I told him I also had reason to believe that Carla's grandmother or grandfather might live in Tunica or had lived here at one time. I told him about the 1967 wreck that Carla's biological mother had been in when she was sixteen. I also told him that the adoption papers indicated that Carla's maternal grandmother may have taught in a private school in Tunica.

"I was superintendent of the Tunica Public School System from 1962–86. I don't know too much about who taught school at the Tunica Institute of Learning, which is the private academy here in town. They organized the institute in the fall of 1967. The principal of that school is Dale Coggins. He was principal at the time they organized, and he is still there. He might be able to tell you who taught school there during the early seventies."

"Do you recall any bad wrecks in this area in 1967 that would have killed one teenager and injured three others?"

"No, I don't, but let me make a few calls."

Mr. Papasan went to his phone and called Patti Tucker and one other person who had lived in Tunica for several years. Neither person remembered a serious wreck that killed a teenager.

Before I left Mr. Papasan's antique clock store, he said, "Give me a call before you leave town. I might be able to give you some teachers' names from the academy."

The first place I went the next day was to the Tunica County Court House. After finding the county registrar's office, I asked if I could see the 1967 book that had all of the *Tunica Times* newspapers. As I was reading the newspaper, a gentleman came in and sat at the table next to mine. From time to time, I saw him glancing at me.

As we made eye contact, he said, "Good morning."

I said, "Good morning,"

"You are not from this area, are you?" he asked

"No, I'm from Warren, Arkansas."

"My name is Bard Selden. I'm the municipal judge here in Tunica County."

"I'm Carl Barger."

"What brings you to Tunica?"

"I am doing some family research."

He told me that he had been born and raised in the area. He said his home was in Hollywood, a little town near Tunica. He attended and graduated from the Tunica Public Schools in 1971.

"Maybe you can be of some help to me," I said.

"How can I help?"

I told him I had adopted a baby girl in 1971, and I had reason to believe her biological mother and maternal grandparents may have lived in Tunica or somewhere nearby in the late 1960s and early 1970s.

"Do you have a name?" Bard asked.

"Does the name Gates mean anything to you?"

"I don't think I know any Gateses living around here."

I explained that in 1967, Carla's biological mother had been in an auto accident. She broke eight ribs in the wreck, one girl was killed, one teenage boy suffered a broken hip, and another teenage girl was injured. I told him that Carla's mother would have been sixteen years old at the time of the wreck.

"I worked in the same office with Mr. Jack Tucker, state senator, around that time. I seem to remember that Mr. Tucker may have represented someone by that name, who had been involved in a wreck. Let me check on something. Come with me, Mr. Barger," he said.

We went to another area of the court house and reviewed a big book that listed court judgments. He found the case that he remembered, but it was a Cates instead of Gates. Mr. Selden made several calls to acquaintances, but no one remembered a wreck of this magnitude.

"After you finish here, you might want to go visit with Mrs. Brooks Taylor, editor of the *Tunica Time*s. She has been here a long time, and she might have knowledge of that particular wreck, or a wreck that might have occurred in a nearby county."

Mr. Bard Selden was such a nice guy and was very helpful. He didn't have to take his time to help, but he did, and I was grateful. Everyone I had met in Tunica had been very kind and willing to help me. I wondered if all the people in Mississippi were like the ones I was meeting here in Tunica.

After reading through the 1967 editions of the *Tunica Times*, I found no record of a wreck that mentioned Gates. I decided to go see Mrs. Brooks Taylor, of whom Brad Selden spoke highly. After arriving at the *Tunica Times* around eleven-thirty in the morning, I met Mrs. Taylor. She was an attractive gray-haired woman in her middle fifties. She had a beautiful smile.

"How can I help you?" she asked.

"I'm Carl Barger, superintendent of the Warren Public School System in Warren, Arkansas," I said as I handed her one of my business cards.

"Mr. Barger, what brings you to Tunica?"

I went through my story with her and shared everything I had shared with Mr. Papasan and Mr. Selden. After I finished my story, I observed tears coming from her eyes.

"Mr. Barger, I think it's wonderful what you are trying to do for your daughter." She told me about being adopted herself and not being able to find her biological father until it was too late. She was very interested in what I was doing.

"I don't remember a wreck like the one you have described, but I was not the owner of the paper in 1967. Let me call the owner and see if he remembers the wreck." She called and described the wreck, but the former owner of the paper said he did not remember a wreck of that seriousness.

I asked her if she knew any Gateses who lived in Tunica.

"I don't know any who live here in Tunica, and I've been here a long time." Mrs. Taylor made several calls to people around town to see if they knew any Gateses, but each time came up empty. She suggested I go to the Tunica Institute of Learning, the private academy on the south side of Tunica.

She said, "The maternal grandmother may have taught school there and lived somewhere else. Students come from all over a three-county area. It's my understanding that many of their teachers live outside of Tunica County."

Mrs. Taylor gave me a new telephone directory and told me to take it with me. The directory listed Tunica as well as places like Marks, Crenshaw, Hollywood, Clarksdale, Robbinsville, Batesville, Sardis, and Senatobia. Little did I know at the time, but this telephone directory would play a major role in my research.

Before I left, Mrs. Taylor said, "You must love your daughter a lot, Mr. Barger."

"I do indeed!"

"Most adoptive parents would fear they would lose their adopted children if they found their biological parents," she said.

I told her that it was because of our love for Carla that her mother and I had decided this needed to be done. I told her that we had no fear of ever losing our daughter's love and didn't fear we'd ever lose *her*. I told her I felt Carla deserved the right to know her biological parents.

"I am going to keep your business card. If I find out anything that might help you, I will certainly call you."

I thanked Mrs. Taylor for taking so much time with me and left for the Tunica Institute of Learning Academy. I arrived at the institute just after noon. It was a nice campus, with well-kept grounds, and the buildings were attractive.

A rain storm was coming when I drove up in front of the school. I was glad I had carried my umbrella with me. I went into the building and asked a student for directions to the principal's office, and he escorted me to it. As I entered the office, the secretary greeted me and asked, "May I help you?"

"Yes, I am Carl Barger, superintendent of the Warren Public Schools in Warren, Arkansas." I always introduced myself as being a superintendent of schools. I found that seemed to carry more weight than just saying, "I'm Carl Barger."

"May I speak to your principal?" I asked.

"Mr. Coggins teaches a class this period. He has already gone to his class."

"When will Mr. Coggins be free to talk with me," I asked.

"Let me see if he's started his class yet," she said.

In a few minutes, Mr. Coggins came into the outer office and, after proper introductions, he asked, "What brings you to the Institute, Mr. Barger?"

"Mr. Coggins, I am looking for a teacher who may have worked at the Institute in the nineteen-sixties and seventies."

"What was her name?"

"Her last name was Gates. I believe her name was Elizabeth Gates."

When I said "Gates" he seemed to tense up. His eyes shifted away from me. He turned and looked at me and said, "Mr. Barger, I am sorry, but I must get back to my class. If I had known you were coming, I could have arranged someone to take my class."

"Does the school have school annuals?"

"No, sir, we didn't have school annuals during that time period. Mr. Barger, I have your business card, if I can think of something, I'll give you a call. I must go to my class."

I asked if I had permission to look at the senior composites that hang on the hallway walls. He looked back at me and said, "Yes, you can look at the composites." I thought the composites might have a picture of a Gates, but the only staff pictures on the composites were sponsors of the senior class and Mr. Coggins.

As I was leaving, I had to pass by Mr. Coggin's office. I was going to tell him that I appreciated his hospitality, but before entering his office, I heard him telling his secretary that he was suspicious of me, and that he was not going to give out any information to a stranger.

As I left the school, I felt that Mr. Coggins probably knew something, but, as he said, he was not going to share anything with me. I would have to try some other avenue in trying to find out if Mrs. Gates ever taught school at the institute.

I went back to Bobby Papasan's antique and clock shop. He asked me how my day had gone. I told him that I had struck out everywhere. He said, "How was your visit at the institute?"

"Not too good!" I replied.

Mr. Papasan had a few choice words to say about Mr. Coggins, who was not one of his favorite people. "Coggins probably knew something, but he's too cowardly to share anything with you," he said. Mr. Papasan gave me a list of three teachers who once taught school at the Institute. "There is one teacher on the list whose husband owned and operated a general hardware store in Robbinsville, Mississippi. You might want to check that one out pretty closely."

Neither of the names was Gates, but I thought it would be to my advantage to check them out. I thanked Mr. Papasan for his kindness to me. Since I had not yet eaten lunch I was getting hungry, so I took Main Street over to Highway 61 where I found one of my favorite places, the Sonic Drive-In.

After finishing my lunch at the Sonic, I decided to call the people on the list of names Mr. Papasan had given me. The first number I called was a Helena, an Arkansas number. I talked to a son of the teacher who once taught school at the Institute. I asked enough questions to determine that his mother was not the teacher I was looking for.

From the second call, I found that the teacher on the list had died and her family did not meet the criteria. The third number was for the teacher who lived in Robbinsville, Mississippi. I reached the number, and her daughter, Sis Draughton, answered the phone. I got a little excited when I started talking to her. I kept thinking, I may be speaking to Carla's mother. I had introduced myself to her as Carl Barger, superintendent of the Warren Public Schools.

"What can I do for you, Mr. Barger?" she asked.

I asked her if her mother ever taught school for the Tunica Institute of Learning.

She said, "Yes, she did. Mr. Barger, what is this all about?"

I explained that I was on a personal mission trying to find the biological mother of my adopted daughter. I had decided that if she was the person, maybe she would want to know and would want to talk to me.

"Mr. Barger, my mother is in a nursing home in Memphis, Tennessee. She is in bad health. Mother is not the grandmother that you are looking for, and I'm not the biological mother you are looking for." She told me how old she was and that she attended the Tunica Public Schools when she went to school. After she revealed her age, I knew she was too young to be Carla's mother.

I asked Mrs. Draughton if she remembered any of her friends having a bad auto accident back in 1967 that would have claimed the life of one teenage girl and injured three others.

"I'm afraid I can't help you. I would have remembered a wreck like that, and I don't." Mrs. Draughton wished me luck with my investigation and said goodbye. I thanked her for taking the time to visit with me.

CHAPTER 34

Striking out in Clarksville

I glanced over at the passenger side of the car and saw the telephone directory Mrs. Brooks Taylor had given me. I opened it to the Clarksdale, Mississippi, section. I looked under the G section for Gates. I notice that Clarksdale had about six Gateses listed in the telephone directory. Something compelled me to drive to Clarksdale, forty-five miles south of Tunica, in Coahoma County. While I was sitting in my car reading the telephone directory, Lena called and asked me how things were going.

"Honey, I'm afraid I've struck out in Tunica."

"I'm so sorry. What are you going to do next?"

"I've found some Gateses in Clarksdale, and I'm going there to check newspapers in their city library.

"That sounds like a good idea. If you don't find anything there what is your next plan?"

"Something tells me I need to go to Sardis and Panola."

Lena reminded me to drive safely, and to let her know when I got settled in.

After I reached Clarksdale, my first stop was the sheriff's department. As I entered the building, I saw a young black lady sitting in an office with an enclosed window with bars on the outside.

"Could I speak to the sheriff?" I asked.

"What is your name?"

"I am Carl Barger, superintendent of the Warren Public Schools, in Warren, Arkansas."

She got the sheriff on the phone and handed the phone to me.

"Mr. Barger, what brings you to Clarksdale?"

"I am researching a wreck that occurred in 1967 and killed one girl and injured three other teenagers."

"I was deputy sheriff in 1967. I remember a bad accident like you are describing that occurred on Highway 61, north of Clarksdale".

"Sir, do you have a record of that accident?"

"We don't keep records that are over five years old."

"Would the state police keep records that are over five years old?"

"No sir, they don't."

I felt dejected! *What now?* I thought to myself. "That's terrible! How does someone like me find out what happened in years past?"

"Mr. Barger, we don't have the space or capacity to store records."

"Why don't you put them on microfilm?"

"That's too expensive!"

"What would you suggest I do to find out who was involved in the wreck you referred to on highway 61?"

"You might try the local funeral homes or the city library. One of them might have a record of the accident."

I was really frustrated. I had gotten a lead on a wreck, but no records were available. I decided to take the sheriff's advice and go to the city library. After arriving at the Clarksdale library, I explored a roll of microfilm for 1967. I found a wreck, but it wasn't the right one. I had again struck out.

On my way back to Robbinsville, Mississippi, where I spent the night, I started reflecting on my conversation with my Little Rock source. I had gone to Tunica, but found nothing. Why did my source tell me to go to Tunica to gamble? Surely, there is a Tunica connection, but what?

I still had a burning desire to continue. I felt God was telling me to hang in there. God knew it was not my nature to give up. I had never been a quitter, and I would not quit now.

As I traveled back toward Tunica on highway 61, I took time to pray. I often did that when I drove places by myself. At that time, I felt a strong desire to talk to my Lord and Savior. He had been good to me all my life, and without Him, I wouldn't be where I am today. I needed His help and since I believed in prayer, I began to pray.

"Lord Jesus, I need your help! I need wisdom to know what to do next. Please give me wisdom, God, so I might know what decisions I need to make to find the Gateses. God, there has to be something I'm overlooking. What is it? Please reveal to me what I need to do." After I had my talk with God, I felt an inner peace come over me again. I knew He heard me.

Before I got out of my car at the motel in Robbinsville, I looked over to the passenger seat and saw the telephone book that Mrs. Taylor had given me. I picked it up and carried it with me to my motel room.

After taking a shower and getting dressed for bed, I decided to take a look at the telephone book. I started flipping through the book looking for the name Gates.

I found Gateses in Crenshaw, Batesville, Jonestown, Marks, and Sumner. All of these places were within eighteen to thirty-five miles of Tunica. I started looking at the yellow pages and noticed that the cities of Batesville, Marks, and Sardis had newspapers.

I got very little sleep during the night. Once I get something on my mind, it's hard for me to get it off. I play it over and over in my mind.

After finding out there were Gateses listed in the Crenshaw phone directory, I decided I would drive to Sardis, which had one of the newspapers that covered Quitman and Panola Counties. The next morning, I left around ten o'clock for the little town of Sardis, Mississippi.

CHAPTER 35

The Elusive Article

After arriving in Sardis, I located the newspaper office on Main Street in the middle of town. The name of the newspaper was the *Southern Reporter*. The editor and owner was Mrs. Betty Fletcher.

As I entered the front part of the newspaper building, I found a nice looking woman sitting behind a desk. She looked up at me and asked, "May I help you?"

"My name is Carl Barger," I replied. "I'm from Warren, Arkansas, and I'm looking for Mrs. Fletcher."

"I'm Mrs. Fletcher. What can I help you with?"

"Mrs. Fletcher, I'm here on a mission. I'm looking for the biological mother to my adopted daughter. I have reason to think that maybe she came from this area of Panola County."

"Mr. Barger, I've been in Sardis almost all my life. Who are the people you are looking for?"

"I don't know their first names, but I have reason to think their surname is Gates."

"Well, there are some Gateses that live in Batesville and some in Crenshaw. I'm afraid I would need to know their first names to be able to help you."

"Mrs. Fletcher, I do have one more bit of information that might help. I'm looking for a newspaper article of a bad accident that occurred in 1967. In the accident, Carla's biological mother was injured badly. She had eight broken ribs. There was one teenager killed, one teenager had a broken leg and hip, and another was injured. Do you have any recollection of an accident occurring in 1967 that fits this description?"

"Mr. Barger, I think I remember that wreck!"

"Do you have a copy of that article?"

"I believe that accident happened at a little place called Sarah, just outside of Crenshaw, Mississippi. If you have time, I'll go in the back and pull the book that will have that article."

"Mrs. Fletcher, I've got all the time in the world."

As Mrs. Fletcher left the front office, I could have danced a jig, I was so happy! I believe God was already working on my behalf. He had earlier impressed upon me to come to Sardis, and maybe, just maybe, this was the article that I'd been looking for.

Mrs. Fletcher came back carrying a big red book that was just the size of the Southern Reporter. "Mr. Barger, I have your article." She laid the book on a nearby office desk and turned to the news article, which was dated Thursday, February 2, 1967. It was titled,

Student Dies from Accident Injuries, Three Other Students Hurt in the Crash

Services were held Sunday afternoon at Crenshaw Baptist Church at two-thirty in the afternoon for Rita Carol Chance, who died late Friday in Methodist Hospital, Memphis, Tennessee, from injuries received in an automobile accident earlier in the afternoon. The accident occurred near Sarah, Mississippi, and three other teenagers were also injured.

Rita was a seventeen-year-old senior at North Panola High School, Sardis, Mississippi, where she had ranked first in a written homemaking knowledge and aptitude test given at the school to senior girls on December 6 and had been named North Paola's 1967 Betty Crocker Home-Maker of Tomorrow. Notification of the award had been withheld, to be announced in the next edition of the *Red Raider* school newspaper.

The Rev. Bob Beckham, local pastor, officiated. Burial was in Long-Town Cemetery under the direction of Sardis Funeral Home.

> She leaves her parents, Mr. and Mrs. Roy Chance of Crenshaw; two brothers, Ronnie Chance and Tony Chance; her paternal grandmother, Mrs. W.W. Chance of Crenshaw; her maternal grandparents, Mr. and Mrs. Roy Jackson of Memphis.
>
> Active pallbearers were Wayne Riales, Gerald Riales, Lawrence Walters, Mike Bright, Larry Bright, and Johnny Morris.
>
> Three other Crenshaw teenagers were injured in the one-car accident near Sarah last Friday afternoon which claimed the life of Miss Rita Chance.
>
> Dane Jaegers, son of Mr. and Mrs. Duane Jaegers of Crenshaw, is recuperating in Baptist Hospital, Memphis, Tennessee. He is a junior at North Panola High School, a member of the Beta Club, and enjoys the highest average of any boy in the tenth, eleventh, and twelfth grades.
>
> Miss Paula Goodnight is the daughter of Mr. and Mrs. H. D. Goodnight of Crenshaw. She is a sophomore at North Panola, where she is drum major of the Red Raider Band, a Y-Teen, and a member of the Glee Club. She returned home from a hospital at Clarksdale, Mississippi on Tuesday.
>
> Miss Gayle Gates, daughter of B. P. and Cornelia Gates of Crenshaw, remains in intensive care at Methodist Hospital in Memphis, Tennessee. A sophomore at North Panola High School, Miss Gates is on the basketball team and a member of Y-Teens.

That last paragraph was what I had been waiting to see! I now had the article, the biological mother's name, and her parents' names. I now knew where they lived. I was so excited, I could hardly breathe! I thought my heart would burst with joy!

"Mrs. Fletcher, that is the article I've been searching for. Could I get a copy of it?"

"Yes, I'll make you a copy," she said.

"Mrs. Fletcher, thank you so much for taking your time to help me obtain this article. It contains the information I need to identify Carla's biological mother and grandparents. I can't thank you enough!"

"I was happy to do it for you, Mr. Barger."

"What do I owe you for the copy of the newspaper article?"

"You don't owe me a thing, Mr. Barger. I have found it interesting that you would do this for your daughter. You must love her a lot."

"I do. She came to us when she was only four days old. She immediately filled the void in our hearts for a child. My wife and I considered her to be a gift from God."

It was still early in the day, so I thought I would spend some time at North Panola High School. There should be school annuals that would have pictures of Gayle. If so, that would give me a chance to see what she looked like as a teenager.

Mrs. Fletcher had given me the name of Jerry Hentz, the high school principal, and the high school counselor, Mr. Don Townie. After getting to the high school, I went directly to Mr. Hentz's office. As I entered his office, the secretary asked if she could help me.

"Is Mr. Hentz in?"

"Yes, he his. Could I get your name?"

"My name is Carl Barger. I'm from Warren, Arkansas."

"Mr. Barger, let me see if Mr. Hentz can see you." She came back and announced that he could see me.

As I walked into his office, he welcomed me and asked me to have a seat. "How can I help you, Mr. Barger?"

"Mr. Hentz, I'm in Sardis doing some genealogy research on Gayle Gates, who went to school here in the 1960s."

"I wasn't here then, but my counselor, Don Townie, has been here for several years. I feel sure he will know Gayle. Would you like to speak with him?"

"Yes, Sir, I'd like that."

Mr. Hentz got up from his chair and said, "Come with me and I'll take you down to Mr. Townie's office. I'm sure he will be able to answer your questions about Gayle Gates." As we walked down the hall, Mr. Hentz still had my business card in his hand. "I see you are the superintendent of schools in Warren."

"Yes, Sir, I am."

"How do you like being superintendent?"

"I like it. I've been a superintendent for several years now. I started when I was twenty-five."

"You were a superintendent at twenty-five?"

"Yes, I was."

"That must be some record?"

When we arrived at Mr. Don Townie's office, Mr. Hentz introduced me.

"Don, this is Carl Barger. He is superintendent of the Warren Public Schools in Warren, Arkansas. He's here to do some genealogy research on one of our former student's, Gayle Gates."

"Mr. Barger, I'm pleased to meet you. What can I do for you?"

"First of all, do you remember Gayle Gates?"

"I remember Gayle well. She was a lovely girl, and smart at that. She lived in Crenshaw and commuted to Panola High. She and her brother, Parker, went to school here in the late nineteen sixties."

"I'm doing genealogy research on the Gates family in Crenshaw and am looking for anything that would be relative to my research. Do you know where Gayle and Parker went to school from here?"

"Mr. Barger, let me pull their drop files." When he came back he said, "It looks like Gayle went to a women's college in Columbus, Mississippi, and Parker transferred to the Institute of Learning Academy, a private school in Tunica, Mississippi. I believe after high school, he went to college at Ole Miss in Oxford."

When Mr. Townie mentioned that Parker had attended the Institute of Learning Academy in Tunica, Mississippi, I realized Gayle's mother must have taught there as well. That was my Tunica connection!

"Mr. Townie, is it possible for me to look at some of your old annuals from that time period?"

"I believe I can arrange that. Our librarian is out today, and right now Coach Taylor has a study hall going on in the library.

Let's go down to the library and see if we can find those old annuals."

I followed Mr. Townie to the library. He asked the coach if he knew where the librarian kept the back issues of the Red Raider annuals.

"I've notice some of the annuals are stored underneath this counter," Coach Taylor said as he bent down and took a look at the annual section.

"There are lots of annuals here. What year . . . or years . . . do you want to see?" he asked.

"Do you have the annuals from nineteen sixty five through nineteen seventy-two?" I asked. Coach Taylor pulled those annuals and handed them to me. "Is it all right for me to look through these annuals?"

"It's perfectly all right, but let's take them back to my office where you won't be distracted, if you know what I mean."

I started with the 1965 annual and worked my way through each one. The first picture I found of Gayle was an eighth-grade picture. I couldn't believe my eyes when I saw the picture! She looked so much like Carla. I marked several pages that Gayle's picture appeared on. She was a popular student. She was in almost all of the clubs and organizations. I found pictures of Parker when he was in the eighth, ninth, and tenth grades. I found Gayle's graduation picture, and the caption had listed her as one of the honor graduates. After looking through all the yearbooks, I asked Mr. Townie if I could copy those pages of the yearbook where I found pictures of Gayle and Parker.

"Our high school copying machine is broken, but I will take you to the superintendent's office, and we can use their copier," he said.

Before I left to make the copies, I asked Mr. Townie how the North Panola High School, once a predominantly white school, became a majority black school.

"In 1970, the school became a public school, and the whites moved to the North Delta Private Academy near Batesville, Mississippi. After that, the Panola High School was taken over by the State of Mississippi as a fiscal and academic distressed school. Do you know what that means?" he asked.

"Yes, I do."

I explained to Mr. Townie that Arkansas had passed a similar law. When schools failed to comply with financial guidelines and academic standards, they too were classified as distress schools. Once a school is declared a distress school, it has three years to correct its deficiencies, or the state will take over and run the school system.

"That's the same law we have here in Mississippi. Does Arkansas appoint a neutral superintendent to run the school?" he asked.

"Yes," I replied.

Mr. Townie walked me over to the central administration office and introduced me to the superintendent's secretary. He informed her that we needed to make some copies of yearbook pages.

The secretary said, "Ya'll come back here."

We went back to the copying machine, and she showed me how to operate the copier. When I saw the machine, my first thought was that they may be a fiscally distressed school, but they have the top-of-the-line copying machine. I didn't have a machine in the entire Warren School System that was as good as that one.

After making my copies, I offered to pay the secretary for the copies. She said, "No, sir. We've never had a superintendent from another state to visit us here at Panola. It's our pleasure to help."

"Everyone here at Panola has treated me very nicely. I truly appreciate all you've done to help me. Thank you."

It was now early afternoon. I had not eaten anything since breakfast, and I was getting hungry. I asked the secretary if she could recommend a sandwich place.

"There's a very nice barbecue restaurant near Interstate 55 on the east side of town that you might try. That is, if you like barbecue!"

"I love barbecue!"

I visited a little longer with Mr. Townie before I left his building. He gave me some teachers' names and telephone numbers who had taught at North Panola High School in the 1960s and 1970s. He said these teachers might know where Gayle Gates currently lives.

The list of names included Pauline Gordon, Margaret Hudspeth, and Betsy Brazil from Sardis. He gave me two names from Batesville, Mississippi: Mrs. William Cook and Mrs. Nelda Bloodworth.

The two hours I spent with Don Townie and Jerry Hentz were going to be very beneficial to me. I gained a lot of valuable information from them. Information that would help me put together pieces of a puzzle.

After lunch, I returned to the *Southern Reporter* newspaper office in Sardis. I wanted to visit once more with Mrs. Betty Fletcher before leaving town.

The purpose of my returning to her office was to get her permission to read some of the back issues of the *Southern Reporter*. Something was telling me I might get to know the Gates family better through the newspaper. When I arrived at the newspaper office, I met Chris Fletcher, Mrs. Fletcher's nephew and co-editor of the paper. I handed Chris one of my business cards and introduced myself to him.

Chris looked at me and said, "My aunt told me about you this morning. She found your story and your mission quite interesting."

"Do you know when Mrs. Fletcher will be back?"

"She should be back here around two o'clock," he said.

"Chris, do you know Gayle Gates?" I asked.

"No, I don't know Gayle."

He proceeded to tell me that he didn't know many of the students who went to the private academy during the 1960s and early 1970s. But he did know two girls who still lived in Sardis and who graduated in 1969. He gave me the telephone numbers of a Meg Woods and a Lynn Porter who lived in Sardis. He said that Meg was currently teaching math at the North Delta Academy near Batesville, Mississippi.

"Chris, does the newspaper have back editions of the *Southern Reporter* that would start around nineteen seventy?" I asked.

"No, all of those copies would be at the North Panola County Court House. Aunt Betty told me she found the wreck article in a nineteen sixty-five book this morning. It just happened that we had all the books from nineteen sixty-five up to nineteen seventy."

"I'm running out of time so if you will kindly give my regards to Mrs. Fletcher, I would appreciate it. Tell her I found some interesting information on Gayle and her brother, Parker, at the North Panola High School today. Tell her, too, that both Mr. Hentz and Mr. Townie were very helpful. Tell her also that I plan to stay in town tonight and might have time to run by in the morning to visit with her."

"Mr. Barger, I'll make sure she gets your message. Good luck to you at the Panola County Registrar's Office. Hope you find lots of good information."

I arrived at the North Panola Court House around three o'clock and went directly to the Registrar's office. I asked the lady at the desk when they closed. She said, "We close at five o'clock."

That gave me two hours before they closed. I had to hurry if I was going to have time to do much reading. I had decided earlier that if I didn't finish up today, I would find a motel in Sardis and spend the night. I was on fire and didn't want to cool off.

From the pictures and articles I had found in the high school annuals, I knew about Gayle's high school experience, but after that, I knew nothing. I wondered if she had gotten married at some point in her life. I wondered if she completed college. Before today, I knew nothing but that she went to Little Rock, Arkansas, and gave birth to our beautiful daughter, Carla.

I first checked the marriage license for Panola County. There was no marriage license for Gayle Gates. This quickly told me that if Gayle got married, she didn't marry in Panola County.

I started with the 1970 bound book that contained weekly articles of several small communities in Panola County, including the city of Crenshaw. The *Southern Reporter* was a weekly paper, and every week there was a column on what was happening in Crenshaw.

I hoped that by reading the "Crenshaw News," I might get to know the Gates family better and just might find out what Gayle's married name was, providing she got married. When I found an article that related to the Gateses, I marked it so I could make copies at a later time.

The following excerpts were taking from the *Southern Reporter* starting on Thursday, November 2, 1972. "The B. P. Gates visited with Miss Gayle Gates in Birmingham School of Nursing, Birmingham, Alabama."

> **Thursday, December 14, 1972**: Gayle Gates, student at Birmingham University School of Nursing, Birmingham, Ala., has arrived home to spend the Christmas holidays with her parents, B. P. and Cornelia Gates.
> **Thursday, February 8, 1973**: Mrs. B. P. Gates visited her daughter, Miss Gayle Gates, in Birmingham, Ala., on Saturday and Sunday.
> **Thursday, March 22, 1973**: Gayle Gates is at home from attending the Birmingham School of Nursing, Birmingham, Ala.
> **Thursday, May 24, 1973**: B. P. and Cornelia Gates spent last Tuesday in Birmingham, Ala., with their daughter, Miss Gayle Gates."
> **Thursday, November 1, 1973**: Mrs. Everett Hathorn of Little Rock, Arkansas, visited in the home of B. P. Gates, Jr.

I later learned that Joann Hathorn was the sister to Mr. B. P. Gates. She is the aunt Gayle went to live with in Little Rock, Arkansas, when she was pregnant with Carla.

> **Thursday, January 10, 1974**: Gayle Gates spent Christmas holidays with her parents Mr. and Mrs. B. P. Gates of Crenshaw.
> **Thursday, November 6, 1975**: Mrs. B. P. Gates went to Little Rock, Arkansas, on Friday and Saturday and

stayed until Sunday visiting her daughter, Mrs. Gayle Gates Elliott, and Mrs. Everett Hathorn. {}

This is the first knowledge I had that Gayle had married. She was now an Elliott. I thought that now it might be easier for us to find an Elliott in Memphis.

Thursday 18, 1976: Parker Gates and Bob D. Crenshaw, students at Ole Miss, Oxford, Mississippi, are home for the spring break holidays visiting their parents, Mr. and Mrs. B. P. Gates and Mr. and Mrs. Jim Crenshaw of Crenshaw, Mississippi.

Parker Gates also attended Northwestern University before transferring to Ole Miss.

Thursday, April 15, 1976: Mrs. Gayle Gates Elliott of Little Rock, Arkansas, spent the past weekend here with her parents, Mr. and Mrs. B. P. Gates.
Thursday, May, 13, 1976: Parker Gates graduates from Ole Miss, Oxford, Mississippi.
Thursday, August 26, 1976: Parker Gates takes job with All State Insurance in Jackson, Mississippi.
Thursday, July 1, 1977: Mrs. Cornelia Gates spent the weekend in Little Rock, Arkansas, with the Everett Hathorns and Mrs. Gayle Gates Elliott.

At four forty-five, I decided to spend the night in Sardis and come back to the registrar's office the next morning. I needed at least one more day in Sardis, and now that I knew the Gateses lived in Crenshaw, I wanted to drive through that little town on my way back to Warren.

I was exhausted from a whirl-wind day, but my attitude was great. I had found Carla's biological mother and grandparents and had learned a lot about them. Anything I found the next day would be icing on the cake, so to speak.

After eating a good dinner, I checked into the Motel 6 in Sardis early enough to make some calls. I wanted to call the women whose names Thomas Townie and Chris Fletcher had given to me. I also needed to call Lena and share all the wonderful news about my findings.

CHAPTER 36

Sardis

The first person I called from the list of women given to me was Mrs. Betsy Brazil. Mrs. Brazil had taught English at North Panola High School for several years. She was now retired and living in Sardis.

Mrs. Brazil answered her phone by saying, “Hello.”

“Mrs. Brazil, my name is Carl Barger. I’m superintendent of the Warren Public Schools in Warren, Arkansas. Mr. Don Townie gave me your number and said that you might be able to help me.”

“What brings you all the way to Sardis, Mississippi, Mr. Barger?”

“I am doing genealogy research on Gayle Gates who graduated from North Panola High School in 1969. Did you know Gayle?”

“Oh, yes, I knew Gayle Gates well. She was one of my best English students at North Panola High School. She was an honor student and was well liked throughout the school.”

“Mrs. Brazil, do you know where Gayle lives today?”

“Mr. Barger, I think Gayle lives in Memphis, Tennessee. I have not seen her in years, but someone told me she lives in Memphis.”

“Do you know if she is still married to an Elliott?”

“No, I don’t know.”

“Mrs. Brazil, did Mrs. Cornelia Gates ever teach at the North Panola High School?

“No, Cornelia never taught at North Panola High School. She stayed in the Crenshaw Public School System where she taught math at the elementary school.”

"Do you know if she taught in a private academy?"

"I believe Cornelia did teach in a private academy in Tunica before she retired."

She was the second person to mention the Institute of Learning Academy in Tunica. I now felt assured that Cornelia was the Tunica connection my Little Rock source meant for me to find by gambling in Tunica.

"Mrs. Brazil, you have been a big help. Thank you for taking your time to visit with me."

"Mr. Barger, call Cornelia Gates in Crenshaw, she can tell you where Gayle is living."

"Thanks again, Mrs. Brazil, for your help."

"I was glad to help!" she replied.

I then called Meg Wood who graduated with Gayle Gates at North Panola High School. Meg lived in Sardis and taught math at the North Delta Academy near Batesville. Meg was Gayle Gates's best friend while attending North Panola High School.

Meg Wood answered the phone with, "Hello."

"Meg, this is Carl Barger, superintendent of the Warren Public Schools. I am in town today doing genealogy research on Gayle Gates. Do you know Gayle?"

"Gayle and I were best friends in high school," she said.

"Do you know where Gayle lives?"

"Yes, Gayle lives in Memphis, Tennessee."

"Meg, would you have Gayle's phone number and address?"

"No, Gayle has moved twice in the past year. Her mother and I play golf together from time to time in Senatobia. It is my understanding that Gayle is in bad health."

"Are Gayle and Mr. Elliott still married?"

"Oh, no, Gayle and Ron Elliott have been divorced for several years."

"Did Ron and Gayle ever have children?"

"No, Gayle never remarried and she had no children."

"I've heard your daughter is graduating tonight at the North Delta Academy with high honors."

"That's right! We are now in the process of getting ready."

"I want to congratulate you on your daughter's honors, and I thank you for taking the time to visit with me."

"I was glad to help. I have B. P. Gates's telephone number if you would like to have it. They live in Crenshaw, Mississippi. Mr. Gates or Cornelia could tell you where Gayle is living in Memphis."

"Meg, I would love to have the Gates's telephone number." I didn't want Meg to know I already had it. After I finished talking with Meg Wood, I called Lena. I intentionally waited to call her until I had all the information. When she answered the phone, I said, "Are you sitting down?"

"Yes, I am. Why?"

"Lena, I have found them. I've found the Gateses!"

"Oh, Carl, tell me all about it. I want to hear every bit of it."

I shared with Lena everything about my visit with Mrs. Betty Fletcher, who owned and operated the *Southern Reporter*. I shared everything with her about Mrs. Fletcher finding the article about the wreck and the details of the wreck.

I shared with her everything about my visit at the North Panola High School and the information I found there on Gayle and Parker. I told her I was bringing home pictures of both Gayle and Parker when they were teenagers. I related to her how I went to the Panola County Court House and read all those papers. I told her about the telephone calls to Mrs. Brazil and Meg Wood. I don't think I missed a thing.

"Oh, Carl, my prayers have been answered. I was afraid you were calling to tell me again that you had struck out. Oh, I'm so happy and so proud of you."

"I'm spending the night here in Sardis. I want to go back by Mrs. Fletcher's office tomorrow and maybe go back and read some more newspapers at the court house. After that, I'm going to drive to Crenshaw and check out that little town and find out where Mr. B. P. and Cornelia Gates live. I've got their address. I just want to see where they live. I will be home sometime tomorrow."

"Everything is going well here. Curt and Patrick have been catching a lot of fish out at Dr. Oxner's big pond. They bring these big fish in, clean them, and then I cook them. They eat everything I cook. I'm telling you, I don't know how they can eat so much."

"You must realize they are big boys, and another thing, football players need a lot of food."

"Carl, you be careful coming home. Remember our agreement. I want to be present when we first meet Mr. and Mrs. Gates. I know you, and I know how tempting it must be for you to knock on their door and introduce yourself to them. You drive by, but don't you stop."

"Yes, boss!"

"I love you," she said.

"I love you more!"

Lena was right. She knew me well. I would like to go by and introduce myself and tell the Gateses we adopted their beautiful granddaughter, but I wouldn't do that. There would be plenty of time to work things through. When I returned to Warren, Lena and I would sit down and work out a plan of action. Until then, I would rely on patience.

CHAPTER 37

The Small Town of Crenshaw

I had another restless night. I was so pumped up that I couldn't get the day's activities and the information out of my mind. I tossed and turned the better part of the night. I finally went to sleep around two o'clock in the morning. I didn't get up until nine. I showered, dressed, ate two donuts and drank my coffee at Motel 6's Continental Breakfast.

I arrived at the *Southern Reporter* around ten thirty. Mrs. Betty Fletcher was having a cup of coffee when I entered the outer part of the newspaper office.

"Good morning, Mr. Barger. Come in and tell me about your day yesterday."

"I can't tell you how thankful I am for all you've done for me."

"Mr. Barger, the only thing I've done is find the article on the wreck and make you a copy. You've done all the rest. But from the expression on your face, I'm assuming you found some good information at Panola County High School and the Panola County newspaper."

"Yes, I did. I know Gayle is living in Memphis, Tennessee. Where, I don't know! I know B. P. Gates and his wife Cornelia live in Crenshaw. I know from the pictures I copied from the Panola High School annuals that Carla favors Gayle. I know where Gayle went to college and that she is a nurse. I know she married Ron Elliott, got a divorce, and never had children. I also know that Cornelia Gates taught in the private academy in Tunica. That was my Tunica connection.

"Yes, I had a great day yesterday! It was all because of the article you found for me. I came by today to thank you once again for helping me. I wouldn't be where I am right now if it hadn't have been for you. I'd like you to do one other thing for me if you will."

"What is that, Mr. Barger?"

"If you were to hear anything that you think I might need to know, would you call me or send me a fax?"

"I will be happy to do that, Mr. Barger. Do you have time for me to make a call for you right now?"

"Yes, please do!" I replied.

"I know this real estate lady who knows a lot of people from Crenshaw. If she knows where Gayle lives in Memphis, she will tell me." Mrs. Fletcher made her call and talked for about three minutes.

"Mr. Barger, my friend knows the Gates family in Crenshaw, but she doesn't know where Gayle lives in Memphis."

"Thanks again for all you've done," I said as I started to leave.

"I can assure you that if I find out anything, I'll let you know."

I decided not to go to Panola County Court House, but to drive to Crenshaw instead. I wanted to check the town out and find the location of Mr. and Mrs. Gates's home. It was something I had to do for my own peace of mind and satisfaction.

The little town of Crenshaw, Mississippi, was divided by a railroad. The blacks lived on the west side of the railroad while the whites lived on the east side. All the businesses were located on the east side of the railroad where the white community lived. As I drove down Main Street, which was Highway 4, I spotted Gates's General Hardware Store. It was an old, two-story building. In its prime, it would have been a very attractive store, but now it was old, like most of the buildings in Crenshaw.

I decided to turn around and go back to see if I could locate Missouri Avenue, the address I found in the telephone directory. The street ran east and west. I turned left on Missouri, which was right by Mr. Gates's General Hardware Store. I continued on Missouri Street when I saw the Gateses' home. It was a red brick home, with well-kept grounds. There were two large magnolia trees in the front yard. The trees had been there for many years. As I drove slowly by, I felt the house and surroundings were typical of the beauty of Mississippi.

Right across the street from house was the First Baptist Church of Crenshaw. I wondered if the Gateses were Baptist and if they attended that church.

I decided to turn around at the next street and drive by the Gateses' home one more time before leaving Crenshaw. This time as I was passing the house, I spotted Mr. B. P. Gates outside in his driveway. Looking at him from a distance, I estimated his age to be late sixties or early seventies. He was about five feet eight inches tall. He was wearing a hat. As I drove slowly by on Missouri Street, I saw him looking at me.

My excitement was high. My first instinct was to turn around, drive back to his house, pull into his driveway, and get out and introduce myself. I wanted so badly to shake his hand and say, "Mr. Gates, twenty-six years ago, I adopted your granddaughter."

Because of my promise to Lena that she would be present when we made our first contact with the Gateses. I drove west on Missouri Avenue until I came to Highway 4. I turned right and drove to a convenience store where I purchased a Panola County newspaper. I wanted something from Crenshaw to carry back home to Warren.

As I was purchasing the newspaper, I asked the proprietor if she knew Mr. B. P. Gates. She immediately said, "I certainly do! He is well respected man in our town. He is known throughout Crenshaw, Panola, and Quitman Counties. He runs a store, just up the street," she said as she handed me my change for the newspaper.

I asked her if she knew where his daughter Gayle lived. She said, "No, but if you'll stop at his store, Mrs. Roberta might be able to tell you, or if Mr. Gates is working, he could tell you."

CHAPTER 38

Back Home in Warren

After arriving home in Warren, I shared my findings with Lena and Curt. They were as excited as I was. Curt said, "I think we should make contact with them as soon as possible." I felt the same as Curt, but felt it was best to wait a few days. We needed time to plan. We certainly didn't want to act on impulse.

I had lots of school work waiting for me when I got back to my office. During the four days I had been gone, Beverly had neatly arranged four working-days of paperwork on my desk. She was a jewel. I felt comfortable having Beverly in charge of my office while I was away.

On Thursday morning, May 22, 1997, I received a fax from Betty Fletcher. The fax message read, "I have some information for you. You can call me at 601-487-5555 before 5 p.m., otherwise, I will be home the rest of the week, and you can call me at my home at 601-487-2222."

I was so excited! What could all this mean? I immediately called Mrs. Fletcher. It was now about nine o'clock in the morning. "Mrs. Fletcher, this is Carl Barger. I just received your fax."

"Hello, Mr. Barger, thanks for calling me. I've got some good news for you," she said.

"What's the good news?"

"Mr. B. P. Gates found out about your being in Sardis on Friday inquiring about Gayle."

"How did he find out?"

"After you left Sardis on Friday, I contacted Mrs. Eugenia Perkins, who is a good friend of the Gateses in Crenshaw.

Mrs. Perkins lived in Crenshaw most of her life. She moved to Senatobia to take a job as dorm mom at the Boudoir Center for the mentally retarded. I know Mrs. Perkins well enough to ask her if Gayle Gates ever had a baby and gave it up for adoption. Mrs. Perkins first said Gayle never had a baby. I told her you had been in my office inquiring as to where Gayle lived in Memphis."

Mrs. Fletcher continued to tell me that on Saturday, Mrs. Perkins called her back and apologized for lying to her. Apparently Mrs. Perkins had contacted B. P. Gates in Crenshaw and had visited with both Gayle and Mrs. Cornelia Gates in Memphis. She said she had shared the information about my being in Sardis.

"Mrs. Perkins explained to me why she lied. She said that no one in Crenshaw ever knew that Gayle was pregnant and had given her baby up for adoption. Mrs. Perkins told me that Gayle had struggled with giving the baby up, but B. P. and Cornelia felt Gayle would be unable to care for the baby properly.

"Mrs. Perkins said Gayle went to live with Mrs. Jo Ann Hathorn, B. P. Gates's sister, in Little Rock, Arkansas. She said Gayle later moved into the Florence Crittenden Home for unwed mothers. She continued that Gayle gave birth to a baby girl in St. Vincent's Hospital on February 4, 1971."

Mrs. Fletcher went on to say that B. P. Gates had contacted her at the *Southern Reporter*. "He wanted me to tell you that they are excited about the news and would like to visit with you and your wife." Mrs. Fletcher said that Mr. Gates wanted me to call him at my earliest convenience.

"Mrs. Fletcher, again, you've been a great asset to me. I really appreciate everything you've done in helping me," I said.

"Mr. Barger, I hope things turn out well for you and the Gates family. This has been one of the best human interest stories I've experienced in all my years of being in the newspaper business. It's been so touching! To tell you the truth, Mr. Barger, it's like I've become a part of something I know is going to play out well. I'm so grateful to have had an opportunity to meet you and see how compassionate you have been in showing your love for Carla.

"There is no other thing that could be any more wonderful than what you and your wife are doing for Carla. I know too, the Gateses will forever be grateful to you for making this possible. I know nothing but good will come from this. In all my years as a newspaper editor and owner, I've never run across a story like this one. What you have achieved will bring great joy into the Gateses' and Carla's hearts. Please let me know how things turn out."

"I will let you know! Do you think Mrs. Perkins would visit with me before I make my call to Mr. Gates?" I asked.

"Mr. Barger, I think Mrs. Perkins would be more than happy to visit with you."

I thanked Mrs. Fletcher once again and said goodbye. I placed a call to Mrs. Perkins in Senatobia, Mississippi.

"Mrs. Perkins, this is Carl Barger. I'm superintendent of the Warren Public Schools in Warren, Arkansas."

"Mr. Barger, I know who you are," she said.

"Mrs. Perkins, do you have a few minutes to visit over the phone?" I asked.

"Yes, I can visit with you, Mr. Barger."

I related to Mrs. Perkins that it was my understanding she knew all about my mission to find Gayle Gates.

"Yes, I am aware of why you were in Sardis last Friday," she said.

"It's my understanding that you, Gayle, and the Gateses are the best of friends."

"Yes, we are and have been all our lives."

She explained to me that she had grown up in Crenshaw with Mr. Gates and taught school with Cornelia. "We are all like family," she said.

"I understand you have had a visit with Gayle about my visit to Sardis."

"Yes, Gayle came over Sunday and we talked. She is at peace with the news and is looking forward to talking with you."

Mrs. Perkins went on to tell me about the time Gayle got pregnant and that she came to her first. She explained that she and Gayle had always been close and that Gayle came to her many times to discuss personal matters.

She continued to tell me that when Gayle discovered she was pregnant, she first wanted to keep the baby but decided that her folks were right in encouraging her to give up the baby.

Gayle told Mrs. Perkins, "I know I'm not able to raise a child in the condition I'm in."

"At that time, Gayle had an alcohol problem and suffered from depression," Mrs. Perkins said.

I asked Mrs. Perkins if the Gateses were upset with me for asking questions in Sardis.

"No, they are not upset with you," she replied.

"I understand Gayle is having some health problems."

"Mr. Barger, Gayle recently had sinus surgery. She got a staph infection and has been pretty sick, but she is much better. Cornelia is in Memphis staying with Gayle until she recovers from her surgery."

"Mrs. Perkins, did Gayle have any more children?"

"No.

Mrs. Perkins shared with me that Gayle married a Ron Elliott, a dentist from Maryland, but the marriage didn't last. She said that Gayle and Ron were divorced by the time Gayle was twenty-two years old. She said Gayle never remarried. She has gone through a lot of depression over the years and had been under psychiatric treatment for depression off and on for several years. Mrs. Perkins went on to say that Gayle was an alcoholic, but had been free from her alcoholic problem for over eight years.

"Gayle is presently doing well with her life. She's now working with the Trinity Home Health Care Association out of Memphis."

"Is Gayle still pretty," I asked.

"Mr. Barger, she is still pretty, but like most of us, she has put on some weight."

"I understand about weight. I have a weight problem myself."

Mrs. Perkins gave me Gayle's address and phone number in Memphis. I asked her who I should call first, Mr. Gates or Gayle.

"Mr. Barger, if I were you, I would call Mr. Gates first. You will be able to get in touch with him at the store. Mrs. Cornelia and Gayle may be out visiting some of Gayle's patients. Try Mr. Gates first."

Finally, I asked Mrs. Perkins if she knew where Parker Gates was living.

She said, "Parker Gates is living in Collierville, Tennessee. He is employed with the DeBold Company. He and Helen have three children. The oldest girl is named Courtney. She is seventeen years old. The second child, Lauren, is thirteen, and Ben is ten years old.

"Mr. Barger, you have made Gayle a very happy person. I wish you well as you visit with Gayle and the Gateses. It's been very nice talking with you, and if you come this way, please come see me. I would love to meet you and show you what I do."

I told Mrs. Perkins that someday when we had the opportunity to come to Crenshaw or Memphis, we would come by and see her.

After visiting with Mrs. Perkins, I placed a call to Mr. Gates at his store in Crenshaw.

When Mr. Gates answered the telephone he said, "Gates Hardware."

"Mr. Gates, this is Carl Barger, superintendent of the Warren Public Schools in Warren, Arkansas."

"Mr. Barger, I am glad you called. How are you?"

"I'm doing well. Mr. Gates, Mrs. Fletcher informed me that you wanted me to call you."

"That's correct, Mr. Barger. We are excited about the news and are wondering if we could set up a time to visit."

"Mr. Gates, Lena and I would be happy to come to Crenshaw or Memphis to visit with you. The Memorial Day weekend is free for us. We could come then if y'all are available."

"I will contact Gayle at her apartment after five o'clock. I will see if Memorial Day weekend is good for us. Gayle has recently had sinus surgery. Cornelia is staying in Memphis with Gayle to drive her around to see her patients. Gayle contracted a staph infection from her surgery and is wearing a pic line so she can take her antibiotic."

I shared with Mr. Gates that we were having high school graduation exercises that night and it would be after nine o'clock before I could take his call.

"Mr. Barger, I will talk with Gayle and Cornelia, and I will call you after nine o'clock. Do you have a few minutes that I could ask you some questions?"

"Mr. Gates, give me a few seconds. I need to tell my secretary to hold my calls." After a moment, I returned to talk to Mr. Gates. "Mr. Gates, I'm back. What is it that you'd like to ask me?"

"Could you tell me a little about your daughter, and what you named her?"

"We named her Carla Lynn. She is now twenty-six years old and lives in Boise, Idaho, with her husband, Brent Lee Phillips. She graduated with honors from both high school and the University of Arkansas at Monticello. She worked three years in the Rogers School System in Rogers, Arkansas, as a kindergarten teacher before moving to Boise.

"After moving to Boise she was unable to find a teaching job so she's working as a safety aide in the Meridian School District. She's about five-feet six-inches tall, has short blonde hair, hazel eyes, and is beautiful. You have a beautiful granddaughter, Mr. Gates!"

"May I ask about your family?"

"My wife's name is Lena. We have two boys younger than Carla. Jeff, our oldest son, is adopted also. He and Carla are two years apart in age. Our youngest son, Curt, is seventeen years old, and he is our biological son. He is a senior this year at Warren High School, and he starts as center on the Lumberjack football team. After we adopted Carla and Jeffrey, God decided to bless us again with a biological son."

"I think that's wonderful!" he said. There was a short pause and then he asked, "What about you?"

"Mr. Gates, this is my thirty-second year in school business. I have been a school superintendent twenty-eight of those thirty two years. We have been in Warren for eight years, and I have previously been superintendent in four other Arkansas school districts before coming to Warren."

"How did you find us?" he asked

"That's a long story! If you don't mind, let us save that story until we meet?"

"Mr. Barger, I'll call you tonight!"

After graduation, we returned home. I quickly changed out of my suit into more comfortable clothes. I had just started watching television when Mr. Gates called.

"Mr. Barger, this is B. P. Gates."

"Good evening, Mr. Gates."

"Did you get those children graduated tonight?" he asked.

"Yes, we did. Those seniors are now officially graduated and out on their own."

"Mr. Barger, if Memorial Day weekend is still available, we can meet with you and Mrs. Barger. We were wondering if y'all could meet us at Gayle's apartment in Memphis, Tennessee, on Saturday, May twenty-fourth, around three o'clock in the afternoon?"

"We will do our best to be there!"

"Mr. Barger, could you call Gayle to get directions to her apartment? She knows Memphis and Shelby County lots better than I do!"

"I'll call Gayle for directions."

"Please know we are looking forward to seeing y'all on Saturday. Be careful traveling. I'm assuming y'all will be traveling Interstate 40 East?" Mr. Gates asked.

"Yes, we do plan to take Interstate 40 to Memphis."

After hanging up the phone, I looked at Lena and said, "It's all been arranged. We are going to Memphis to meet Carla's biological mother and grandparents."

CHAPTER 39

Face to Face at Last

Before returning to Boise, Carla knew I had started my investigation to find her biological mother. It had been my intention from the beginning not to tell Carla that I had found her biological mother unless she was willing to meet Carla and pursue a relationship. If the biological mother decided she didn't want to meet her, then everything stopped. Carla wouldn't know that I'd found her biological mother.

Lena and I previously agreed that we would make the first contact with the biological mother. At this point, Carla had no knowledge that I'd found her mother and grandparents. If Gayle and her parents decided they didn't want this to go any further, I would end my journey, as if nothing ever had happened, and Carla would never know I had found them.

After I hung up the phone, Gayle Gates Elliott called me. "Mr. Barger, this is Gayle Elliott. Daddy said I needed to call you and give you directions to my apartment."

"I was getting ready to call you about that very thing."

"Mr. Barger, my apartment is easy to find. If you follow my directions, you won't have any problems."

"Gayle, we look forward to meeting you and your parents."

"We are looking forward to meeting you also. Mr. Barger, I've been praying about this for years. I'm so happy. This is the best news I've ever gotten."

"Lena and I are excited as well. We should be there around three o'clock. If I have any problems finding you, I'll give you a call."

"We look forward to your visit. Please travel safe. Those big trucks on Interstate 40 are killers."

We arrived at Gayle's apartment on Friday, May 23, 1997, at three o'clock. We had no problem finding it, because she had given excellent directions. As we drove to the street of Gayle's apartment, I saw B. P. Gates standing on the corner. I knew it was him, because I had seen him previously washing his pickup in his front yard in Crenshaw. I stopped at the curb where he was standing. He saw the Arkansas license plate and immediately came up to our car.

"Are you the Bargers?" he asked.

"We are the Bargers," I replied.

"I'm B. P. Gates. Welcome to Memphis!"

We greeted each other with a friendly handshake.

"You can call me BP, if you'd like."

"Please call us Carl and Lena."

"Well, Carl and Lena, let's go inside. Gayle and Cornelia are waiting for us."

Lena and I followed Mr. Gates. As we entered the front door, a tall, attractive woman wearing a blue pantsuit greeted us at the door.

"Cornelia, this is Carl and Lena Barger. Carl and Lena, this is my wife, Cornelia Gates, and this is my daughter, Gayle."

We shook hands as Cornelia directed us to the large dining area where a big coconut cake was sitting in the middle of the table. *Oh, my goodness*, I thought, *does it taste as good as it looks*. I love coconut cake. The trip from Warren had been long and I was hungry. Driving always makes me hungry. *I could eat a fourth of that cake*, I thought. I knew Lena was watching me. She had warned me to watch my manners.

"Did y'all have any trouble finding Gayle's apartment?" Cornelia asked.

"We had no problem. Gayle gave good directions."

"Let's all sit down and have some coffee and cake. I hope y'all like coconut cake."

"Carl loves coconut cake, don't you, Carl?"

That was Lena's way of telling me that I could have some cake. "Coconut is my favorite of all cakes. How did you know that, Cornelia?"

"I didn't know that, Carl, but I'm glad it's your favorite. What would you like in your coffee?"

"I'll take some cream in mine, but no sugar," I said.

"I'll take mine black," Lena said.

During the time that Cornelia and Gayle were serving cake and coffee, Cornelia was talking. I loved her and B. P.'s southern accents. They sounded just like one of our past Presidents, Jimmy Carter. They weren't from Georgia, but they sounded just like him.

Because Cornelia dominated the talking, B. P. and Gayle had a hard time breaking into the conversation. B. P. tried, but Cornelia was always finishing his sentences. Gayle wasn't very talkative at first. When she did talk, she seemed to nasalize. I learned later that this was due to the sinus surgery she'd had three weeks prior to our visit.

I could see some resemblance between Carla and Gayle. Carla resembled Gayle more during Gayle's teenage years. The pictures I copied from the Panola High School annuals of Gayle showed a stronger resemblance.

We had finally met! We were sitting in the dining room with Gayle Gates Elliott, our daughter's birth mother, and her parents, B. P. and Cornelia Gates! It didn't take Lena and me long to see that these people were genuine and down to earth, Southern people. In no time, we felt right at home with them. There was not a minute of silence. We were sharing information back and forth. Everyone was craving new information. I didn't mind the busy conversations. I had feared we would get in the meeting and run out of something to say. Then what would we do? I quickly saw that my worries had been in vain. Our conversations were nothing but interesting and good. We were having a wonderful time getting to know each other.

After finishing my cake, Gayle looked at me and asked, "Carl, we want to know how you found us."

For some reason, I knew this question would come up, so I was ready for it. "It's a long story, so we may need some freshly brewed coffee and maybe some more of that delicious coconut cake." Everyone laughed, but Cornelia took me up on it and put more coffee on to brew.

"Last March when Carla was in Warren on her spring break, I was sharing with her my genealogy findings from Missouri relating to the Bargers and Heiples. After sharing with her, she looked at me and said, "Dad, now you can see why I have always wanted to know who my biological parents are."

I spent about an hour filling them in on the steps I had taken to find them. I shared the disappointments and the feeling of joy and success when I finally learned who the biological family of my daughter was.

I think there were four things which actually made my journey a success. First, knowing Carla's given name was Susan Ann Gates. Secondly, the help of a good friend in Arkansas telling me I should go to Tunica to gamble. The third thing was the article in the Sardis newspaper telling about Gayle's wreck, and last, but certainly not least, was God's guidance and patience. If it hadn't been for God, this meeting wouldn't be happening.

The Gateses went on and on about what a good detective I was. I said, "No, I had a lot of help from God. He was with me all the time. He opened many doors and closed a few."

"Tell us about your and Lena's background," Gayle said.

"I grew up in a little place called Higden, later called Greers Ferry, Arkansas. I came from a large family of eleven children. My parents were Edward and Mamie Barger. My mother had her first baby when she was sixteen years old. She was a tough lady.

"My family was considered a migrant family. From the time I was three until I was seventeen, we went to the fruit harvest in Benton Harbor, Michigan, and in early fall, we picked cotton in Monette, Arkansas. We were considered poor folks. Experiencing the hard times convinced me that there was something better in life than remaining a migrant worker."

After I finished my story, I looked at Lena and said, "It's your time!"

"My father died when I was nine years old. I am the oldest of four girls born to Joseph Leonard Dollar and Milbra Stone Dollar. Like Carl's family, we were poor. My mother raised all four of us girls by herself. I have three sisters. Earlene and Virginia received college degrees in education and are presently teachers. My baby sister, Patsy, received a two-year vocational degree. I am presently teaching English at the Monticello Junior High School in Monticello, Arkansas."

After sharing our stories, Gayle said, "Carl, could we see those pictures you and Lena brought."

"Give me a few minutes," I said. "I have to go to the car and get them." It was raining a little when we arrived at Gayle's apartment, so we had left the pictures in the car. Mr. Gates and I went back to the car and got the pictures. Lena had made Gayle an album with pictures of Carla from babyhood to adulthood.

"Gayle, do you want to see baby pictures first, or do you want to see Carla as she is today?" Lena asked.

"I want to see her as she is today!" Gayle said excitedly.

Lena pulled out Carla's wedding pictures, and as soon as Gayle and her parents looked at them, Gayle said, "Oh, she is so beautiful! Look at her! Isn't she beautiful?" B. P. and Cornelia were in full agreement.

Lena and I enjoyed seeing the expressions on their faces. I was thrilled that this album of pictures made them happy.

Gayle said, "Look at those teeth! How beautiful they are!"

Lena and I looked at each other and smiled. We had spent a small fortune on Carla's teeth. It took two years to correct her teeth problems. But thanks to braces, her teeth are beautiful.

Gayle said, "Now let's see her baby pictures."

Lena handed Gayle the album she had put together for her. Gayle opened the album with Mrs. Cornelia and Mr. B. P. looking over her shoulder. As soon as she saw the baby pictures she said, "Oh, she looks just like my baby pictures, doesn't she, Mother?"

"I cannot believe this," Cornelia said.

Gayle went into her bedroom immediately, and got a picture album she had made for us to take back to Carla in Boise. We looked at her baby pictures and, sure enough, Gayle and Carla looked so much alike as babies.

Gayle's cellular phone rang. It was her friend, Sandra, who was aware that we were coming to Gayle's apartment. She was calling to see how things were going. I heard Gayle say to Sandra, "Oh, Sandra, Carla is so beautiful! I cannot wait for you to see the pictures. She's everything that I imagined she'd be. . . . It's going very well. They are good people."

I could tell this day had become a good day for Gayle Gates Elliott, one she would long remember. The news about Carla was definitely what the doctor had ordered for Gayle.

CHAPTER 40

Biological Father Revealed

After talking to Sandra, Gayle came back to the table where we were all sitting. She looked at me with her hands on the table, and said, "Carl, have you had any luck finding the biological father?"

"Gayle, I'm glad you asked me that question, because I have run into all sorts of problems finding a lead on who he is and where he lives.

"Carl, I can tell you who Carla's father is," she said.

With the information Gayle provided to me, I was able to locate him, visit with him, both by phone and personally at my home in Warren, Arkansas. During his visit to Arkansas to meet Carla, we spent the biggest portion of two days getting to know him.

Because of his request that he and his family not be included in this story, I am ending that part of the story here.

Our visit with Gayle, B. P., and Cornelia couldn't have gone better. It was like everyone was craving more and more knowledge of what had gone on since the birth of Carla. In late afternoon, since we were getting tired, Lena and I left Gayle's apartment for the Hampton Inn. The next two hours were spent resting and getting ready to go to dinner with Gayle and her family.

About six-thirty, Gayle and her parents picked us up at the Hampton Inn, and we went to the Embassy Suites in Memphis which, according to them, had the best Italian food in the city.

It was at dinner that Cornelia shared with us that she had taught math at the Institute of Learning in Tunica. She had been teaching school at the Institute when Gayle gave birth to Carla. During the two years she taught there, she took her son, Parker, with her. Parker graduated from the Institute of Learning in 1972. Cornelia's story reaffirmed that she was my Tunica connection.

Our visit with the Gateses at the Embassy Suites was enjoyable and informative. We learned a lot about Gayle's home life growing up in Crenshaw. Gayle shared with us the problems she had as a result of the accident. In spite of the problems, and with the help of a good psychiatrist, Gayle graduated with honors from Panola High School. In the fall of 1969, Gayle entered her freshman year at the University Women's College at Columbus, Mississippi.

Our dinner with the Gateses was one of the niceties nights we'd spent with anyone. We never seemed to have a silent moment visiting with each other. We took several pictures sitting around the table. After dinner they dropped Lena and me off at the Hampton Inn for the night.

Lena and I rejoiced over our exciting day. We had met the biological mother and maternal grandparents of our daughter. We were pleased that they were Christians, and we were excited that they wanted to see Carla. What a wonderful day it had been! We looked forward to Sunday when again we would meet with them for Sunday brunch at Shoney's.

I struggled with sleeping on Saturday night. I kept thinking about how blessed I had been by God helping me locate these wonderful people. I kept thinking about how I would continue my search for Carla's biological father. I thought about how I would break the news to Carla when we went to Boise on May 31.

After falling asleep sometime during the early hours of Sunday morning, Lena and I got up at eight-thirty. About nine-forty, Gayle and Cornelia came by and picked us up. B. P., who was a deacon and teacher at First Baptist in Crenshaw, had gotten up early and gone to Crenshaw to teach a men's Sunday school class. He would return to Gayle's apartment around noon to spend the afternoon with us.

We arrived at Shoney's about ten o'clock. It was there that we learned more about Parker Gates and his family, who lived in Collierville, a suburb of Memphis. Parker's wife, Helen, home schooled Courtney, their eldest daughter, who was seventeen. Parker and Helen also had a thirteen-year-old daughter, Lauren, and a ten-year-old son, Ben.

Parker was employed with the DeBold Manufacturing Company in sales. From listening to Cornelia, it was apparent that she was very proud of her son.

After finishing brunch, Gayle drove us back to the Hampton Inn to get our car. Lena and I had already checked out of the hotel and had put our luggage in the car. Lena rode with Gayle and Cornelia back to Gayle's apartment while I followed in my car.

Before we separated at the Hampton Inn, we informed Gayle and Cornelia that we would be flying to Boise on May 31 and would then break the news to Carla that we had found her biological mother and maternal grandparents. We went on to say that if Carla was up to talking to them after hearing the news, we would place a call to Gayle and let her and Carla talk. This excited Gayle!

I had explained to them that Carla had no knowledge of my having found them. I had kept this a secret. I didn't want Carla to be hurt should we make contact and the biological parents expressed no interest in knowing her.

It was hard saying goodbye to these newfound friends. They were great people who had received us with open arms. As we were leaving Gayle's apartment, I said, "Gayle, how do you feel about the past twenty-four hours?"

"I think I'm still in shock! I just can't believe all of this has happened. It's been wonderful! It's a prayer that's been answered. I just want you and Lena to know how much I love you for giving Carla a good home. I've worried about her for so many years. I prayed that God had given her good Christian parents, and that she was happy. God has answered many prayers for me this year, especially the prayer I prayed in February, when I said, 'God if I ever know my daughter, it will be because you will work it out.' After I prayed that prayer, I felt an inner peace I had never before experienced. In March, one month later, you started your search for me. I know now that God has answered my prayers."

After a mid-afternoon snack, which included another big piece of Cornelia's coconut cake, we took several more pictures before leaving for Warren. Gayle must have hugged us at least three times on the way to the car. We finally said goodbye and left for home.

On the way home from Memphis, Lena and I both agreed that this first part of our journey had been a success. We had found a Christian family who wanted to meet a daughter and granddaughter they hadn't seen in twenty-six years.

We were emotionally exhausted but felt an inner peace just knowing that soon our promise to Carla would be fulfilled. We left Memphis with the photo album that Gayle was sending to Carla, a prayer written by B. P. Gates to Carla, and a letter Gayle had written to "Susan" on her twenty-second birthday. My faith in God was reinforced knowing that God has His own time for everything. Praise the Lord!

CHAPTER 41

A Wonderful Time with Family

On Saturday, May 31, Lena, Curt, and I left the Little Rock airport on Delta Airlines for Boise. This was Curt's first airplane ride. Everything went well until we experienced some turbulence. At this time, Curt got a little uptight. It didn't take the pilot long to make the necessary adjustments to get us out of the turbulence. I must confess that flying in turbulent weather gets to me as well. I've read that there has never been a plane fall apart because of turbulence, but at the same time, I'm thinking, *What if we are the first?*

When we arrived at the Boise airport, Carla and Brent were waiting at the gate for us. As we entered the waiting area, I couldn't believe my eyes. Carla had gotten her hair cut short. Her beautiful long hair that I adored and loved was gone. Although the beautiful hair was gone, her beautiful smile was not.

As we hugged, Carla asked, "Dad, how do you like my hair?"

"Carla, what did you do with all your beautiful hair?"

"You don't like it, do you?" she said.

"I liked your hair long better, but if you like your hair short, I guess that's what's important!"

Although her hair was short, it was still beautiful. To me, Carla would be beautiful if she were bald. I have learned over the years not to get upset about something that has already occurred. It's too late, so why fuss? It was Carla's hair, and she could do anything she wanted to do with it.

We left the airport and went straight to Carla and Brent's home on the west side of Boise. They lived in a rental house.

Carla was so excited to show us their home. As I walked through the front door, I began to see Carla's touch. She loved flowers. She had live flowers in both the living room and the kitchen. She had family pictures in both rooms, as well. She had done a great job making their home beautiful and personable. The atmosphere was filled with warmth.

Carla was also a good housekeeper, maybe a little too good at times to suit the men folks. The first thing we did before unpacking was take a tour of the house. We started with the downstairs and finished by climbing several steps leading to the upstairs where Carla and Brent's master bedroom was located. The entire house was clean and smelled good. I don't know what fragrance she was using, but it was heavenly. After touring the house, Carla suggested that we go out to eat. She didn't cook much, so she and Brent often ate out.

Carla and I had never agreed on the importance of eating meals at home. I always thought it was cheaper to cook than eat out. She always said, "Dad, Brent and I like to eat out, and besides, by the time you buy everything to prepare a meal, you have spent as much as you would by eating out."

Carla and Brent took us to their favorite place in Boise, TGI Fridays. As we pulled up in the parking lot, we noticed people standing in the lobby of the restaurant. Carla said, "We won't be able to get a table here for probably an hour. Do ya'll want to go somewhere else?"

"I have a suggestion. Let me out at the door, you circle around with the car while I go in and see how long before we can be seated. You can drive back by and get me."

"That sounds like a good idea, Dad," Carla said.

I went inside and walked up to the reservation desk and inquired about a table for five. The young lady said, "You are in luck!"

"Great! How long will we have to wait?"

"We can seat you right now. What is your name?"

"Barger," I replied."

"Mr. Barger, give us a minute."

I told her I'd be right back. I had to let my party know that we could be seated.

I went outside, and Brent pulled the car right up close to the door, anticipating that I would say, "Let's go somewhere else." Instead I said, "I've got a table. They are waiting to seat us."

"Oh, Dad, quit your kidding," Carla said, laughing.

"Brent, park your car and let's eat," I said.

As we got inside the waiting area, the receptionist said, "Mr. Barger, your table is ready!"

After we were seated, Carla said, "Dad, how did you get a table so fast with all of these people waiting?"

"Carla, the young lady liked my looks, my Southern charm, and she also liked my Arkansas accent!"

"Come on, Dad. You slipped her some money, didn't you?"

"Carla, I'm telling you again, it's that Southern charm. It works for me every time!"

Everyone had a good laugh, and we all enjoyed our delicious meal at TGI Fridays.

"I hope y'all don't mind, but we've got to run by Wal-Mart and get some groceries. We don't have anything to cook for breakfast."

I looked at Lena and she looked at me. We were hoping we could go back to Carla's after dinner. We were tired and we wanted to share our good news with Carla before going to bed. After shopping at Wal-Mart, we returned to Carla and Brent's home around ten o'clock. After the groceries were put up, we all went to the living room where we started watching television.

"Carla and Brent, Lena and I have something to share with you. Is it all right to turn off the television?"

Brent turned the television off and sat down by Carla. "What's this all about, Dad?" Carla asked.

"Carla, do you remember when you were home in March on spring break, and you and I went to Little Rock to do some research on your adoption?"

"Yes, I remember that quite well. We were not very successful."

"Yes, that's right. We weren't successful, but I decided I would continue the search. I started my own search the week after you returned to Boise, and, Carla, I have found your biological parents."

Carla's face lit up. I could feel her excitement! "You have found my biological parents?" she said, unbelieving.

"Yes, I have found your biological parents. Your biological mother is a registered nurse, and she lives in Memphis, Tennessee. She works for Trinity Health Care Services. Her name is Katherine Gayle Gates Elliott.

"She was married and divorced by the time she was twenty-two years old. She never remarried, and she had no other children after giving birth to you."

"Dad, how did you find her?" Carla questioned.

"It wasn't easy, but I had four things going for me. First, I had the name Gates. Second, I had paper work which described a bad automobile wreck that Gayle was involved in when she was sixteen. The paperwork went on to say that Gayle was the driver and had eight broken ribs. The paper work revealed that there was one girl killed, one girl injured, and a boy who had a broken hip.

"The third thing I had was that the maternal grandmother taught in a private academy. Fourth, and certainly not least, I had God helping me. Without His help, I wouldn't be sitting here in your living room right now sharing this with you.

"I researched a month or more in Arkansas before I found out from a friend that neither of the biological parents was from Arkansas. After finding out they were from Mississippi, I went to there to conduct my research. After one trip to Tunica, Mississippi, and one trip to Sardis, Mississippi, I was able to find out who she was and where she lived. It has been a wonderful experience for both Lena and me."

Carla just sat there listening and not saying a word. I continued to tell her that Lena and I went to Memphis on Memorial Day weekend to meet Gayle and her parents, B. P. and Cornelia Gates. I explained that B. P. and Cornelia lived in the small town of Crenshaw, Mississippi, located about forty-five miles south of Memphis. I told her that we found Gayle and her parents to be very nice people, and they were looking forward to talking with her by phone and meeting her when arrangements could be made.

Carla was elated! She didn't really know what to say. I told her that when we visited Gayle in Memphis, she gave us the name of her biological father.

"Dad, I just can't believe you really have found them," she kept saying.

"Carla, Gayle sent you a photo album that has pictures of her when she was a baby, a teenager, and as an adult. Do you want to see the album?" Lena asked.

"Yes, I would like to see the pictures."

Lena gave the album to Carla. We moved over by her to point out who the people were in the pictures. Gayle's baby pictures looked a lot like Carla when she was a baby. The adult pictures of Gayle didn't favor Carla as much.

Lena also gave Carla the letter that Gayle had written to "Susan" on her twenty- second birthday. Susan was the name Gayle had given Carla at birth. Lena also presented Carla with B. P. Gates's written prayer for her.

We spent several minutes answering questions for her about our trip to Memphis. By that time it was getting late, and I suggested we go to bed. We were all tired from our plane trip, and a good night's rest would feel good to this old man of fifty-three years.

When Lena and I got in bed, I said, "Well, honey, what do you think?"

"I think Carla took the news well," Lena replied.

"That's how I saw it as well," I said.

"Have you given any thought about Carla wanting to go back to Arkansas with us to see Gayle, B. P., and Cornelia?" Lena asked.

"If she wants to go back to Arkansas with us, I'll buy her a plane ticket. If she talks to you about it, let her know we will be happy to purchase a ticket for her."

"If I know Carla, she will want to go back to Arkansas with us," Lena said.

There were still things to do, like getting them together, but it was a great day for Carla and the rest of us.

God opened many doors in my search, and closed only a few. I believed it was God's will that everything developed as it did. We had brought joy into the hearts of Gayle, B. P., and Cornelia. Joy that they hadn't known before. Gayle now knew what had happened to the daughter she gave up, and B. P. and Cornelia now had their first grandchild to love and cherish. What could be better than that?

This reunion with Carla's biological mother and maternal grandparents would certainly resolve a lot of unknowns in Carla's mind. She, too, would have a peace of mind knowing who her biological mother is, and, maybe, who her biological father is.

"All the questions Carla asked me as she was growing up can now be answered. That's a good thing, Carl," Lena said.

Before going to sleep, Lena and I prayed and thanked our Lord and Savior, Jesus Christ, for His goodness and love and providing us an avenue to make others happy.

On Sunday morning, we got up and went to church with Carla and Brent. They attended the United Methodist Church in downtown Boise. It was a beautiful old church with lots of personality. They have been regular in their attendance since moving to Boise.

Although we were Southern Baptists, we found the Methodist church to be warm and receptive. The people were very nice, and we felt right at home there.

After returning to their house after lunch, we changed into walking shorts and headed to the Boise race tracks. Brent, Carla, Curt, and I liked watching the horses run. Lena went along just for the ride. We spent a relaxing afternoon at the tracks.

After the races, Brent took us on a driving tour of Boise, a beautiful city situated in a valley surrounded by mountains. The valley has two different rivers flowing through the city of Boise. They are the Boise River and the Snake River. There are several farms in the valley around the city of Caldwell. That part of the valley reminded me of my migrant days because of the different fruits and vegetables being grown in that area.

Boise is one of the leading technology centers in the United States. The two largest industries in Boise are Micron and Hewlett Packard. Those two industries employ lots of people and pay good salaries. Brent was an employee of Hewlett Packard. He was recruited by HP right out of Dartmouth University where he graduated with an MBA.

The first week we were in Boise, Brent went to work every day at Hewlett Packard. Carla wasn't working at that time, so she had time to take us places. She knew I enjoyed seeing schools and colleges. She took us to Boise State University, home of the Broncos. Their football stadium was a work of art.

We enjoyed staying up late, watching movies, sleeping until ten o'clock in the morning, getting up and eating a late breakfast, and just lounging around.

On Tuesday, Carla asked me if she could talk to me in her room. "Dad, I've been thinking a lot about Gayle. Do you think you could get her on the phone and let me talk with her?"

"Sure I can, but we will have to wait until she gets off work this afternoon. Is that going to work for you?"

"Yes, that will work for me, and, Dad, when you get on the phone, I want you to talk first and stay on the phone while I am talking."

"I don't have any problem with that," I said.

Carla was still insecure in a lot of ways. However, I might be the same way if I were making a call to my biological mother for the first time in my life.

It was five-thirty when I reached Gayle on the phone. "Gayle, this is Carl Barger, I'm calling from Boise, Idaho."

"Carl, it's good to hear from you. How are things going?"

"Everything is going well. We are having a good time."

"How is Carla taking the news?" she asked.

"Very well," I said. "Would you like to talk to her?"

Carla started shaking her head and saying, "Dad, no, I don't know what to say right now."

"Carla, I will stay on the line, pick up the phone."

“Gayle, here is Carla!” I said.

“Hello,” Carla said.

“Hello, Carla. I’m Gayle, how are you?”

Carla was so nervous. It didn’t take Gayle long to make Carla feel comfortable while talking with her. I stayed on the phone and enjoyed the dialog between a mother and daughter who had never seen or talked to each other.

As I listened to their conversation, I could feel both of them reaching out to the other. There was so much to be said and so much to look forward to. When it became apparent that I was no longer needed, I broke in and said, “Gayle, I am going to hang up now. I will say goodbye and let you and Carla visit in private.”

“Carl, thanks for calling.”

“You are welcome,” I said with tears in my eyes as I hung up.

I left Brent and Carla together upstairs and joined Lena and Curt downstairs. As I was leaving, I saw Carla rocking back and forth on the floor. That was a sign of the nervous tension coming out in her. I had seen it all through her life. When she was nervous, she would rock and pick at her lip, or kick her right foot in and out. Although I knew she was nervous, she was doing quite well talking with Gayle as I left her bedroom.

On Thursday morning, Carla came to me and asked, “Dad, do you think you could afford a plane ticket for me to return to Arkansas with ya’ll to meet Gayle and her parents?”

Lena was so right. She knew Carla well. I hadn’t tried to push Carla toward going back with us. That had to be her decision, but I was glad she wanted to.

“Yes, Carla, I will pay for your ticket. I first need to call Gayle and find out about her schedule for the week after we return home.” I knew Gayle had already paid for a vacation cruise and was going to leave on June 15.

I knew how much this meant to Carla. I knew she needed to see Gayle as soon as possible. Carla is the type of person who cannot stand not knowing what’s going on! Her curiosity has to be resolved in a short period of time, or she gets really emotional.

I called Gayle at her home in Memphis. "Gayle, Carla has decided she wants to return to Arkansas with us to see you and your folks. I know you are planning to leave on your cruise on Sunday, June fifteenth. Since we will return to Arkansas on June eighth, we were wondering if we might get together on Thursday, Friday, and Saturday."

"Carl, that's a great idea. I'll make arrangements to be off from Thursday through Saturday. This is just great!"

"Okay, we will plan accordingly," I said.

"I will make all arrangements here in Memphis," she said.

Carla called Delta Airlines and was able to get a ticket on the same flight with us to Arkansas.

On Friday, June 5, Brent, Carla, Curt, Lena, and I left Boise for Yellowstone National Park for a three-day, two-night stay in the park. Lena, Curt, and I had never been to Yellowstone. We had always heard about how beautiful it was, and we had been looking forward to seeing Old Faithful erupt into its glorious beauty and the many varieties of animals that run wild in the park.

We spent our first night at the Teton Mountain Village in Jackson Hole, Wyoming. We stayed at the Best Western Hotel near the base of the Teton Mountains. The Teton Mountains shade the village area where we stayed, so it was nice and cool there. After settling in at the hotel, we traveled six miles to Jackson Hole for dinner.

Jackson Hole is a unique little tourist town that has something for everyone. Many visitors go to Jackson Hole during the winter months to enjoy the ski slopes.

Our time at Teton Mountain Village turned out to be too short. It was so quiet and peaceful. Before leaving the village, Brent, Curt and I had an opportunity to ride the tram to the top of the Teton Mountain, which proved to be an experience I shall not forget. From the top of the mountain, we could see God's beautiful creation for several miles.

After leaving Teton Village, we traveled to Jackson Hole for lunch and on to Yellowstone National Park. The National Park was everything I had heard people talk about. The winding roads prevented us from speeding and gave us more time to enjoy God's beauty. We saw many of the wild animals that roamed the beautiful valley and mountains in the national park.

We arrived at Old Faithful about two-forty in the afternoon. As we pulled into the parking lot, we heard some people say, "Old Faithful is to blow again in fifteen minutes." People were headed toward Old Faithful in droves. We took our seats on a bench constructed on a board walk that went around the geyser area. As we waited impatiently for Old Faithful to do her stuff, she teased us by shooting up a little steam from time to time. Just as we thought she would blow, she would settle down. Finally, she blew! It was beautiful! I had read about Old Faithful in history books and had seen pictures of her but never truly understood what it was all about until now. I really couldn't believe I was standing there watching Old Faithful entertain the many people who had come to see her. I will never forget the beauty I observed on that day. We spent our second night in West Yellowstone at the west entrance to the park.

West Yellowstone is an interesting resort town. Unlike Jackson Hole, it had millions of mosquitoes. Those mosquitoes were everywhere.

On Sunday morning we re-entered the west entrance of the park and traveled to the Grand Canyon of Yellowstone. Before leaving the park, we drove to the high country in hopes of seeing some grizzly bears, but no luck. Even with that disappointment, we agreed it had been a wonderful three days.

CHAPTER 42

Carla Meets Gayle

On Tuesday, June 8, we left Boise and returned to Arkansas around seven-thirty in the evening. Our son, Jeffrey, met us at the airport. After collecting our luggage, we went to supper at Chili's. We had a good time visiting with Jeff, who would soon go to work for the Arkansas Nature Conservancy in Little Rock. He was excited about his new job. He had returned from Alaska the last part of May and had several job interviews before being hired by the Nature Conservancy.

It was good to be home from an enjoyable trip to Boise and Yellowstone National Park, but what I found waiting for me at my office made me want to go away again. I had ten days of mail to go through and several telephone calls to return.

Carla was busy at the house putting together picture albums that would be gifts to Gayle, B. P. and Cornelia. On Wednesday night, Carla was trying on clothes. She would come into the living room where I was watching television and ask my opinion about what she should wear to meet Gayle for the first time. I didn't realize the dress thing was so important to her. Carla wanted to remember exactly what she wore when she first met Gayle. I thought she looked good in everything she tried on.

She finally decided to wear a light-blue, denim blouse and navy-blue slacks to meet Gayle. She chose a beautiful pink dress with white dots for the reunion dinner. I felt she had made some really good choices.

Carla was up late getting ready for the next day. She was nervous about meeting Gayle for the first time. I knew things were going to be all right, but Carla didn't know that. She was worried that they wouldn't like her.

We left for Memphis on Thursday, June 12. We decided to eat lunch in Pine Bluff, which was on our way to Memphis. Before getting into Pine Bluff, I asked, "Does anyone have a preference on where they want to eat lunch?"

"I do," Carla said. "I want to eat at Sonic. I've not eaten at a Sonic since leaving Arkansas."

"The Sonic it is!" I said.

After eating lunch, we drove on to Memphis. We arrived at Gayle's apartment around three o'clock in the afternoon.

"Carla, what's wrong?" Lena asked.

"Mother, I'm scared!"

"I know, baby, but believe me, everything will be all right. I can assure you that Gayle, B. P., and Cornelia will make you feel welcome. You will see!"

"You go first, Dad. Mom and I will follow you."

As I led the way to Gayle's apartment, I noticed that Lena and Carla had fallen about fifteen feet behind me. "Come on, y'all," I encouraged.

I rang the doorbell, and Cornelia came to the door. She said, "They're here!" She came out and hugged Lena and me. By that time Gayle had burst through the front door, brushed right by me and Lena, and headed straight toward Carla. She embraced Carla and said, "Hi, it's so good to see you!" Gayle grabbed Carla's hands and just stood and looked at her. She was smiling all the time. She said, "Carla, you are so beautiful! You are more beautiful than your pictures."

It was one of the sweetest things I have witnessed in my lifetime. I had seen television shows where adopted children were united with their biological mothers at airports, but I had never personally witnessed a mother and daughter being reunited for the first time. It was beautiful! There were signs of excitement and emotions running high that particular day. Gayle and Cornelia were bursting with joy. Although B. P. wasn't showing the same emotions, you could still see signs of happiness in his smile.

I shall always remember that day. The day we brought joy and happiness to a mother and grandparents who had wondered for years what had happened to that little baby they left behind at St. Vincent's Hospital in Little Rock, Arkansas, twenty-six years earlier.

As the celebration continued, Carla would look at me and grin when Cornelia and B. P. spoke. She, too, loved their Southern accents. I had previously told her that she would love hearing them talk.

We had been at Gayle's apartment for about thirty minutes when Carla reached in her bag and pulled out the picture albums and pictures she brought as gifts to Gayle and the Gateses. She handed Gayle her picture and album first, and then proceeded to give B. P. and Cornelia theirs. They were very appreciative of her gifts.

"These are gifts that I will treasure for the rest of my life," Gayle said.

After visiting for another thirty minutes, Gayle asked Carla to take a walk with her. After Gayle and Carla returned, Gayle shared with us the plans for the next two days.

"We have planned a reunion dinner at Jim's Place, a popular restaurant in the northern part of Memphis. Parker and Helen will be meeting us at Jim's Place for dinner.

"We will have a light breakfast here at my apartment. After breakfast, Mom and Dad will be taking you on a tour around Memphis on Friday morning while I attend a meeting and luncheon at Trinity Health Care.

On Friday afternoon Mom and Dad can bring ya'll to the Parkway Shopping Mall, where I will meet you. I want Carla to spend the afternoon with me shopping. While Carla and I are shopping, Mom and Dad will be entertaining Carl and Lena.

"On Friday night, we will cook an Italian dinner here at my house. My aunt, Joann Hathorn from Little Rock, will be joining us for supper. Joann is the one I went to live with in Little Rock when I was pregnant with Carla. She is Dad's sister.

"On Saturday morning, we will have breakfast at the Blue Plate Restaurant on Popular Street, near the Hampton Inn, where you are staying. You will love this restaurant. They have one of the best breakfasts in Memphis.

"Parker and his family will join us at the Blue Plate Restaurant for breakfast. This will give Parker's children an opportunity to meet Carla, Lena, and Carl.

"How does this all sound to ya'll?" Gayle asked.

"It all sounds good to me," I said.

"Me too," Lena said.

I must admit, Gayle had carefully crafted a full schedule of events. I actually needed a pocket calendar to remember the times and events that she had planned.

We left Gayle's apartment around five-thirty in the afternoon for the Hampton Inn on Popular Street in the northern section of town near Interstate 40. We checked into our room, showered, and dressed for dinner. Carla wore her beautiful pink dress with white dots. Lena wore a red flowered dress, and I wore a navy pin-stripe suit. My two ladies looked beautiful. I was so blessed! This, too, would be a night we'd all remember.

About seven-thirty, Gayle and her parents arrived at the Hampton Inn to pick us up. We arrived at Jim's Place at seven forty-five. Parker and Helen had not yet arrived. We were seated at our table and the waiter was taking our drink order when Parker and Helen arrived. They were running late due to a little league baseball game that Parker coached. Parker's son, Ben, played on the little league baseball team. After we were properly introduced, Parker and Helen ordered iced tea.

After placing our dinner orders, we enjoyed getting to know each other. Parker told us he graduated from Ole Miss., at Oxford, Mississippi, with a degree in marketing. He was presently employed with DeBold Manufacturing Company of Collierville, Tennessee. He and Helen had been married fifteen years, and had three children: Courtney, 17; Lauren, 13; and Ben 10. Courtney is Helen's daughter from a previous marriage. Parker adopted her as his own daughter when she was eighteen months old.

We learned that Helen and Parker were members of a Fellowship Bible Church in Collierville. They both were active in their church.

Lena and I shared our backgrounds with Parker and Helen. Our conversation soon was directed toward Carla. She became the focus of the remaining part of the night. Our dinner was served and it was delicious.

After dinner, B. P. insisted that he was paying for the meal. I didn't expect him to pay for ours, and I insisted that I pay for our part of the dinner. But B. P. said, "Carl, this is one of the greatest celebrations of our lives, and we want to pick up the tab for this dinner. You have done a great job raising our granddaughter, and this is just a small way for us to say thank you."

After dinner, we took several pictures inside the dining area and then went outside and took additional pictures. Gayle had brought her camera, which she thought was loaded with film. She had snapped several pictures with her camera before realizing she had no film in it. She kept saying. "My camera shows thirty-six exposures, but it's been sitting on that same number for a long time. It keeps flashing."

Parker looked at Gayle's camera and discovered that she had not added a new roll of film. We all had a good laugh, and to this day, I've not let Gayle forget the camera incident.

After returning to the Hampton Inn, Carla said, "Gayle's invited me to spend Friday night with her and at her apartment. What do ya'll think about that?"

"Carla, if you feel okay with that, I don't see anything wrong with it," Lena replied and I concurred!

We retired to bed around one o'clock in the morning. Carla was all wound up and couldn't sleep. Lena went right off to sleep, as usual. I've never seen anyone who goes to sleep faster than my wife. I lay there listening to Lena snore and Carla toss and turn. It had been a big day for Carla. It was both exciting and emotional for her. She's a lot like me. When I experience new things, it takes me a while to wind down.

On Friday morning we ate breakfast at the Hampton Inn, loaded Carla's luggage, and went to Gayle's apartment.

We visited with Gayle for a while before she had to leave for her meeting at the Trinity Health Care Center. After she left, B. P. and Cornelia took us for a tour of Graceland, the famous downtown Peabody Hotel, and the Titanic exhibit at the Pyramid. We enjoyed our time with them.

We had dinner at Gayle's apartment, where we were introduced to Joann Hathorn, B. P.'s sister from Little Rock. We enjoyed meeting and getting to know her. She shared with us the story of Gayle's stay in Little Rock when she was pregnant and the birth of Carla at St. Vincent's Hospital.

After a very nice Italian dinner, which was prepared by Cornelia and Gayle, Carla was presented a beautiful birthstone ring by Gayle, who wanted to give Carla something of personal value that she could remember.

On Saturday morning, Lena and I were the first ones to show up at the Blue Plate Restaurant. The waiter seated us in the back dining area where two large tables had been reserved for our party. There would be twelve people present for breakfast. Lena and I ordered coffee as we waited for the others to arrive. The Parker Gates family showed up about five minutes later. We had already met Parker and Helen, but it was our first time to meet their children. Ben sat at the end of the table across from me. When Parker introduced Ben to me, he reached out and shook my hand like an adult. He was ten years old. Courtney, Parker and Helen's oldest child, was a very outgoing person, full of personality. Lauren was a little quiet. She was a cute girl but didn't talk as much as Courtney.

Parker and I really hit it off. I liked Parker, and he was interesting to talk with. The last ones to arrive were Carla, Gayle, Joann, and the Gateses. Gayle and the Gateses were correct: the Blue Plate Restaurant was an excellent place to eat.

As Parker was introducing Carla to his children it appeared to me that they liked Carla. They now had a first cousin, one they never knew existed until a few weeks ago.

After breakfast, Bill and Earlene Brecheen joined us at the Blue Plate Restaurant. Earlene (Lena's sister) and Bill taught school nearby in the Blytheville and Gosnell School Districts. Earlene wanted to come to Memphis to meet the Gateses and visit with Carla before she returned to Boise.

After introductions were made, we visited and took pictures both inside the restaurant and outside. This time Gayle had a roll of film in her camera.

On our trip back to Warren, Lena asked Carla how she felt about our visit with the Gateses and Gayle.

"It's been good. My only regret is that we didn't get to spend long enough."

"I know it was short, but there will be more opportunities over the years to get to know them better," I said.

The meeting between Carla, Gayle, and the Gateses had gone very well. Carla had met her biological mother and the Gates family. Ever since Carla was old enough to realize what adoption really meant, she lived with many questions that couldn't be answered. These questions had haunted her for years. She now could find some inward peace knowing there were good reasons why we were her parents and why Gayle had given her up for adoption. She felt good knowing that Gayle and the Gateses had opened their hearts to her and welcomed her back into their family. As I see it, that was the best gift Lena and I could have given Carla.

After returning to Warren, we received a nice card from Cornelia. It read:

> Dear Lena and Carl,
>
> I want to thank you for bringing Carla back into our lives. Last week was filled with so many of God's blessings. It was one of the best weeks of our lives. Already I have seen a wonderful change in Gayle. She gets up happy and cheerful each morning. I look at her and say to myself, Praise the Lord!
>
> The time Gayle and Carla spent together was just what Gayle needed. Gayle has a new lease on life. She is now ready to tackle about anything. We love you guys, and let's stay in touch.
>
> Cornelia Gates.

CHAPTER 43

A New Search Begins

It was the weekend of Father's Day that Jeffrey said, "Dad, now that you have found Carla's biological parents, maybe you could find mine. I've been thinking that, since you have turned into a pretty good investigator, I might need to take advantage of your skills. What you have done is pretty exciting and remarkable stuff."

Jeff had not said anything about his adoption for several years. The successful meeting with Carla's biological mother and father must have sparked an interest in his own biological parents.

"Jeff, give me a few weeks' rest and time to catch up at the office, and I'll start searching for your biological parents."

"I understand perfectly, Dad."

After finding Carla's biological parents, I thought my mission was completed. It now appears my mission is only half completed. I pray God will once again open necessary doors for me to find Jeff's biological parents.

On Tuesday, July 1, 1997, I started my search for Jeffrey Christopher Barger's biological mother. I had two documents that might be beneficial to me in finding her. I had a court document that listed the baby's name, Peter Anthony Patrick. I had always thought that name was just a fictitious name, but I would use it to see what I could find out. The other bit of information was that Jeff's maternal grandmother was listed as being an employee of the Arkansas Department of Vocational Education.

The court document read, "In the Probate Court of Columbia County, Arkansas, let it be known in the matter of the adoption of Peter Anthony Patrick, an infant, under the age of fourteen years, by Carl Junior Barger and Lena Lorene Barger vs. Ivan H. Smith, Guardian."

The judgment rendered in Columbia County on September 23, 1973, gave us sole custody of Peter Anthony Patrick. It was on that date that Peter Anthony Patrick's birth certificate was changed to Jeffrey Christopher Barger.

Several weeks prior to starting my search for Jeff's biological mother, I was going through a large, black-leather briefcase full of keepsakes. I never throw things away that might be important in the future. As I was going through the keepsakes one by one, I came upon the court document. When I read it, I thought, *Now how did we get this document? Is this document authentic?* I had no idea how the document got in my keepsake file. For years, every piece of adoption information that we got when we adopted both Carla and Jeff was in our safe deposit box at the bank, or so I thought. Why was this not in the safe deposit box?

I put the document on top of my chest of drawers to take to our safe deposit box at First State Bank. One day Lena noticed the document lying on my chest of drawers. She picked it up and brought it to me.

"Carl, have you seen this document?"

"Yes, I found it in my keepsake stuff the other day, and I was going to put it with the other adoption stuff at the bank."

"Carl," she said, "I think the name on this document may be Jeff's real name."

"I thought the same thing when I found it. Do you remember when we would have gotten this document?"

"No, this is the first time I've seen it," she said.

"Lena, a few weeks ago, God laid it on my mind to go through that old leather briefcase and see what I had put back. I can't explain why I did it, but I believe God was telling me something, so I did it. As I was going through all the documents, one by one, I found this court document. My first thought was *Could this be Jeff's given name?*, and if it was, why did we have such a document in our possession? I placed it on the chest thinking that if Jeff ever wanted me to search for his biological mother, I would check to see if this document was authentic."

"Carl, now that Jeff wants you to look for his biological mother, why don't you check it out?"

"I plan to do that," I said. "Lena, if Patrick was Jeff's last name, his grandmother must have been a Patrick. Since the biological mother was only sixteen years old when she gave birth to Jeff, she would have been a Patrick as well.

"According to the adoption papers we received from the Arkansas Social Services Department, Jeff's grandmother was a school administrator. If she was an administrator in Arkansas, she would have been a member of the Arkansas Teacher Retirement System. I am going to the Arkansas Teacher Retirement System and check out the name, Patrick. But first, I am going to the Division of Vital Statistics at the Arkansas Department of Health to see if I might get lucky and get a birth certificate on Peter Anthony Patrick. Since I have the court document, they might let me have a birth certificate."

"That sounds like a good plan. Carl, I do believe you are getting good at this," Lena laughingly said.

"I may want to become a private investigator after retiring from my school superintendent job." Naturally, I laughed!

"I'm not kidding," Lena said. "I think you have a good plan."

On July 1, 1997, I left Warren for Little Rock. Little did I realize that on this day, God would bless me with all the information I would need to find Jeff's biological mother. My first stop was at the Arkansas Department of Health on Markham Street. I took the court document to the Vital Statistics Office and handed it to the woman at the desk. "I would like to get a birth certificate for Peter Anthony Patrick," I said.

She looked at the document and then asked, "Mr. Barger, are you the father?"

"Yes, I am the father," I replied.

"May I see some ID?" she asked.

I showed her my driver's license, and she looked at it and noticed my name was Carl J. Barger. "Mr. Barger, she said, this court document is an adoption document. Are you the adoptive father?"

"Yes, I am," I replied.

"Mr. Barger, do you have a judge's court order that gives me permission to open this file?" she asked.

"No Ma'am, I don't," I answered.

"Mr. Barger, it takes a judge's court order originating from the county where the adoption took place for me to open the file on an adopted child. I can't help you without a judge's court order."

"I was afraid of that!"

"I'm sorry, but it's the Arkansas law."

For some reason, I didn't feel disappointed. I never had my hopes built too high on getting a birth certificate by using the court decree, but what now gave me hope was the lady in Vital Statistics told me I had a legal court document. Now, I could go to the Teacher Retirement System and start my search.

After lunch I went to the Arkansas Teacher Retirement complex, arriving at about one-thirty in the afternoon. I asked to see Bill Shiron, director of Teacher Retirement. His secretary informed me that he was out. I then asked to see Angelo Coppolo, his assistant, but he wasn't in either. I explained to the receptionist what I needed, and she said, "I believe Nona Comer can help you with that."

The receptionist took me to Mrs. Comer's office and introduced me to her. I explained to Mrs. Comer that my mission was trying to find my son's biological mother. I told her I believed that Jeff's grandmother was a school administrator in Arkansas. I also told her I thought the grandmother's name might be Patrick.

Mrs. Comer was very nice. She said, "Let's see what we have on Patricks." She pulled up all the Patricks who were members of the Arkansas Teacher Retirement System. There were several.

"Mr. Barger, do you have the age of the grandmother you are looking for?"

"Yes, I have her age at the time her daughter gave birth to my son." We eliminated a lot of the Patricks due to their being males. Finally, we hit upon one person who looked as if she might be the one. Her name was Mrs. Peggy Patrick Johnson. She worked as an administrator for the Arkansas Department of Vocational Education. She listed a daughter as her beneficiary. The daughter's name was Susan W. Patrick. Susan's birth date would put her at sixteen years old when Jeff was born. I said, "Mrs. Comer, I believe we have found the person I'm searching for." I was so happy!

The retirement records showed that Peggy was living in Santa Maria, California. She was married to a Wayne E. Johnson. The records also showed that at one time Peggy was married to a Jones and later to a Carl Patrick. Her daughter Susan was born a Jones, but later was adopted by Carl Patrick.

"Mrs. Comer, I truly appreciate your help with my mission."

"Mr. Barger, it was my pleasure. I think it's great what you are doing for your son. I don't think many adoptive parents would do what you are doing. I hope the rest of your search turns out to be successful and that Peggy is the grandmother you are looking for."

I said goodbye to Mrs. Comer and left for the Arkansas Department of Education's Vocational Division. Since I had been a superintendent in Arkansas for twenty-eight years, I knew several people in the Vocational Department. I knew Charles Brown, the deputy vocational director, well. Charles was once a staff member with the Arkansas Department of General Education but had changed over to the Vocational Department several years ago.

As I entered Charles Brown's outer office, I was greeted by his secretary.

"May I help you?"

"Yes, you may. I'm here to see Mr. Brown."

"Did you have an appointment?" she asked.

"No, I don't have an appointment, but if I can see him, I would appreciate it."

"He has someone with him right now. Take a seat, and as soon as he is free, I will tell him you are here."

"Thank you," I said.

I waited about ten minutes, and a woman came out of Charles's office. Charles's secretary immediately buzzed his office. In a matter of seconds, Charles came to the door and said, "Carl, come in here. Have a seat and tell me what you've been up to."

"Charles, I am not here on school business, but rather a personal one. I need your help."

After a brief explanation concerning my mission, Charles leaned forward in his chair and said, "Carl, that's wonderful. How can I help you?"

"I have every reason to believe my adopted son's grandmother worked here in the Vocational Division. Her name was Peggy Patrick. It could be Peggy Johnson. Do you know her?"

"I've heard that name, Carl, but I don't think I ever worked with her. I believe she worked here before I came over from General Education. I know someone who will know her." Charles phoned upstairs to Helen Lee and said, "Helen, what are you doing?"

"Nothing that can't wait," Mrs. Lee exclaimed.

Charles continued, "My good friend, Carl Barger, superintendent of the Warren Public Schools is in my office. If you have some time to spare, we would like to come up and visit with you."

"Come on up," Mrs. Lee replied.

As soon as I saw her, I remembered her from my Emerson, Nashville, and Bentonville days. She also remembered me.

Charles related to Helen my mission and said, "Do you remember Peggy Patrick?"

Mrs. Lee said, "I remember Peggy very well. She and I worked together for several years."

"Carl, I need to go. I'll let you and Helen visit on this subject. I need to do a few things in my office before I leave for the day. Good luck with this."

"Thank you for your help, Charles!"

"It was my pleasure," he said.

I turned to Mrs. Lee and said, "What can you tell me about Peggy Patrick?"

"Mr. Barger, Peggy was very good at what she did. She was what I would consider a perfectionist. She left the Vocational Department for a position in California."

"Mrs. Lee, I have reasons to believe that Peggy may be a biological grandmother to my adopted son, Jeff. Do you know anything about her daughter?"

"I remember that Peggy had a teenage daughter," she answered.

"Do you know where Susan is today?"

"Yes, I believe she still lives in North Little Rock."

I asked Helen if she knew anything about Susan's having had a baby at age sixteen.

"No. If she did, Peggy never talked about it. But I know someone who might know something. If you give me a few minutes, I'll see what I can find out."

Helen made two calls to two different women, neither of whom knew anything about a baby. Both women also thought that Susan lived in North Little Rock but didn't know what her married name was. Helen continued to tell me what she knew about Peggy's life at the time she had known her.

"Peggy was once married to a Hugh Caple Jones. They divorced, and Peggy married Carl Patrick. Carl still lives in North Little Rock. He officially adopted Susan while he and Peggy were married. Peggy got a divorce from Carl and is now married to a Wayne Johnson from Santa Maria, California.

"Carl, I just thought of another person who might know Susan's last name: Francis Rudd, a retired administrator with the Vocational Education Division. If you have time, I'll call her. I have her number. Francis was a very close friend of Peggy's. She now lives at the Parkway Village Estates. She suffers with Lou Gering's disease."

Mrs. Rudd told Helen that she couldn't think of Susan's husband's last name, but his first name was Will, and he worked for AP&L. She said Susan and Will had a daughter named

Emily, who was ten years old. Mrs. Rudd went on to tell Helen that another co-worker, Genevieve Blanchard, might know Susan's last name.

Mrs. Lee put in a call to Mrs. Blanchard.

"Genevieve, this is Helen Lee with the Vocational Department. I've got Carl Barger, superintendent of the Warren Public Schools, in my office, and he is trying to locate Susan Patrick. Could you visit with him?"

"Yes, I can," Mrs. Blanchard said.

Mrs. Lee handed me the phone, and Mrs. Blanchard and I talked. I asked her if she knew Susan's married name.

"I don't remember Susan's married name, but let me give you Peggy's telephone number in Santa Maria, California. You might call her and get Susan's married name."

I thanked Mrs. Blanchard and wrote down the telephone number for Peggy Johnson.

"Helen," I said, "you have been a great help. I want to thank you for taking all this time with me."

"It's my pleasure, Carl. I think it is so nice what you are trying to do for your son. I hope you find Susan and that she is the biological mother of your son."

I said goodbye to Helen and left for Warren.

CHAPTER 44

Mission Accomplished

After returning to Warren on Tuesday night, I e-mailed my friend in Little Rock. He had helped me earlier by giving me a clue on which state I should search to find Carla's biological family. Without his help, I may have never found them.

I e-mailed information to him relating to Peggy Patrick and her daughter, Susan. The question I asked him was, "Am I on the right trail by pursuing these two people as Jeff's biological mother and grandmother?"

On Wednesday, July 9, I called and asked him if he could confirm my findings.

"Mr. Barger," he said, "again you have done excellent work. If I were you, I would stay on this trail. I believe you will be successful."

I loved the way he gave me clues without giving me the answer. This was his way of helping me but without divulging the source of his information. I felt great! I had been blessed again. Now, how do I find out Susan's last name?

I was sitting in my office trying to decide if I should go ahead and contact Peggy Johnson, Susan's mother, in Santa Maria. I was getting ready to call her when something impressed upon me not to call. Until I found out Susan's last name, it might be premature to call her.

My thoughts turned back to Genevieve Blanchard. Maybe she could tell me more this time.

When Mrs. Blanchard answered the phone I said, "Mrs. Blanchard, this is Carl Barger. I visited with you last week about Peggy Johnson and her daughter, Susan Patrick."

"I remember you, Mr. Barger."

"I hate to keep bothering you about Susan, but I feel certain that Susan is the one I'm looking for. I was wondering if you knew someone else who might know her last name."

"Mr. Barger, after we talked last week I got to thinking about who else I knew who might know Susan's last name. I realized that I know Susan's Uncle Bill Winchell. I can call him, and I will call you back."

"Good," I said.

Mrs. Blanchard called me back within a few minutes and said, "Susan's last name is Benson. She is married to Will Benson, and they live in North Little Rock. Will works for Entergy. Susan and Will have a ten-year-old daughter named Emily." Mrs. Blanchard gave me Susan's phone number and address.

I had received the information I needed to start making my contacts. I was so relieved, I felt this might be a good time to call Peggy Johnson. I wanted to see how she felt about my contacting Susan. I didn't want to ruin a marriage if Susan hadn't told her husband about having a baby and giving him up for adoption.

After getting home, I shared my new information with Lena. She, too, was excited.

"I thought I would first call Susan's mother in California. I think it's best for me to start with the grandmother."

"I totally agree, the grandmother should be your first contact."

As we sat down for dinner, we received a call from Jeff. Lena answered the telephone and passed it to me.

"Dad, have you made any progress in finding my birth mother?"

"Jeff, don't get your hopes up too high, but I may have found her."

"Are you serious?"

"I'm about ninety-nine percent sure, but I'll know more after I place a couple of calls tonight."

"How did you find her so quickly?" he asked excitedly.

"I don't have time right now to tell you, but I've got to believe it was another one of God's blessings. If all goes well tonight, I should know for certain that I have the right person. If I do, I'll give you a call. How is that?"

"Dad, you are a true detective! I'm so proud of you!"

"Thanks! It has been my pleasure to do this for Carla and you."

My first call was to Peggy Johnson's home in Santa Maria, California. A man answered the phone.

"Is Mrs. Johnson home?" I asked.

"No, I'm her husband, Wayne Johnson. Can I help you?"

"Mr. Johnson, I'm Carl Barger, superintendent of the Warren Public School System in Warren, Arkansas. Do you know when I might be able to speak to her?"

Mr. Johnson said, "She's not here. She's in Sacramento at a reading conference."

"When do you expect her home?"

"It will be another two days."

"I really need to talk with her."

"What's this all about, Mr. Barger?"

"I need to visit with her about her daughter, Susan."

"Has something happened to Susan?"

"No, it's nothing like that. I believe Susan is fine, but I need to discuss a personal matter with Mrs. Johnson."

"Mr. Barger, I can give you her phone number at the hotel. Wait until about eight-thirty tonight, California time, before calling her. She should be back in her room by then."

"Does she call you at night?"

"Yes, Sir, she calls me every night."

"When she calls, could you ask her if she's talked with me? If she says no, would you give her my telephone number and ask her to call me at her earliest convenience?"

"Yes, Sir, I can do that."

"Thank you, Mr. Johnson!"

After being unable to talk to Peggy, I decided to call Susan. She was forty years old, and by now she should be able to handle a call of this magnitude. Lena was on the phone in another room. I called Susan's number, and Emily, her ten year old daughter, answered the telephone.

"Hello," she said.

"Hello. Is your mother at home?"

"Just a moment please," Emily said.

When Susan picked up the phone, I said, "Susan, this is Carl Barger, superintendent of the Warren Public Schools. You don't know me, but I need to visit with you about something that is personal in nature. Are you where you can talk privately with me?"

"Mr. Barger, what is this all about?"

I could tell she was apprehensive.

"I need to take you back to March 15, 1973. My wife and I adopted a baby boy in Little Rock whose name was Peter Anthony Patrick."

"Oh, my God!" She started crying and said, "I need to sit down. Let me get the phone in my bedroom."

"Okay," I said.

Susan picked up the phone in her bedroom and said, "Mr. Barger, can you hear me?"

"Yes, I hear you well."

"I gave him up as a baby. How is he? Is he okay?"

"Yes, he is fine. He is in good health and doing well. Susan, I want to apologize for approaching you in this manner. I was afraid you may not have shared about the baby with your husband and daughter, and I didn't want this call to hurt you in any way."

"Don't apologize, Mr. Barger. This is the best news I've ever gotten. Emily and Will are both aware of the baby I gave up for adoption. In fact, Emily was going through pictures one day and found a picture. She said, 'Who is this?'

"I told her the whole story. She was so excited to know she has a brother. She wanted to know if we could search for him. I explained to her that I had given him up for adoption, but someday, we would find him.

"Emily put the picture on her dresser mirror and she guarded it as if it was the most important thing in her life. The picture got misplaced once, and Emily wouldn't stop looking until we all pitched in and found it."

"I'm glad they know about Jeff," I said.

"What is Jeff's full name?"

"We named him Jeffrey Christopher Barger."

Susan asked me one question after another. She wanted to know his whole life history. Some of the questions she asked were: Does he have dark complexion? Did he go to college? Where did he go to college? Is he married? Does he have children? What is he working?"

I thought Susan wouldn't ever finish asking questions. She kept saying, "This is wonderful news! Too good to be true!"

"Mr. Barger, about one year ago, I actually went to the Arkansas Social Services Department and picked up papers to get on the Arkansas Registry, but I never filled them out. My husband, Will, has encouraged me time and time again to do it. For years, I've been in fear that he might hate me for given him up for adoption. I just didn't know what to do."

Lena had been listening in on our conversation and responded to Susan's last statement. "Susan, you don't have anything to worry about. Jeff is an easy going young man, one who has a personality that warms the hearts of everyone he comes into contact with. He would never hate you!"

"Oh, I do want to see him. When do you think we could get together?" she asked.

"We are supposed to call Jeff back tonight. Why don't you and Will talk things over, and let us find out when Jeff would be available to meet you," Lena said.

"That's a good idea. I'm not working right now on Friday, Saturday or Sunday, so any weekend would probably be okay with us."

Lena and I were grateful that Susan was receptive to meeting Jeff. Before calling him, I called Peggy Johnson in Sacramento, where she was attending a reading conference.

"Is this Peggy Johnson?" I asked.

"Yes, this is Peggy Johnson."

"Mrs. Johnson, I am Carl Barger, superintendent of the Warren Public Schools, in Warren, Arkansas. You don't know me, but I have something of a personal nature to discuss with you."

"What is it, Mr. Barger?" she asked.

I told her I had just gotten off the phone from visiting with her daughter, Susan. I explained that we had adopted Susan's baby twenty-four years earlier and now we wanted her to know that Jeff would like to meet his biological family.

"I have wondered about the baby off and on for twenty-four years. How is he?" she asked.

"Jeff's fine," I said.

"You named him Jeff?"

"Yes, Jeffrey Christopher Barger."

"I like that name. What is he doing now?"

Lena and I were both on the phone so Lena began telling Peggy about Jeff's returning from Alaska in early June and now had a job with the Nature Conservancy. Peggy asked several questions about Jeff's background. We shared memories with her about his early childhood, his teenage years, and what he was doing at the present time. We told her he had graduated from the University of Central Arkansas in Conway with a degree in biology.

"That's interesting. Susan majored in biology when she attended the University of Central Arkansas in Conway. I'm really impressed. It appears that you have done a good job of raising Jeff. I am so glad the Arkansas Social Service Department placed him in a good home. It always bothered me not to know what happened to him. We had a difficult time deciding to give him up for adoption. How did Susan take the news?"

"She was excited and seemed joyful at hearing the news," Lena said.

"Susan wants to meet Jeff in the near future," I said.

"This is all so wonderful! I just can't believe this has happened. I have been planning on coming to Arkansas in November for Susan's birthday, but since all of this has happened, I may come before then. I would like for all of us to get together when I come. Do you think that would be possible?" she asked.

"Yes, I think that could be arranged," I said.

"Do you think you could send some pictures of Jeff?"

"Yes, we will get some together in the next few days and send them to you."

"I'm going to call Susan as soon as I can, to see if she, Emily, and Jeff can fly out here to see us sometime."

We said goodbye to Peggy. After hanging up the phone, Lena and I both agreed that Peggy seemed to be excited about Jeff as well. Emily had been Peggy's only grandchild; now she had two.

We tried several times to get Jeff on the phone, but no one answered. Finally, about eleven o'clock he called.

"I'm sorry for calling this late, but I've been working tables at Shorty Smalls. Dad, did you find out for sure who my biological mother is?"

"Yes, I did. Her name is Susan Benson. She lives in North Little Rock with her husband, Will Benson, and their ten-year-old daughter, Emily. We've also visited with Susan's mother, your biological grandmother, Peggy Johnson, who now lives in Santa Maria, California. She and Susan both are elated about the news. They can't wait to see you. In fact, Susan wants us to give them a date when she, Will, and Emily can meet with us in North Little Rock. Susan says she is free on Friday through Sunday for the next few weeks. We are trying to set the date around your working schedule."

"I'll take a look at my calendar and let you know. May I ask a few questions?"

"Yes."

"What is Susan's full name?"

"Her full name is Susan Patrick Benson."

"Where does she live?"

"She lives in North Little Rock."

"What is Susan's mother's name?"

"Her name is Peggy Johnson. She lives in Santa Maria, California. She's a retired vocational education administrator from the Arkansas Vocation Education Department. Jeff, we told Susan we'd call her back after visiting with you to set up a meeting between her family and us."

"Dad, I would like to do this myself!"

"No, this has to be a family thing. This is something Lena and I agreed to before I set out to find your and Carla's biological parents. We agreed if I was successful finding your and Carla's biological parents, we, as a family, would meet together the first time."

"You're right, Dad. That's the way it should be."

I asked him if he could meet with Susan and her family on Saturday, July 12.

"July twelfth would be a good time for me."

"Susan sounded very nice. She's a Baptist and says she's a Christian. You have a little sister. She is ten years old and her name is Emily," Lena said.

We told Jeff we would visit with him some more after talking to Susan. Lena called Susan the following night. Susan said she and Will would feel more comfortable meeting somewhere neutral for the first time and suggested we meet at the Dixie Cafe in North Little Rock on Saturday, July 12. We agreed to meet there for lunch at twelve-thirty in the afternoon.

After finalizing the meeting arrangements, we continued talking over the telephone. We found out that, after Susan gave birth to Jeff and gave him up for adoption, she went to live with her adoptive father, Carl Patrick. She lived with him throughout high school; she had attended Sylvan Hills High School in the Pulaski County School System.

Susan told us that her biological father, Caple Jones, died a year earlier without her having seen him for thirty-six years. She said she was four years old when her father and mother got a divorce. She went on to say that her adoptive father still lived in North Little Rock, and they had a wonderful relationship. She told us that she had stepbrothers and stepsisters on Carl's side of the family, but none from her mother's side of the family. Susan said she had a fourteen-year-old niece who was adopted and was best friends with Emily.

"There is just something special about an adopted child," Susan said.

"We can agree with you on that one hundred percent," Lena concurred.

"Emily is very involved with youth activities at our church. I regret, due to my work schedule, that I don't get to attend regularly."

Susan worked at the North Little Rock Veterans Hospital as an assistant dietitian. She had to work several weekends during the month. She gave us her home address and invited us to come by when we were in North Little Rock.

CHAPTER 45

Fears Allayed

On Saturday, July 12, Lena, Curt, and I left Warren for the Dixie Cafe in North Little Rock. We were to meet Jeff and the Bensons at twelve-thirty. Jeff was living in Little Rock, so it was going to be convenient for him to meet us at the Dixie Cafe.

Jeff was the first one to arrive. He had gone inside and was sitting in the reception area waiting for all of us to arrive, which we did at about twelve-fifteen. After greeting Jeff, I went to the receptionist and asked if he could arrange a large table for seven people.

"Mr. Barger, we will get you fixed up," he said. He escorted us to a large table in the corner of the dining area.

Susan had described what her family would look like. She had said, "You cannot miss my husband, Will. He is six-feet-five, wears his hair in a ponytail, and weighs about three hundred pounds. My daughter comes to my shoulders. She has blond hair and blue eyes. I'm five-six and have brown hair, brown eyes, a dark complexion, and am overweight!"

I said, "We don't talk about being overweight. I am overweight myself."

At about twelve twenty-five they walked through the door and headed for the waiting area. I said to Jeff, "I think that is them."

"Yes, I believe you are right," he said.

I was sitting at the end of the table, so I got up and headed in the direction of the waiting area. Jeff, Curt, and Lena followed along behind me. As I approached the waiting area, Will Benson saw me and got up from where he was sitting.

"Are you Will Benson?" I asked.

"Yes, I am," he said coming toward me.

"I am Carl Barger and this is my wife, Lena, and our sons, Jeff and Curt."

Susan and Emily had been looking out the window. They turned toward us, and Will introduced them. Jeff and Susan smiled at each other, and then Jeff crossed the room and gave Susan and Emily hugs. That was all it took. The ice was broken! Susan's fear of Jeff hating her had been in vain. Jeff set that straight really fast!

"We've already got a table. If you will follow me, we will go have lunch." Jeff got in first on the right side of the table. Susan sat next to Jeff, and I sat at the end next to Susan. Lena, Curt, and Emily sat across the table from us. Will sat at the other end of the table.

The waiter took our orders, and we then began to look at pictures that Susan and Lena had brought. Susan and Jeff favored each other a lot. Both had dark brown hair, brown eyes, and a dark complexion. Susan's pictures of her consisted of baby, childhood, teenage, and adulthood. She also had pictures of Emily, Will, and her mother, Peggy Johnson. We enjoyed looking at and talking about the pictures while waiting for our lunch to be served.

Emily was really a talker. She could talk on about any subject that came up. The topic of President Clinton came up, and Emily said, "I met President Clinton one time in Washington DC, and he came up to me and said, 'Hello there, Cutie Pie.' I said, 'Hello, Mr. President.' I knew what he wanted all the time. He just wanted my vote!"

We all laughed! What an amazing ten-year-old girl! I told Emily I had known President Bill Clinton personally for several years. He had spoken at our graduation ceremonies two times while I was superintendent of the Nashville Public Schools.

We found Emily to be a very intelligent kid. She was going into the sixth grade in the fall of 1997. She liked basketball, and Jeff volunteered his time to teach his little half-sister the skills of the game.

We had an excellent lunch together and spent at least two hours talking about our families. Susan informed Jeff that she was a graduate of the University of Central Arkansas in Conway. She told him that she majored in biology as well.

By mid-afternoon we were getting tired of sitting. Susan suggested we go to the park near the Dixie Café so we didn't have to move our automobiles. There was a fountain and an outdoor theater in the park.

I carried my 35 mm Canon camera and my movie camera with me to the park. While we were there, I shot both stills and movies of this grand occasion. Emily was so proud of her big brother, Jeff. She was climbing all over him. I was so proud of Jeff, too. He displayed so much patience with and understanding of his little sister. It was as if he understood that Emily needed to make up for lost time, and she needed a big brother.

"Emily, what do you think about your big brother?"

"Oh, he's the best big brother a sister could hope to have! I love him!"

"I think she loved him from the day she saw his picture and knew he was her brother," Susan said.

It was obvious that Susan had spent time with Emily telling her about her brother and about the adoption.

Lena, Curt, and I spent a lot of time with Will and Emily while Jeff and Susan sat off from us visiting with each other. From our observation, they seemed to be hitting it off well.

Will at one time said, "Ya'll, this has been the greatest gift that Susan has ever received. Ever since you called, she has been on cloud nine. She has not smiled and laughed like this in many years. Look at her! This is the best medicine she could ever get!"

Will said he tried to persuade Susan several times in the past few years to go put her name on the registry at the Arkansas Social Service Department.

"She would start to do it, but then would back out. She was afraid she might upset your lives. She was also afraid that Jeff might hate her for giving him up. But now it appears she had nothing to fear."

Emily came over and visited with me a while. She talked about her school and about her basketball interest. I asked her when her birthday was.

She said, "August seventeenth."

"Really? My birthday is August seventeenth as well."

"You are just kidding me, aren't you?"

"You ask Lena if you don't believe me."

"Dad, Mr. Carl and I have the same birthday." Emily and I decided that some time we would have to celebrate our birthdays together.

We left the fountain area and headed back to our automobiles around four-thirty in the afternoon. Lena was getting tired. She had had gall bladder surgery on July 8, and the trip to North Little Rock had been tiring for her.

As we said our goodbyes, Susan came up to me and Lena and said, "Carl and Lena, please know how wonderful this has been. I've dreamed this would happen someday, but to tell you the truth, I had just about given up hope. Y'all have done a good thing for Jeff and me. Jeff is such a nice, polite, and handsome, young man. I've always thought he'd be good looking, but I never dreamed he would be as good looking as he is.

"I've lived with guilt for so many years. I've questioned myself so many times about consenting to adopt him out. I now know why! God planned it that away. He placed Jeff with a Christian couple who loved, cherished, and raised him well.

"I know now that I couldn't have done the things you and Lena have done for Jeff. I am now at peace knowing my son has been well taken care off. You have made me a very happy person today. Most adoptive parents would never have done what you and Lena have done. I can't thank you enough. I know both of you love him very much!"

"Yes, we do," Lena said.

We said our goodbyes with the understanding that we would stay in touch with each other. Susan invited Jeff over to her house for supper and he accepted.

When we got back to our car, Jeff told us he had something to say to us. "I want both of you to know how much this all means to me, and, most important, I want both of you to know you will always be my number one parents." He embraced Lena and me and said, "I love you both!" It was like Jeff was reassuring us that we had nothing to fear about losing him as a son or his love for us. He would always be our son, and I think he wanted us to be assured of that.

"We love you too, son."

Needless to say, Lena and I shed a few tears over Jeff's remarks. It had been a good day. God had provided another great day of celebration by allowing two people separated by circumstances to come together to establish a loving relationship. It was all worthwhile! As I drove away from the Dixie Cafe parking lot I told myself, "Carl, you have done a good thing in bringing Jeff and Susan together."

After Susan and Jeff got to know each other better, Jeff came to me and said, "Dad, I don't think I want to know who my biological father is. I think it's best that my search ends with Susan. She's a nice lady, and I really am not interested in finding out who my biological father is."

"Jeff, I will certainly honor your wishes. If you ever change your mind, you know where to find me."

"Dad, I love you. Thanks for what you've done for me."

CHAPTER 46

Normalcy . . . Almost

After finding Carla's biological mother and father and Jeff's biological mother in 1997, things became normal again at the Bargers' household in Warren.

During the times I was gone from Warren trying to find Carla's and Jeff's biological parents, I left two able-bodied young men in charge of seeing after Lena and doing chores around the house. Those two young men were my son, Curt, and Patrick Ellis. In order to better understand how Patrick came into our household, I need to go back to the year 1994.

In the fall of 1994, one day after football practice, Curt came home and asked if he could talk to Lena and me about a problem.

My first thought was, *Oh, what has he done?*

Lena, right away said, "What is it, Curt?"

"Don't worry, I'm not in trouble."

With that statement, Lena and I began to breathe more easily. "What's going on, Curt?" I asked

"Y'all both know my friend, Patrick Ellis?"

"Yes, he's a very nice young man," Lena said.

"Patrick's mother has cancer and has been hospitalized. His younger brothers are going to stay with their grandparents out in the country. Patrick doesn't want to stay with them because he would have to quit football. Can he come stay with us?"

I looked at Lena and she looked at me. What could we say? We knew Patrick and knew him to be a fine young man. He had been in our home several times. We knew Curt had a heart as big as a mountain and had feelings for those in need. What else could we say, other than yes?

"Curt, you can tell Patrick he can move in with us, but you need to explain to him that he has to abide by our rules. He has to study, get in at a certain time, go to church with us, and pull his share of the chores around here. If he can do that, he will be welcome in our home," I said.

"Pops, I know he'll do what you want him to. When can I tell him he can move in?"

"You can tell him as soon as he wants."

To make a long story short, a few weeks turned into five years. We enjoyed having Patrick and treated him like one of our own sons.

Patrick abided by our rules except for one time when he broke curfew. I locked the door on him, forcing him to have to climb through the window in the laundry room. After he got inside, he and I had a little talk. He never broke curfew again.

Patrick was one of the best young men we have ever known. He was well-mannered and had a good work ethic and followed rules well. He and Curt were the best of friends and enjoyed sports together. Patrick and Curt were known around Warren as two of the best fishermen in Bradley County. They loved to fish and always came home with some big bass. Patrick never drank alcohol or used drugs, as far as we knew.

After he started dating Stephanie Burns, he pretty much withdrew from running around with Curt and his buddies. Some of his friends accused him of being "hen-pecked" by Stephanie. However, Stephanie played a major role in keeping him in line. She came from a wonderful family in Warren, and she and Patrick were cut out for each other from the beginning.

The five years Patrick lived in our household were very good years. Our lives were enriched by having him in our home. He became one of our sons whom we grew to love and respect.

Patrick and Stephanie later married, and Patrick went into the Air Force. He decided to make the Air Force his career. He and Stephanie have lived in North Carolina; Anchorage, Alaska;

Great Falls, Montana; and are presently living in Conway, Arkansas. He is now stationed at the Jacksonville Air Force Base in Jacksonville, Arkansas.

He and Stephanie have one child, a little boy, Cohen, whom we consider our grandson.

In the year 1999, Lena and I moved one of the sweetest ladies we ever knew into our home in Warren. Her name was Retha Snider. "Mom Snider," as I called her, was the bounciest ninety-one year old lady I had ever met. During the ten years we had known her, she invited us out to her house for Sunday dinner on many occasions. She was an excellent cook. At times we treated her to Sunday lunch at our house in Warren. She also loved eating out, and, like us, she loved pizza. Before moving in with us, she made a twelve-day trip to Scotland with a tour group. She was ninety years old at that time.

She was one of the most traveled ladies we had known. She always told people that she had traveled to all fifty states and eighteen foreign countries. Mom Snider had outlived all her relatives and friends.

After her trip to Scotland, she had fallen victim to pneumonia and had no one to care for her. She had to spend two weeks in the Bradley County Hospital. When it was time for her to be released from the hospital, her doctor said, "Now, Mom Snider, you know you can't live by yourself." She started to cry and said, "What in the world am I going to do?" Lena was with her at the time, and she said, "You are going to come live with us." We brought her home from the hospital, and she spent the rest of her life with us.

She certainly was a blessing to us. I learned a lot from that wonderful lady. I took her all over Arkansas to see acquaintances. I took her to Ouachita Baptist University on several occasions for appreciation luncheons with those who had set up an endowment scholarship for a loved one. She had set up a scholarship to recognize her late husband. Everywhere we went, she introduced me as her son. I always enjoyed being her son.

One day we were sitting around the dining table, and I was talking about the building lot I had purchased in Conway and how we would be building our home and moving within a year.

We all looked at Mom Snider when she dropped her fork into her plate and took a big breath. She started crying, "What about me? What are you going to do with me?"

We hadn't told her about changing our floor plan to include a bedroom downstairs with a walk-in shower, just for her.

I looked at Lena and she smiled and said, "Tell her what we've got planned for her."

I laid my hand on hers and said, "Mom, you are going with us. We've already decided to build you a bedroom downstairs. You will live with us until God comes and takes you home. Is that going to be all right with you?"

Mom Snider put her hands together, raised them in the air, and shouted, "Hallelujah, praise the Lord! Thank you, thank you. I just didn't know!"

"Mom, you didn't think we were going to put you in a nursing home, did you?"

"I didn't know what you planned to do."

"We would never do that. You are going with us to Conway, Arkansas."

We didn't realize it at the time, but Mom Snider, who was suffering from spleen cancer and a rare kind of blood disease, would die before our house was completed in Conway.

I had set a goal in life to retire from being a superintendent at the age of fifty-six. If nothing unforeseen happened, I would retire at the end of the 1999–2000 school year.

I heard several retired superintendents say, "You better have other interests to keep you busy after you retire. If you don't, you will be bored to death."

My goal after retiring was to write novels. I loved historical books, especially about the Civil War. I had some good ideas about getting started; I just needed the time to do it.

The Arkansas Teacher Retirement System is one of the strongest retirement systems in the nation. I had made some good investments over the years, and, according to my calculations, there would be ample money for Lena and me to live comfortably for the remainder of our lives.

After I retired, Lena continued to teach in the Monticello School District. While she taught school, I spent most of my time going back and forth to Conway to supervise the building of our new home.

My brother-in-law, Bobby Bittle, who was married to my baby sister, Leona Faye, was building our house. I had seen some of the homes he had built and liked what I saw. After showing him my architectural plans, I asked him, "Can you build this house for me?" After studying the plans, he said, "I can build your house, but it's going to take a while."

Bob started our house in March 2000 with an anticipated completion date of June 30, 2001. We moved in on June 17, 2001.

Because of several change orders required by the city of Conway's building codes, I found myself needing seventy-five thousand dollars more in order to finish our house. This was a big problem for us. I could go into my investments, which I didn't want to do, or I could cut several square feet out of our new home, and I didn't want to do that either.

One day I was at the new house working on landscaping my yard when I received a call from Jim Hill, superintendent of the Arkansas School for the Blind. He related to me that the superintendent of the Arkansas School for the Deaf resigned and the board, which governs both schools, authorized him to locate someone who could come to the deaf school for the 2000–2001 school year. He asked me if I would be interested in coming and visiting with the school board.

I immediately had a good feeling that God was blessing me once again. I needed seventy thousand plus dollars to complete our new house. I thought maybe this was an answer to my prayers. I asked Jim Hill what the job paid, and he said, "Carl it's a grade ninety-nine, which pays somewhere around eighty thousand dollars a year, plus benefits, such as insurance, a house with maid service, food, and reimbursement for all travel related to your job."

"Jim, I would be interested in talking to the school board."

To make a long story short, the Arkansas School for the Deaf Board of Education hired me as their new superintendent. I went to work on October 1, 2000.

CHAPTER 47

Deaf School

In early October, 2000, I moved into the superintendent's home on the campus of the Arkansas School for the Deaf in Little Rock. I had officially accepted the responsibilities as superintendent and was ready to get started.

The superintendent's house was completely furnished and had maid service. This was going to be ideal for me, since Lena was still in Warren fulfilling her last year of teaching responsibilities in the Monticello School System.

In early January 2001, I returned to my home in Warren to remove leaves and pine needles from the gutters on the steep roof of my house. While working on an eighteen foot retracting ladder, I had a serious accident. The lock on my ladder failed, and it started retracting with me on it. When the top of the ladder reached the edge of the roof system, it fell into the wall of the house, throwing me from the ladder onto a fifteen-foot concrete patio. The fall knocked me out cold.

Lena and Curt heard the ladder falling and came rushing out the back door to find me unconscious with a pool of blood under my left ear. The ambulance was at my house in no time at all. They picked me up and carried me to the hospital, which was only about five blocks from my house.

After an extended examination by my family doctor Kerry Pennington, he found I had broken my left collar-bone and four ribs and had cracked the hard bone behind my left ear. That was the reason I was bleeding out of my left ear. He was afraid I was bleeding from the brain, but with further tests, he ruled that out.

My doctor kept me in the hospital for five days to see how I was doing. After that five days and a weekend at home, I returned to my job at the deaf school.

I was never the same after that fall. I started having vertigo badly and wasn't able to walk straight. I was sent to a doctor at UAMS in Little Rock. He diagnosed me as having Post-Concussion Syndrome. For months, I had to take therapy to train myself how to walk properly again. I had vertigo for over six months. The fall hurt my back as well, and I had to get treatments from a chiropractor off and on for months.

Although I was suffering from these medical problems, I never lost sight of what was expected of me as far as doing my job at the Deaf School.

During the spring semester of 2001, the school board asked me if I would consider staying on permanently. I reminded them of a policy that the school board had adopted a few years before I came. The policy made it mandatory for the school superintendent to live on campus in the superintendent's house. I informed Mr. Bill Payne, the president of the deaf school, that I would gladly stay on as the school superintendent if that policy changed. I explained to Mr. Payne that this was Lena's last year of teaching at Monticello, and we wanted to be in our new home in Conway in June.

"I want to live in my new home with my wife," I said.

To make a long story short, the school board voted to change their policy and granted me the right to commute from Conway on a daily basis. I would spend the night in the superintendent's house on special occasions, such as student activities and basketball games.

During my second year at the Deaf School, I still suffered the effects of my ladder accident. I continued to have vertigo attacks from time to time. I never knew when the attacks were coming. I had two vertigo attacks during school board meetings in my second semester and had to be carried to the hospital emergency room to get a shot to stabilize me. I would get deathly sick to my stomach when my head started spinning.

In January 2002, after going through lots of health problems, I resigned as superintendent of the deaf school. I agreed to stay on until June 30 to help with the new superintendent's transitional process.

Resigning was one of the hardest decisions I had to make. I had fallen in love with the deaf school children. I loved my job and my administrative staff. I had to weigh what was best for the children attending the deaf school. My health was declining, and I knew it was only a matter of time before I would have to leave. I felt the school board needed to hire someone healthy who could continue the good things we had accomplished during my two year tenure at the school.

The school board was made up of a wonderful group of men and women. They were dedicated to being the best they could be and always had the interests of the children at heart. They were always seeking better ways to serve both the deaf and blind schools.

It was people like Bill Payne's and Houston Nutt's dedication as school board members, and Jim Hill, superintendent of the blind school, who made a real difference in supporting the needs of the deaf and blind students. They went far beyond what was required of them in serving the needs of these special children. They were super people whom I grew to love and respect.

EPILOGUE

The move to our new home in June 2001 was wonderful. We had more space than we knew what to do with. The space has come in handy many times for family celebrations, such as a fiftieth wedding anniversary reception that our children hosted to honor Lena and me in December 2014. The five bedrooms and four and a half baths have been very useful in hosting overnight guests over the years.

Each time Carla and her family visited us from Boise, B. P. and Cornelia Gates were always here, along with Gayle. I don't remember a time we've had to sleep anyone on the floor. There was always a bed or couch available for sleeping.

Many times when Jeff comes, we invite Will, Susan, and Emily Benson to our house so they can share time with Jeff and his family.

Since retirement Lena and I have traveled to Europe two different times. We've visited Austria, Bavaria, Scotland, Wales, England, Switzerland, Scotland, and Ireland. We have also traveled to Israel, a country we never dreamed we'd have an opportunity to visit. Israel gave us a firsthand experience to actually see the city of Bethlehem where Jesus was born, where he lived in Nazareth, where he was crucified, and where he was raised from the dead. We were also able to spend a lot of time in Jerusalem, the Mount of Olives, Capernaum, the Sea of Galilee, and the Valley of the Doves. We also saw the ancient caves where the Dead Sea Scrolls had been found.

Israel, no doubt, was the most fascinating nation we've seen. It was a total blessing for Lena and me. I had said before going to Israel that there were three things I wanted to do when I got there: ride a camel, be baptized in the Jordan River, and float in the Dead Sea. All my life I've wanted to float on water. I had tried many times in rivers and lakes, but never could accomplish the task.

When I got to the Dead Sea, I waded out until the water came up to my chest. I then threw myself backward and my feet rose to the top. I stretched out on my back and lay there looking up at the beautiful blue sky. I had finally accomplished something I could never do in rivers, lakes, or pools back home in America. If I had wanted to, I could have just lain there and slept all night long. I found it to be both peaceful and remarkable. As I lay there looking up at the blue sky, I said, "Thank you, Jesus!"

Carla still lives in Eagle, Idaho, a suburb of Boise. She and Brent now have three children: Hannah, age eighteen; Hayden, age sixteen; and Houston, age fourteen.

Hannah graduated from Bishop Kelly High School, a private Catholic school in Boise. We are proud of her accomplishments. She graduated as one of fourteen valedictorians at Bishop Kelly during the 2016 spring commencement. She made a thirty-four on her national ACT and was named a national merit finalist. Being ranked a national finalist put her among the top 1 percent of students in America. She was offered and accepted a scholarship to attend Colby College in Waterville, Maine.

Hayden is now a junior at Bishop Kelly. He likes sports of all kinds and is currently running cross country. He hopes to play basketball at Bishop Kelly this year. His younger brother, Houston, graduated from the Galileo STEM School in the Meridian School System and has joined Hayden at Bishop Kelly.

While at the Galileo STEM School, Houston received the overall leadership award during his seventh and eighth grade years. During his eighth grade year, he was elected and served as the President of the Student Council.

Our son, Jeff, lives in Austin, Texas, where he works for a non-profit organization, The Ocean Conservancy. He's been with them for several years. He and his biological family have a good relationship. He continues to make contact with them when he visits us in Conway.

Our son, Curt graduated from Warren Public School System in 1998. He went on to graduate from the University of Arkansas at Monticello, with a major in physical education. His first coaching job was with the Ashdown Public School System.

After coaching in Ashdown for five years, he applied for and was awarded the high school principal's job in Foreman, Arkansas. He left Foreman for the junior high principal's job in Benton, Arkansas. Benton school system is one of the larger 6 A schools in Arkansas.

After spending three years as junior high principal in the Benton School System, he was promoted on July 1, 2016, to the Benton senior high school principal's position.

On April 2, 2006, Curt married Donica Dodd from Crossett, Arkansas, and they have two unique and beautiful children. Addison is ten years old and Jonathan Curtis Barger II is nine years old. Donica is presently one of the junior high councilors at the Benton Junior High School.

As of this writing, Curt plans to start work on his superintendent's certification in the spring of 2017 at the University of Central Arkansas, Conway, Arkansas.

Patrick and Stephanie and their eight-year-old son, Cohen, currently live in Conway, Arkansas. Patrick has been wonderful in helping Lena and me when we need something. It is so nice to have him and his family within five miles of us. He is currently in the U. S. Air Force and is making that his career. He and his family enjoy the outdoors and make frequent trips to see and experience new things. Patrick loves fishing, and, when his job lets him, you can find him in his fishing boat somewhere on a nearby lake. He also enjoys duck hunting.

For seventeen years, B. P. and Cornelia Gates played a major role in the lives of their first born grandchild, Carla Lynn Barger Phillips, and their great-grandchildren, Hannah, Hayden, and Houston.

At the ages of ninety-one and eight-nine, B. P. and Cornelia were still enjoying life to its fullest. They enjoyed playing golf and watching Ole Miss play football. They were devout supporters of Old Miss. Cornelia was an alumnus of Old Miss and their son, Parker, graduated from there as well.

I was amazed at how active both B. P. and Cornelia were. Every time Carla and her family came home from Boise, the Gateses and Gayle drove up from Crenshaw to spend a few days with them and us.

In 2013, B. P. suffered major injuries from an auto accident. He never could regain his health. He was pretty much confined to his wheel chair. Although his physical condition was not good, his mental outlook on life was the very best. The automobile accident he was involved in never dampened his spirit or his intellect. He could still talk about any issue anyone wanted to discuss.

On May 5, 2014, B. P. went to be with his Lord and Savior, Jesus Christ. He was a deacon and teacher in his church, First Baptist of Crenshaw. He had touched the lives of many people during his ninety-one years. Friends and acquaintances from far and near came to pay their respects to this wonderful man. B. P. was buried in the Longtown Cemetery in Crenshaw, alongside his grandfather and two great-grandfathers.

Cornelia Gates continued to live in their home in Crenshaw and continued to play golf and travel to see friends and family. Three months before she died, she fell in her bath tub and broke her hip and injured her back. Her health went downhill after her accident.

On May 16, 2015, Cornelia Gates died. She was buried alongside her beloved husband, B. P. Gates III, in the Longtown Cemetery in Crenshaw.

Gayle Gates Elliott is now retired from a nursing career, and, in July 2016, she moved into an assisted-living complex in Olive Branch, Mississippi.

For a poor hillbilly boy growing up in the foothills of the Ozark Mountains, I have had a good life, better than I deserve. I have accomplished things in my life that I never thought I could. God has been supremely good to me. I know the things I've accomplished could not have been accomplished if God hadn't loved me and shown me the way.

I've heard people say, "Anyone can do anything they want and accomplish anything they want in life, if they set their mind to it." That statement is true to a certain degree, but in my opinion, one needs more than relying on oneself. We all need God in our lives. I have never felt overly intelligent, but with God, I was able to achieve the goals that I set for myself.

Everything that's happened to me has happened for a purpose and because of His love. I've not always made Him happy when following worldly desires instead of His. He's taught me valuable lessons along the way. I'm still learning and hope He never gives up on me.

The best advice I could give to anyone is to include God in your decisions, set realistic goals, pursue professions and areas of life that you are interested in, and work hard to accomplish those goals.

Our life is short, but the life hereafter is eternal.

Carl J. Barger, age 2, 1945

Edward, Carl J., and Roy Barger (Those in wagon)

Roy, Ella Mae, Jimmy & Carl J. Barger

Leona, Jimmy, Roy, and Carl J. Barger

Back, L-R, Minnie Robinson, Nancy Jane Bradford Totten, Carl J. Barger: front, L-R, Ella Mae Barger, Joyann Davis, and Cora Jane Robinson

Roy, Loudeen, Ella Mae & Carl J. Barger; Front, Joy Ann Davis

Edward, Mamie, Ella, Carl, Roy, and Jimmy Barger

Carl J. Barger

Edward and Mamie Ann Totten Barger (top)

Edward Barger (right)

Edward and Mamie Barger

Edward Barger

Milbra Stone Dollar and Children: L-R, Earlene, Virginia, Patsy, and Lena Dollar

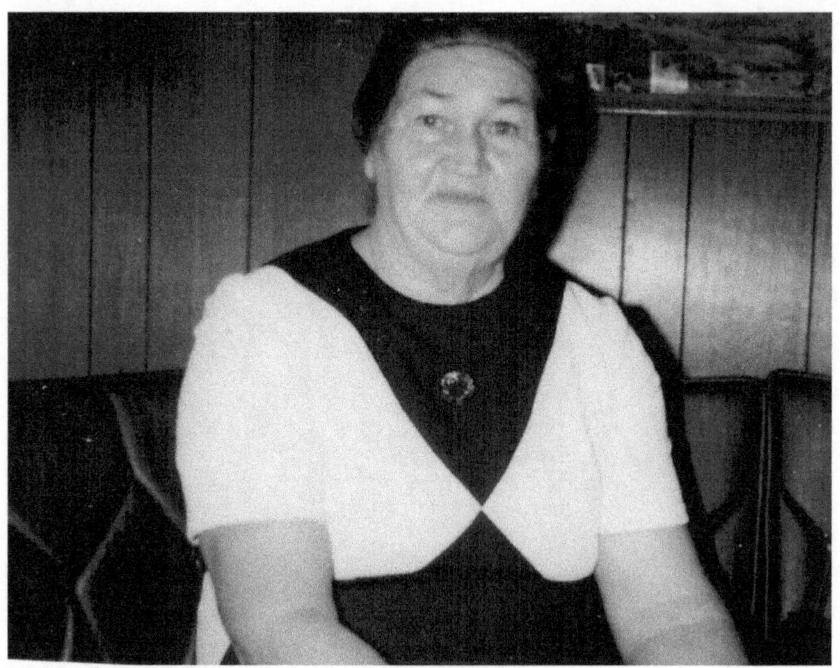

Mamie Ann Totten Barger

Roy and Carl J. Barger, and Minnie Robinson

Lena Dollar Barger & Carl J. Barger

Betty, Carl, and Harvey Barger

Carl J. Barger

Lena and Carl J. Barger

L-R: Carl, Roy, Jimmy, Willie, and Harvey Barger

L-R: Carl, Roy, Leona, Jimmy, Ella, Willie, Chester, Harvey, Loudeen, and Imogene Barger

L-R: Jonathan Curtis Barger, Lena Barger, Carl J. Barger, Jeffrey Christopher Barger, and Carla Lynn Barger

L-R: Houston Lee Phillips, Lena Barger, Addison Layne Barger, Hayden Carl Barger, Jon Curtis Barger III, Carl J. Barger, and Hannah Phillips

Willie, Jimmy, Harvey, Chester, Carl, Roy, Loudeen, Imogene, Faye, Betty, & Ella Mae Barger

Our 50th wedding anniversary

ABOUT THE AUTHOR

Carl J. Barger lives in Conway, Arkansas, with his lovely wife, Lena. After a career in public school administration, he started writing historical fictional and non-fiction books. Since retiring in 2002, Barger has written five novels: *Swords and Plowshares*; *Mamie, An Ozark Mountain Girl of Courage*; *Dark Clouds Over Alabama*; *Blue Skies of El Dorado*, a sequel to *Dark Clouds Over Alabama*; and his latest, a biography, *Arkansas Hillbilly: One Man's Memoir of a Blessed Life*. Barger has also written and published a comprehensive history on Cleburne County: *Cleburne County and Its People, Vol. I* and *Cleburne County and Its People, Vol. II.*

Barger credits his upbringing as a poor country boy growing up in the foothills of the Ozark Mountains and his faith in Jesus Christ as the two main reasons he's had a Blessed Life.

Review Requested:

If you loved this book, would you please provide a review at Amazon.com?

CPSIA information can be obtained
at www.ICGtesting.com
Printed in the USA
BVHW070801240619
551796BV00002B/218/P